LIBERATION AND DEVELOPMENT

LIBERATION AND DEVELOPMENT

Black Consciousness Community Programs in South Africa

Leslie Anne Hadfield

Michigan State University Press
East Lansing

♾The paper used in this publication meets the minimum requirements of ANSI/NISO
Z39.48-1992 (R 1997) (Permanence of Paper).

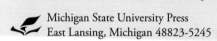 Michigan State University Press
East Lansing, Michigan 48823-5245

Printed and bound in the United States of America.

22 21 20 19 18 17 16   1 2 3 4 5 6 7 8 9 10

Book design by Scribe Inc. (www.scribenet.com)

LIBRARY OF CONGRESS CATALOGING-IN-PUBLICATION DATA

Hadfield, Leslie Anne, author.
Liberation and development : Black Consciousness community programs in South Africa /
Leslie Anne Hadfield.
     pages cm.—(African history and culture)
     Includes bibliographical references and index.
     ISBN 978-1-61186-192-1 (pbk. : alk. paper)—ISBN 978-1-60917-479-8
(pdf)—ISBN 978-1-62895-252-0 (epub)—ISBN 978-1-62896-252-9 (kindle)
1. Community development—South Africa. 2. Economic development—Social aspects—
South Africa. 3. Blacks—Race identity—South Africa. 4. Black Community Program (South
Africa)—History. 5. South African Students' Organisation—History. 6. Black Consciousness
Movement of South Africa—History. I. Title. II. Series: African history and culture.

     HN801.Z9C6374 2016
     305.896'073068—dc23   2015022464

Cover design by Shaun Allshouse, www.shaunallshouse.com
Cover image: The humble beginnings of Njwaxa Leather Home Industry. From left
to right: unidentified man, Nomust Mpupha, unidentified man, Sarha Papu, Vuyo
Mpumlwana, unidentified man, Niniwe Mamase, Esther Mpupha, and Nothemba Sinxo.
(BCP, "1974 Report," 14, Unisa Archives, Documentation Centre for African Studies,
ACC 20 Black Community Programmes.)

g green Michigan State University Press is a member of the Green Press Initiative and
press is committed to developing and encouraging ecologically responsible
INITIATIVE
publishing practices. For more information about the Green Press Initiative and the use of
recycled paper in book publishing, please visit www.greenpressinitiative.org.

Visit Michigan State University Press at
www.msupress.org

Contents

Acknowledgments

When the Xhosa thank someone by saying "*Isandla sihlamba esinye*" (one hand washes the other), they are expressing the sentiment, "I would be glad to do the same for you." This conveys my feelings to all of those who have helped make this book possible. It has been a long time in coming. Many people have contributed to who I have become as a historian and have tirelessly provided various forms of assistance along the way. I wish I could repay them all and hope that they will gain some satisfaction in seeing *Liberation and Development* in print.

There are many individuals I would like to thank in particular. My brevity (or accidental omission) should not be taken as a reflection of the depth of my gratitude, but my own inadequacies in expressing it. First, I thank the many people in South Africa who guided and supported me in my research. I would like to thank all those who graciously agreed to be interviewed (some multiple times) and helped me contact others, including residents of Zinyoka and Njwaxa (such as Mama Nondalana and Mama Cola), and former activists Nontobeko Moletsane, Malusi Mpumlwana, and Thoko Mpumlwana. I am particularly grateful for Bennie Khoapa, who spent many hours answering my questions, and for Peter Jones's encouragement and help over the years. Many people in academic and archival institutions facilitated my research and gave me a home in South Africa: Cornelius Thomas (at the time the director of the National Heritage and Cultural Studies Center at the University of Fort Hare); Qondi Malotana, Nokwezi Ganya, and staff at the Eastern Cape Archives and Records Service in King William's Town; and Stephanie Victor, Lungisile Ntsebeza, Luvuyo Wotshela, and Sifiso Ndlovu, who all imparted knowledge and wisdom on Eastern Cape history and the Black Consciousness movement. Ammi Ryke at the Unisa Library Archives has always kindly offered help, but especially as I was preparing images for publication.

The Steve Biko Foundation and its employees in the King William's Town office supported my research with contacts and introductions, office space, intellectual engagement, and an opportunity to video-record many interviews. I also found a family there. *Enkosi kakhulu* Mama Ntsiki Biko, Nkosinathi Biko, the late Mncedi Ngoloyi, the late Andile Jack, Obenewa Amponsah, Noshumi Kekana, Lucia Baepile, Jongi Hoza, Lungi Malgas, Milisa Mganu, and many others. It was a privilege to work with Lindani Ntenteni, my teammate, colleague, and friend who spent many hours traveling, interviewing, and discussing my research with me. Mandisi Aplom made much of this research and my experiences in King William's Town possible from our first meeting in 2002. He facilitated various research visits and meetings and remained a friend and counselor after he left the foundation.

I have many mothers, fathers, sisters, brothers, and extended family members in South Africa. They all have enriched my life and played significant roles in my research and understanding of South Africa. These people include my Xhosa tutors and friends: the late Lindile Magewu, Siyabonga "Togie" Thetho, Nomalanga Grootboom, and Lindile Ndlebe. Hlumela Sondlo, my wonderful first formal Xhosa teacher, and her family in Pretoria and Johannesburg have provided me with a home base in Gauteng and valuable language training and assistance—Palesa Mothlabane transcribed most of my interviews in Xhosa. Numerous members of the Church of Jesus Christ of Latter-day Saints in East London and King William's Town acted as my family, including Linda Smith and Fundiswa Mnyaiza, who were always willing hosts. I can never thank the Mnyaiza family enough for their hospitality and love. Zoliswa Mhloma introduced me to the Xhasumzi and Nosidima Mrwashu family in Zwelitsha (including Spoki, Siba, and Gugu), who allowed me to join their family in 2008. I will always be grateful for their help in speaking Xhosa, fixing my car, going to the gym, and connecting with people and their rural villages. The Sihlalo and Pumla Booi family in Beacon Bay has been an anchor and blessing since I first stayed with them in 2000. Their home has remained a haven and a strength for me over many years, and Pum Pum first introduced me to Ntsiki Biko. I owe much to Pum Pum and Tata, along with Masande, Xhanti, Sino, Koleka Wofa, and many extended family members. *Maz'enethole, bantu bam basekhaya.*

This book would also not have been possible without my African studies and African history family at Michigan State University (MSU). I am greatly indebted to Peter Alegi for having faith in this project and for pushing me to improve my research, writing, and thinking. He has been a continuous example of a thorough, creative, energetic, and engaged scholar, and I am deeply grateful for his careful attention and guidance. Walter Hawthorne taught me what the field of African history is as I began my master's program at Ohio University. He continued to be a trusted adviser and friend at MSU, along with Peter Limb, who has graciously given of his time and insights and faithfully kept watch for sources related to my research. I must also thank MSU African Studies Center staff, John Metzler and David Wiley, and Chris Root for their guidance and help. My fellow students in East Lansing gave me their companionship and expanded my understanding of African history, particularly those in my initial cohort: Assan Sarr, Harry Odamtten, Bala Saho, Lumumba Shabaka, and Jill Kelly. Special thanks goes to my twin brother Assan for his invaluable friendship and help, ranging from typing up interview questions on the road to Athens, Ohio, to offering intellectual and moral advice.

I must also thank crucial sources of financial support and those who helped further this book along while I worked at Brigham Young University (BYU). A Fulbright IIE grant funded the bulk of my research in South Africa. I also received funding from Michigan State International Studies and Department of History sources, plus generous research funds from the BYU College of Family Home and Social Sciences. My department and colleagues at BYU also importantly provided an encouraging working environment. A number of friends helped in preparing my Xhosa interview transcripts to be deposited in archives, especially Nkosinathi Vezi, Lindani Ntenteni, and Sonto Pooe. I am also grateful to many colleagues, friends, and anonymous reviewers who read various drafts and offered constructive feedback. I am especially indebted to Dan Magaziner for graciously sharing valuable contact information, ideas, and research tips as I began my research and for tirelessly providing constructive feedback many times after.

Finally, I would like to thank my biological family. My sister, Natalie Hadfield Bowen, has long served as my in-house editor. All of my siblings, their families, and my grandparents have encouraged and supported me in various ways. My brother-in-law, Chris Greenmun, used his graphic design skills to create the maps for this book. Good fortune added my cousins Ed and Candice Stratford and their family to this group when I began working at BYU. Throughout, my parents, Randy and Kathryn Hadfield, have encouraged and helped me in my research, writing, and schooling. They built a sound home base for me and have remained steady examples and counselors. Thank you for nurturing my ideas and passions, even when it meant eating a grasshopper for extra credit, being the only girl in my seventh-grade shop class, and living on the other side of the world. And thanks goes to the God whom I know, who has guided me.

Note on Terminology

APPROPRIATE SOUTH AFRICAN RACIAL TERMINOLOGY AND PLACE names have changed over time, and some terms are still up for debate. In this book I use "Coloured" spelled with the South African spelling and capitalized to show that I refer to a mixed-race group of people historically, politically, and socially defined by this term. "African" refers largely to Nguni- and Sotho-Tswana–speaking people, though the term can also include the people known as the Khoe-khoe and the San. "Black" refers to all people of color in South Africa as Black Consciousness activists used it, as explained in the text.

When referring to places, I have used the modern spelling of Xhosa place names but have referred to places as they were known in the time period of this study. I have spelled the names of individuals as they were written by the individuals themselves, although some of the spellings may not be correct according to modern Xhosa orthography. Direct quotations retain their original spelling. In cases where people share the same surname with another person discussed in the text, I have used both first and surnames in every instance of mention to avoid confusion.

Introduction

IN THE HEART OF NJWAXA, A VILLAGE NEAR MIDDLEDRIFT IN SOUTH Africa's Eastern Cape, stands the St. Augustine Anglican Church. One can easily see the church from the top of the hills on the east, where the main road descends into the village. When one moves closer to the church, a large concrete slab becomes visible in the churchyard. Aloes, shrubs, and grass grow in the cracks of what was once the foundation of a small building. Cut-off wooden pillars line the edges. Njwaxa is generally a quiet village today, but in the mid-1970s the building that once stood in the churchyard was bustling with activity. It was the site of the Black Community Program's (BCP) leatherwork factory that produced shoes, book covers, and purses. At the height of its production, it employed up to fifty villagers and could produce fifty to one hundred pairs of shoes per day. It attracted business from neighboring villages and tapped into nearby tourist markets. A former employee of the factory, Nontozande Nofence James, remembered that the factory made their village important. "It was valued by the other villages in the area," she said, "because of the factory."

More than just raising the profile of the village, however, the factory had a profound material and social impact on the individuals who worked in it. For example, for James, its real significance lay in how it changed her family's economic position. Soon after the factory opened in 1974, she was recruited for her skilled beadwork. For her and her family, this was a godsend. Her husband was sick and no longer able to work. With the wages she earned at the factory, James bought food for her family, purchased medicine for her husband, and paid her children's school fees. This led James to later declare that by providing jobs at the factory, Steve Biko "saved my life."[1] Others who worked at the factory experienced a similar dramatic change in their lives. In the 1970s, Njwaxa was part of the Ciskei, a largely rural region of the Eastern Cape, between the Kei and Fish Rivers, deemed an apartheid homeland. Like other South African colonial "Native Reserves," the

1

apartheid government turned the region into an ethnically defined future nation, designed to exclude Africans from political participation in South Africa. The territory suffered from underdevelopment and the negative effects of migrant labor. In Njwaxa, much like today, few residents could make a living on agricultural production and livestock. The majority were women, children, and the elderly unable to work in the cities where many of the middle-aged men had gone. By establishing the small leatherwork factory in the village, the BCP brought much-needed economic opportunities to Njwaxa. Over thirty years later, villagers testified to the positive impact this had on them: not only did it improve their economic condition, it also helped to increase their sense of human dignity. As another Njwaxa resident, Nokukwaka Cola, put it, the factory worked "to make us people"—in other words, real human beings.[2]

The BCP was closely tied to Steve Biko and South Africa's Black Consciousness movement of the 1970s. Yet these stories from Njwaxa are not the kind of stories or setting people associate with the movement or Biko. Most know Black Consciousness as a liberation movement confined to the 1970s and characterized by its bold politics and intellectual production. Few scholars have explored the community development dimension of this movement and its impact; yet the BCP's history holds powerful lessons for today that go beyond the political history of Black Consciousness and South African liberation movements. By analyzing the history of the BCP, this book brings a new perspective on the movement to the history of development in Africa. It examines the ideas, practices, and various actors who took part in BCP activities—including the crucial role of youth, women, and churches in BCP work on the ground. As opposed to better-known histories of antipolitical, macroeconomic, state-led development, it argues that this history demonstrates that people and ideas from the so-called global South have led development in innovative ways that promised to increase social and political participation.[3] Indeed, at the core of the Black Consciousness approach was a focus on liberation—helping black people reach their full potential by improving their self-reliance and sense of human dignity. The book thus causes us to rethink aspects of African history while also offering lessons about the power of youth, women, and churches to shape communities and the importance of people-centered leadership focused on liberatory development.

These are valuable insights for present-day South African and African societies. South Africans are increasingly reexamining their relationship with their government and searching for political alternatives. The South African government is still working to spread economic security and prosperity more broadly. Violently suppressed strikes at Marikana in 2012, along with probes into the self-supporting ventures of political leaders, have called into question the ruling party's commitment to ordinary people. At the same time, opposition parties struggle to reach a broader population. Political forces linked to Black Consciousness are themselves criticized for being too intellectual at the expense of connecting with ordinary workers or have stumbled with egotistical politics. The history of the community development aspect of the movement, however, demonstrates the possibilities of participatory methods that aim for both a social-psychological liberation and material self-reliance. It highlights the need for grassroots action and political and intellectual aspects of movements to inform each other in order to have a concrete impact on daily life. Furthermore, this history also speaks to African societies still dealing with serious developmental challenges similar to those faced during apartheid. Many—including South Africans—live in societies where a minority enjoys prosperity while the majority suffers from poverty, ill-health, a lack of education and political freedoms, geographic segregation, or exclusion from industrial concentration. Black Consciousness community development exemplifies how young Africans themselves can address these challenges under oppressive circumstances.

The book explores Black Consciousness community development primarily through the history of the BCP organization and its three major projects: the annual publication *Black Review*, the Zanempilo Community Health Center, and the Njwaxa Leather Home Industry factory. As a work of history, it is not just about what did and did not work in these projects (though it does seek to address these questions). It is about how ideas and practices developed and changed over time, how people responded to the challenges in front of them, and how they sought to change their circumstances with limited opportunities. It is also about what happened to people in the process. This last aspect was perhaps the most important aspect of Black Consciousness community development. The apartheid state shut down the BCP on October 19, 1977, the day police tore down the Njwaxa factory building. However, oral history evidence indicates that the BCP's projects had begun to accomplish its goals from various angles. In the words of Xhosa Eastern Cape villagers, BCP projects restored their human dignity (*isidima*) and improved their ability to stand on their own (*ukuzimela*). These successes, along with projects that continued along Black Consciousness principles after 1977, make the BCP's historical implications reach beyond its time and South Africa.

DEVELOPMENT, LIBERATION, AND
BLACK CONSCIOUSNESS HISTORY

Historians have helped us understand the discourses, assumptions, and institutions driving development in Africa in historical context. The meaning of "development" has been subject to much debate. Throughout the late colonial period up through independence, the term generally meant economic progress that would result in high agricultural and manufacturing production, improved infrastructure, access to basic social services, and increased consumer power. From the 1970s onward, historians asked questions about Africa's relationship to world economic systems and how colonial states molded African economies and agricultural practices.[4] They explored these topics when the hopes of postcolonial economic development seemed to dissipate. African state initiatives followed roughly the same state-led, top-down colonial patterns, and many countries eventually accepted the structural adjustment demands of the International Monetary Fund (IMF) in return for financial relief. Frederick Cooper, along with Randall Packard and others, subsequently traced the history of the development concept itself. These works have examined the colonial and independent developmentalist state and its failures to "resonate with the local context" or cultivate political participation.[5] James Ferguson, for example, argued that the work of state and international development agency initiatives in Lesotho resulted in the entrenchment of bureaucratic state power at the expense of local participation.[6]

Few historians have been concerned with the history of community development as a framework for inquiry. Community development can include increased agricultural and manufacturing production, improved infrastructure, access to basic services, and increased consumer power, but for a small, geographically defined group. An important element of this concept is also improving the ability of a community to work together to become self-reliant. In line with this aspect—indeed, one of the most important for Black Consciousness activists—I further distinguish community development as initiatives not led by the state or foreign agencies. Accounts of particular projects and organizations that take this approach abound, but are not written for the purpose of African history, and histories of health and environmental initiatives involving communities need to be brought more into direct dialogue with development history.[7] Exploring the history of community development as I have defined it here causes us to rethink the history of development. It provides insights into the variety of practices, networks, ideas, and relationships with states of those working at different levels. For example, the history of Black Consciousness community development shows that Africans practiced a type of participatory development before the international community started to widely discuss, debate, and practice it. Shaped by the apartheid context, this approach promised to increase the social and political participation of black South Africans, as opposed to the state-led initiatives on which historians have tended to focus.

The ideas and practices of Black Consciousness development were wrapped up in a liberation project that emerged under a highly repressive South African state. By the late 1960s, the apartheid government had banned major organizations such as the African National Congress (ANC) and the Pan Africanist Congress (PAC), and imprisoned or forced their leaders into exile. State security forces had adopted more ruthless and extralegal tactics to suppress opposition. This created a climate of fear and a vacuum in aboveground anti-apartheid black leadership. With the formation of the South African Students' Organization (SASO) in 1968–69, black university students embarked on a project of psychological liberation and building self-reliance that they believed would enable the black oppressed to bring about meaningful change. These were not necessarily new ideas—Africanists of past generations like Anton Lembede and Robert Sobukwe or those in Ethiopian Christian movements had spoken of the same need for African affirmation and self-reliance.[8] Yet SASO students operated in a different context and offered new interpretations. At a time when people generally feared the repercussions of resistance, carrying on less political activities such as economic, educational, and health projects was safer and viewed as preparation for a future political liberation. Yet activists also hoped to develop the whole black person. For them, liberation meant having the ability to reach one's full potential—psychologically, socially, materially, spiritually, and politically. In this sense, Black Consciousness community work is an example of development initiatives that have stemmed from overarching ideologies of liberation, which should be a part of development initiatives, as Amartya Sen has similarly argued.[9]

The way scholars and the broader public have situated Black Consciousness and Steve Biko in South African history has obscured the significant combination of liberation and development in the movement. An emphasis on the movement's political influence and intellectual production has particularly eclipsed its envisioned and realized impact on people's material lives. In the late 1970s and early 1980s, political scientists who analyzed the origins and evolution of Black Consciousness helped establish a narrative of the movement's political contributions. For example, Gail Gerhart situated Black Consciousness as the latest and most diffused strand of orthodox

African nationalism, and C. R. D. Halisi aligned it with what he defined as the black republican tradition.[10] This focus on political thought and organization almost entirely left out Black Consciousness community development and gave the impression that the movement was made up of an urban intelligentsia who "spoke to people very like themselves, most of the time."[11]

More recent scholarly work has added breadth to the initial narrative with explorations of the accompanying cultural movement, intellectual history, and philosophy.[12] These works have shown how the student movement evolved into a social, cultural, and political movement. Daniel Magaziner provided the first historical monograph of the movement with his examination of the way black university students formulated their philosophy in their time and how the movement bequeathed a sense of fearless sacrifice to the 1980s. He argued that activists first explored existential questions, significantly engaging Christian theology, before Black Consciousness took a political turn.[13] As the movement became more political, activists formed the Black People's Convention (1972) and increasingly clashed with the state. O. A. Tiro's scathing critique of the University of the North's administration led to his expulsion and widespread student strikes in mid-1972, followed by the banning of many leaders to their home magisterial districts in 1973. Further arrests, trials, and imprisonment came in 1974, after SASO and the Black People's Convention staged rallies supporting the national liberation movement of Mozambique, FRELIMO. Another wave of state repression came in 1976, after the student uprisings began in Soweto. Throughout these well-known political events, activists continued to put their philosophy into action through community development projects. And yet only one chapter in the literature to date has examined this element of the movement. Authors have discussed the impact of Black Consciousness in Soweto and cultural and theological circles; yet few have gone beyond activists to explore the impact of the movement on ordinary South Africans.[14]

Furthermore, a focus on Biko has obscured the depth of people and networks involved. A narrative centered around the powerful figure of Steve Biko has most widely dominated the history of the movement. Biko's biography is often used to chronicle Black Consciousness history. His death at the hands of the security police in September 1977 often marks the end of an era, especially since one month following Biko's death, the government banned all Black Consciousness–related organizations, including the BCP.[15] This pattern is reinforced by its popular appeal and the work of the Steve Biko Foundation.[16] The focus on Biko is not fully unwarranted. He was one of the drivers and foremost writers of the movement. His charismatic personality drew people to him socially and politically, and his death made him a national and international martyr. Yet centering the narrative on Biko and his political writings often eclipses Biko's own community work. While this study is not centrally about Steve Biko, by looking at what consumed much of his time in the last four years of his life, it does contribute to our understanding of Biko—both real and remembered. In December 1973, Biko wrote to Anglican priest and friend Father Aelred Stubbs of his intention of "finding expression for my skills" in the context of his BCP work. He continued: "Over the years I have developed a strong liking for the kind of work done by the Black Community Programs."[17] For Luyanda ka Msumza, a neighbor to the Biko family in Ginsberg in his youth, scholars have not yet captured who Biko really was. Msumza argued, "This you'll not find in any academic journal. You will not find it in any library," but "etched in the hearts of ordinary people" who were influenced by Biko "in quiet little corners where Steve came alive."[18] In many ways, the history of the BCP in the Eastern Cape is the history of what happened in those "quiet little corners." And while oral histories related by those "ordinary people" offer an overly celebratory history of Biko, they reveal important aspects of Biko's life and the way he is remembered.

Most important, the history of Black Consciousness community development ideas and practices deepens our understanding of the movement's broader significance. It goes beyond Biko and the political level to examine the people, ideas, challenges, and networks that shaped activists' work at the grassroots—including women, Christian activists and churches, and the young rank and file. Through this history, the movement emerges as a liberation project that included theorizing about as well as addressing people's immediate material needs. Viewing a people's material position as tied to their sense of human dignity and ability to change society makes the Black Consciousness movement more akin to social justice movements in Latin America related to liberation theology than movements focused primarily on political power or membership numbers.[19] This is why Brazilian Paulo Freire's methods of raising people's critical consciousness while teaching them to read appealed to Black Consciousness activists in South Africa. It also gives the movement broader significance in the history of development and in current debates.

YOUTH, WOMEN, CHURCHES, AND STATE REPRESSION

During my investigation of Black Consciousness development and the workings of the BCP, youth, women, and churches emerged as particularly important. The role and impact of each of these categories of historical actors will be explored together throughout the chapters. These actors, their characteristics, and how they were received were often influenced by their position in one or more of these categories. Their participation also related to the obstacles and opportunities created by the political context of the time—they acted in response to or in spite of state repression. Thus, analyses of youth, women, and churches in Black Consciousness community development ought to be woven together as part of the historical analysis of the BCP and its major projects. Here, I outline broader arguments that will be illustrated in the chapters that follow.

There is a growing literature in African and South African history on youth and generational tensions.[20] Scholars of the Black Consciousness movement have explored similar questions. For example, Magaziner analyzed how SASO students claimed adulthood through their assertion of a positive black identity in opposition to apartheid and the previous black generation.[21] This study takes the analysis of youth in the movement further by arguing that Black Consciousness activists' position as youth—defined here simply as those of an age and position in society between childhood and adulthood—was critical in shaping their community work, the BCP's projects, and their interactions with local communities. These activists did not carry responsibility, caution, or the memory of state repression against anti-apartheid movements like older generations. Thus, they were generally unrestrained and uninhibited in embarking on community work. Their eagerness and overconfidence initially led to frustrating results. They learned the need to refine and improve their efforts. Yet youthful energy and self-assurance also helped them carry out their work in a politically hostile climate.

As university students in the late 1960s and 1970s, Black Consciousness activists were well positioned to access resources and significantly contribute to the communities in which they worked. At universities, they engaged with different ideas and networks that influenced how they formed their own philosophy and methods. Higher education also gave them skills to provide much-needed service to poor black communities, such as medical care. At the same time, the BCP accelerated their transition into adulthood and mature professionalism by giving them valuable work opportunities. Under apartheid, BCP employees in their mid-to-late twenties or early thirties found themselves thrust in positions that, under different circumstances, older individuals with greater experience and training would have filled. Moreover, many of these activists were young educated women who filled both supporting and leadership positions. Much like radical youth in other times and places, Black Consciousness activists boldly questioned authority and societal conventions, including some gender norms. Yet they were also driven by a philosophy that stressed the value of the customs, ethics, and beliefs of black or African cultures. When working in the Eastern Cape, activists and BCP employees recognized the importance of following certain cultural rules regarding age and communication (particularly important in rural areas). Activists also worked with key community elders who would give these outsider youth credibility or permission to operate under their jurisdiction. The way that young activists interacted with villagers despite their status as university students lessened generational tensions that may have arisen as the BCP moved into local communities to run projects.

The history of the BCP also complicates previous analyses of women in the Black Consciousness movement. It is true that in general the movement failed to address issues of gender adequately. Female activists and other scholars have written about its male-dominated and even sexist nature, as well as its lack of a political focus on gender.[22] These views reflect broader trends in the history of women in South African resistance organizations. Aside from acknowledging the accomplishments of women's movements in the mid-1950s, scholars such as Denise Walsh and Pamela Scully have concluded that participation by women in liberation movements was too often directed by men and "rarely mobilized to express" the needs and interests of women.[23] This literature overemphasizes women in formal political organizations and feminist agendas. The history of the BCP begs the question: do women have to organize around gender directly to have a legitimate political consciousness, a wider gender consciousness, or an impact on the position of women in society?[24] Scholars are right to point out the contradictions in movements that did not take women's liberation seriously despite women's contributions or a philosophy of total liberation. Yet there is something to Oshadi Mangena's argument that the Black Consciousness movement "inadvertently and tacitly endorsed" gender as an issue and that women within the movement "could be leaders in their own right."[25] In the BCP, women assumed numerous leadership positions—especially as police harassment and detentions forced the BCP to rely on committed and skilled young women. This had the effect of altering perceptions of the abilities and roles of women, even if unintentionally. It increased respect for women in social relations and professional positions both within the movement and in the communities where they worked.

The BCP also empowered women as it addressed women's practical issues in the Eastern Cape. In response to criticism that the Black Consciousness movement did not address women's issues, Nohle Mohapi (Eastern Cape

BCP branch administrator) asserted that the BCP recognized women and helped them gain independence. She pointed out that not only did the BCP employ women in managerial positions, but it catered mostly to women who bore the brunt of rural homeland poverty.[26] In responding to the needs of the people in the Eastern Cape, the BCP could not help but work with women. They constituted the majority of the population in rural areas while their young and middle-aged male relatives worked most of the year in mines on the Rand or in other major urban areas. The BCP's projects thus arguably had their greatest impact on the economic position of rural women like those in Njwaxa. Furthermore, having female staff members in professional and leadership positions helped the organization work with village women. The history of the BCP then demonstrates the importance of women's networks and the recognition of gender differences in development work, even if the BCP itself did not explicitly do so.

Finally, the history of the BCP highlights the crucial role of Christian churches and radical priests in providing material support to both liberation movements and development initiatives. Christian churches and missions have a long history of providing social services and disaster relief in Africa. These efforts have often been fraught with paternalism and cultural chauvinism. In the 1970s, activists criticized churches for giving charity without empowering. At the same time, ecumenical organizations such as the Christian Institute of Southern Africa, the South African Council of Churches, and radical or progressive clergy provided much-needed support to activists.[27] The resources ecumenical organizations, local parishes, and international churches gave to the BCP are an example of how churches often have the resources to provide crucial support to social movements or development initiatives in the absence of state support—or when acting in opposition to the state.[28] Like those inspired by liberation theology in Latin America under military regimes a decade earlier, South African churches and clergy occupied a relatively safe space in society, which allowed them to mobilize resources and speak out against a repressive regime. Whether it was regional ecumenical organizations, the Anglican Church in the Eastern Cape, the Methodist Church in Soweto, or the Congregationalist Church in Durban, churches and individual clergy provided space, entry points into communities, and human resources. This allowed the BCP to establish itself where otherwise a lack of resources or opposition from local authorities would have acted as barriers. Without all these forms of Christian action, the BCP would have ceased operations long before the government shut it down in 1977.

SOURCES AND METHODOLOGY

Oral testimonies proved crucial in constructing the history of the BCP and its impact. Finding archival sources for the BCP was difficult. As an organization deemed a threat to apartheid, the BCP lost much of its documentation to police raids in the 1970s. Aside from BCP pamphlets and a few archived papers, so far none of the BCP records and personal files confiscated by the state have surfaced in government archives. Because the BCP was part of the Special Project on Christian Action in Society (or Spro-cas 2) until 1973, the archives of the sponsoring organizations, the Christian Institute and the South African Council of Churches, yielded important documents. Yet the Spro-cas records end when the story of an independent BCP begins, and other relevant church and publishing records have been lost or destroyed by fire.[29]

In contrast to this thin paper trail, I found a largely untapped group of people who could provide rich oral testimonies. From the time oral history and oral traditions became accepted as legitimate sources for African history, scholars have analyzed the manipulation of these sources, the frailties of memory, and the dynamics of interviewing. Yet as in the case of the BCP, oral sources necessarily form the source base for many liberation movement histories. Moreover, scholars have proven the efficacy of oral testimonies when critically interpreted along with other sources.[30] In my investigation of the BCP, I found I could gain valuable evidence from interviews by conducting numerous interviews from different perspectives, respectfully challenging and probing interviewees, and analyzing interviews as individual interpretations of the past.

I conducted most of the seventy-plus interviews for this study in 2008 while based in the King William's Town area. I interviewed former Black Consciousness activists, BCP employees, and villagers in English and Xhosa. This diverse group of interviewees ranged from Bennie Khoapa, the director of the BCP, to clinic nurses and village residents who worked as factory employees or attended the BCP's clinic as patients. I also interviewed various activists and community members not directly involved with the BCP. Throughout, I had to negotiate the influence of nostalgia and the present context on the interviews. Memories of a time filled with the promise of improved health care and economic opportunities contrasted with the economic suffering of villagers in 2008. Steve Biko, the movement's most famous leader, and the BCP shared a martyr status that carried iconic power, elevating them above criticism aimed at present politics and government. Praise of Biko often overshadowed memories of tensions or difficulties and the role of other historical actors. I also had to manage my position as an outsider and hopes that my interest in the BCP's history would lead to the revival of its programs in the villages.

In order to deal with the weaknesses of memory, influence of nostalgia, and emphasis on Biko, I adopted a number of strategies. First, I interviewed people with various perspectives. For example, I sought out the wife of a former headman who had opposed Biko in the village of Zinyoka. I also found ways to probe interviewees. Often, I let people praise Biko then followed up with questions about other people, interpersonal relationships, BCP challenges, or specific aspects of the daily work of the projects. For example, I asked Zinyoka residents about views of Dr. Mamphela Ramphele working as a black female doctor or asked factory employees in Njwaxa about the consequences of arriving late at work. I also frequently referred interviewees to documents and newspaper articles or showed photographs from surviving BCP reports to invite responses about divergent viewpoints and trigger memories.

I also returned to a number of interviewees. This allowed me to explore issues I previously had not and to hear stories told a second time. Working with the Steve Biko Foundation to video record interviews opened up this opportunity and brought new challenges. My female gender, ability to speak Xhosa, and young age played to my advantage. For example, older village women seemed to view the interview as an opportunity to teach the younger generation as they addressed me and my companions as *abantwana*—children. Yet, as a white American, I had to negotiate the influence of my outsider status on the interviews. Partly because of this, I asked Lindani Ntenteni, serving as the Social History and Leadership Development Officer at the Steve Biko Foundation at the time, to accompany me in the Zinyoka and Njwaxa villages and act as a Xhosa translator when needed. The foundation eventually proposed that we formally team up to video record the interviews in the villages for a future audiovisual archive (I conducted most other interviews in English by myself). My research and questions remained the focus, and I continued to audio record the interviews.[31] Conducting interviews with a video camera led some interviewees to become stiff and reserved. I once returned to the wife of the headman who opposed Biko without Lindani or any equipment because I suspected she might feel free to answer a potentially sensitive question without a recorder and an employee of the foundation (though she did not elaborate on the source of contention between her husband and Biko beyond declaring it was just politics). Others may have been more prone to praise Biko with an employee of the foundation present and with the prospect of appearing on video. Yet video recording allowed us to return to interviewees a second time and probe further.

The greatest benefit of video recording the interviews, however, was presenting videos to those we interviewed to give back to them and invite their responses. Near the end of 2008, I presented a brief summary of my research and roughly edited videos I had compiled with a local filmmaker at functions the foundation and I organized in Zinyoka and Njwaxa. This gave villagers an opportunity to see the end product and respond to others.[32] I similarly put the interviews in conversations with each other when I examined their content after conducting all of the interviews. As with the feedback I received from the villagers that brought out conflicting viewpoints, certain aspects of the interviews indicated that nostalgia did not distort every memory. While villagers and rank-and-file BCP employees were more apt to praise Biko uncritically, those who worked with Biko as his peers or who had evaluated the BCP's work as employees in the 1970s offered more critiques. I also analyzed the silences—what did it mean, for example, that female employees of the Njwaxa factory denied that there were any personal tensions between them? Other interviews provided glimpses of challenges as people narrated similar stories, elaborated on statements made in passing, or speculated as to the causes of police harassment.

Finally, analyzing *how* people remembered in addition to *what* they remembered helped me understand the interviews as individual historical interpretations of personal, community, and BCP history. While I initially saw praise of Biko and nostalgia as obstacles for getting at what really happened, I later looked for what this told me about the meaning this history had for people in their present context. As Sean Field and Jacob Dlamini have demonstrated, nostalgic reminiscences give us clues as to what people long for in the present and thus how they interpret their present and their past. It is also important to take the emotions expressed in these interviews seriously, even when happy memories contradict views of apartheid times as completely oppressive and disruptive of black life and initiative. Emotions can determine what is available in memory and what people are willing to narrate. They can also help us understand the lived experience and impact of certain events over time.[33] Since Black Consciousness activists sought to change the way black people felt about themselves, emotions are important to understanding if activists succeeded in doing so. In the case of BCP history, positive emotions expressed in interviews reflected the relationships and success interviewees enjoyed in the past. Memories and praise of Biko symbolized what the Black Consciousness movement meant to many so-called ordinary individuals—an affirmation of racial equality, human dignity, and the potential for black self-reliance—at times when they did not otherwise experience those affirmations (whether in the 1970s or 2000s). The perspective of these individuals has not previously featured in Black Consciousness history but is crucial to measuring its significance for African history and current societies.

RACE, COMMUNITY, AND PLACE

The book moves both chronologically and thematically through the history of Black Consciousness community development. As it does so, it deals with various notions of black communities. The construction of the idea of a "black community" was important to the way SASO and the BCP approached their work. The way activists defined "black" geographically and politically led them to involve people of color in South Africa from different classes, in both rural and urban settings. For them, "black community" at once referred to bounded settlements of black people as well as a broad grouping of those discriminated against by the government on the basis of their skin color who shared similar cultural characteristics and historical, political, and socioeconomic experiences. This definition included the different groups divided into three categories under apartheid—Africans, Coloureds, and Indians. Young Black Consciousness activists from these different groups imagined and created this black community.[34] They learned, however, that not all black people held the same perspective, as tensions within communities at times hindered their work. Throughout, this book explores the way activists interacted with different black communities at various levels and how that affected their work. The difficulties SASO and the BCP had in working with communities demonstrates the importance of recognizing the complex dynamics of groups of people when defining and working with communities, even if activists themselves did not always do so.

The first two chapters analyze the relationship between community work and the Black Consciousness philosophy and chart the evolution of the methods and strategies activists employed. Chapter 1 examines the way that Black Consciousness activists conceptualized community development in the South African and African context of the late 1960s and early 1970s. Chapter 2 looks at what happened when activists attempted to put these ideas into practice—how SASO adapted the methods of Brazil's educationalist Paulo Freire, how SASO and the BCP mobilized resources, and how circumstances and timing shaped the BCP. The chapter particularly examines the birth and evolution of the organization. It analyzes the impact of state repression on the BCP's turn to local communities and how activists balanced their efforts to build black self-reliance with the use of what could be viewed as white resources.

The next three chapters explore the BCP's work with in-depth histories of its most important initiatives. This work was largely carried out in the Eastern Cape, where King William's Town became a hub of Black Consciousness community development activity. Each chapter reveals the role of the various networks and actors involved and examines the change people experienced as a result. Taken together, the chapters also help in evaluating the success of the BCP's different approaches to building critically aware black communities capable of working together to change their circumstances. Chapter 3 focuses on the BCP's production and dissemination of knowledge, primarily through its most successful publication, *Black Review*. The BCP saw this yearbook as an important tool for both practical development and a social-psychological liberation—or "conscientization." Analyzing the messages and impact of the publication illuminates the vision activists had for their community work and brings into relief the successes and limitations of different conscientization approaches when compared to the BCP's other programs. The history of *Black Review* also illustrates how the BCP relied on youth and women, who in turn changed through their involvement.

The next two chapters focus on BCP projects concentrated on black physical welfare run in the Ciskei—projects that arguably had a more profound impact on people than the BCP's publications. The local dynamics of these communities and the Ciskei region determined the needs of the people and the opportunities and limitations with which the BCP worked. Chapter 4 explores BCP health initiatives through the history of the Zanempilo clinic in the village of Zinyoka. It introduces the challenges posed by the Ciskei homeland context as it discusses local politics and the poor state of health and health care in the region. It examines the innovations the BCP made as it sought to address root causes of ill-health, including establishing economic programs for village women. The chapter also explores community tensions, gender dynamics, and the role of churches and youth in the Zinyoka village.

Chapter 5 uses the history of the Njwaxa leatherwork factory to examine the BCP's economic initiatives. It compares the BCP's effort to establish a home-industry in this marginal village to state "separate development" policies. Like the other chapters, it highlights the connections the BCP had with Christian activists and ecumenical organizations, the role of BCP and village women, and the impact the BCP had on villagers' self-perceptions and material conditions.

After recounting the closure of the BCP and its projects, the conclusion evaluates the effectiveness of the BCP's three major projects and describes post-1977 initiatives that followed BCP principles and strategies. Although the BCP ended when the state dismantled the organization in October

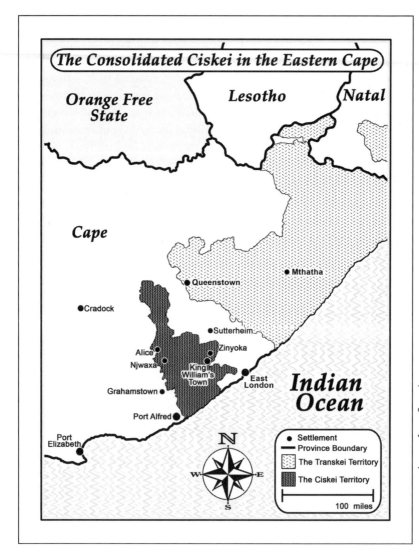

The Consolidated Ciskei in the Eastern Cape

1977, the ideas and practices it employed survived as activists and former BCP employees invented and reinvented projects. The conclusion then comments on how BCP history relates to debates in development studies, including approaches based on liberation and conscientization, leadership and participation, and the role of foreign aid.

CHAPTER 1

Liberating Concepts

MALUSI MPUMLWANA REMEMBERED ONE OF THE SIGNIFICANT MOMENTS in his own "conscientization" as when University of Fort Hare students such as Barney Pityana and Lindelwe Mabandla came to Mthatha after being expelled for participating in a student strike in 1968. Malusi Mpumlwana was a high school student at St. John's College at the time. He recalled that Pityana, Mabandla, and others went around, "almost like evangelists," asking people in the streets, "Have you ever stopped to consider how much you owe to your people—how you owe your language, your [socialization], everything you have and you are—and what that means for your responsibility to society?" These questions particularly struck Malusi Mpumlwana, whose family background in the Ethiopian movement of the Anglican Church had primed him for involvement in black-led community outreach. He later played an in important role in both SASO and BCP projects. His memory represents how integral community action was in Black Consciousness in the minds of SASO's early leaders.[1]

SASO students and BCP employees formulated their ideas about development in the late 1960s and early 1970s, a time when people across the African continent believed African political independence and economic development went hand-in-hand. Political circumstances in South Africa were different, however. Oppression grew worse, even as the South African state engaged in economic development. While community work began as a way to address the poverty so many of their people experienced under apartheid, SASO leaders and later the BCP also came to see "community action and development" as "inherently liberating concepts."[2] Facing an oppressive state, community action was a way to develop people in preparation for a future political liberation. For Black Consciousness activists, liberation meant reaching one's full potential, and development meant obtaining the tools and capacity to do so. They believed that, if geared toward helping "the humblest of black people" cultivate human dignity and self-reliance, health, education, and public works projects would help them reach their goal of totally transforming individuals and society.[3] Tying their concepts of liberation and development together in this way pushed against the fear and paternalistic practices in South Africa at that time.

DEVELOPMENT AND LIBERATION IN AFRICA IN THE MID-1960S AND EARLY 1970S

Kwame Nkrumah's adage "seek ye first the political kingdom" (and all things will follow) reflected the high hopes of the 1960s that African countries that had just gained independence could now enjoy real economic prosperity and growth. Many African leaders like Nkrumah saw political independence as the gateway to entering the world economy in a competitive position. They eagerly planned to mobilize local resources for the benefit of their own people rather than colonial powers. National strategies formulated in top-tier government offices promised to redirect economic and agricultural activities and organize communities to reach a higher level of development—a higher level of production, consumer power, and basic services. This included increased industrial manufacturing, major infrastructure projects, expansions in education and health care services, and even state-supported cooperative movements. It also included mobilizing peasant agricultural production for national and international markets.[4]

One of the boldest experiments in charting a new course for independent African development was Tanzanian president Julius Nyerere's *ujamaa* (or "familyhood"). In a postcolonial Cold War context, Nyerere touted *ujamaa* as a unique socialism that drew upon deep roots of African communalism. Taking a leading nonaligned position, Tanzania also planned to function independent of foreign capital or monetary aid tied to global rivalries. This kind of fettered financial support could compromise Tanzanian independence. In 1967, the Tanzanian African National Union (TANU) adopted the Arusha Declaration, which outlined the principles of *ujamaa*. Echoing Nyerere's writings and speeches, it focused on self-help and agriculture. TANU leaders acknowledged that Tanzania had made mistakes in the past in thinking that industrialization and money (in the form of foreign aid or capital) would bring about development. In the first few years of their independence, they had learned that instead of money, "the development of a country is brought about by people." Once the people were self-reliant and assured of their human dignity, they would bring about economic development rooted in their own society. The declaration made it clear that TANU leaders recognized they could not go entirely alone without money; but it established that their focus should be on developing the self-reliance of people in order to maintain their independence. It emphasized the importance of intelligent hard work and local agricultural resources in developing that self-reliance.[5]

Tanzania inspired many who looked to Nyerere and TANU's socialism as holding to African independence. Gilbert Rist argued that Nyerere also changed international development discourse by bringing the concept of self-reliance into its vocabulary in a concrete way.[6] The irony was that while Tanzania made a unique contribution to development with its focus on self-reliance, once it came to implementing the Arusha Declaration in the 1970s, the country also followed the continental trend of state-led development that often turned autocratic. *Ujamaa* most notably found its practical application in the grouping of people into cooperative villages with communal farming. State-enforced relocation to these villages inspired resentment rather than increased communal production. Along with the failure of business initiatives and global and environmental factors, *ujamaa*'s agricultural failures led Tanzania to depend heavily upon international aid in subsequent decades.[7]

In the mid-to-late 1960s, the South African state acted much like newly independent African developmentalist states that designed, implemented, and controlled national development initiatives. Yet the apartheid government carried out its development programs for rather different purposes. In other words, South Africa was "an African country with specific differences."[8] Whereas African governments looked to secure black African national independence, the white minority government in South Africa worked to restructure society to support Afrikaner economic, social, and political interests. The Afrikaner-led National Party had been in power since 1948, when it began implementing policies that intensified racial segregation. Historians have revealed how the apartheid state evolved over the years, influenced by various racial and religious ideologies, economic dynamics, and political groups. The state grew and morphed as it extended its reach into the daily life of black South Africans, classifying and segregating races, further restricting black movement, and seeking to control black labor and urbanization.[9]

A boom in economic growth, increased white support, and silenced black opposition allowed for greater implementation of large-scale restructuring in the mid-to-late 1960s. One of the main programs was that of grand apartheid—separation of the races on a large scale, even as separate nations that administered their own governments and basic services. The apartheid state targeted ten so-called homelands to become independent countries for specific ethnic groups. Africans who belonged to these groups would no longer be citizens of South Africa (helping the government quell black opposition) but could still work in South African industries.[10] The apartheid state used development discourse to gain support for this policy. Hendrik Verwoerd, the Afrikaner-led National Party politician considered to be the father of apartheid, used the term "separate development" to describe grand apartheid, explaining it as "the growth of something for oneself and one's nation, due to one's own endeavors."[11] This echoed the sentiments of new African nations of the time. Yet in reality, separate development meant that white South Africans could develop South Africa for themselves and relegate Africans to small, rural backwaters. More honestly, Verwoerd explained to other government leaders, "This was the only way of buying the white man his freedom and the right to retain domination in what is his country."[12]

As it began to implement grand apartheid, the government had to make adjustments. For example, it had to balance economic interests with its desire to curb black urban migration. The country experienced rapid economic growth in the 1960s, spurred on by strong international investment. At the same time that it tightened pass laws to restrict movement to the urban areas, the government recognized that many black communities were entrenched in those areas and that industry and business needed educated black workers. The state thus encouraged manufacturing near rural homelands (and later within homelands) to make it easier for black workers to live in the regions and still work for South African industries. The state also adopted top-down agricultural policies in order to accommodate increasing concentrations of people in the homelands. In urban areas, the state created new black urban city councils, which were elected but were linked to apartheid homelands and expected to carry out apartheid policies. The government also continued to implement what became known as Bantu Education. Starting in the 1950s, the government took over most mission schools and controlled school curriculum, orienting it toward putting black students into semiskilled jobs that could support white economic interests. In the 1960s, the government focused on implementing Bantu Education to bolster grand apartheid (to educate black people to provide segregated services, particularly in the rural homelands) and increased higher education segregation. As discussed below, this both served apartheid and worked against it, extending education to more youth who often became politicized through their schooling experiences.[13]

While many black people benefited from South Africa's economic boom and increase in school enrollments, black South Africans in general remained economically disadvantaged in the 1960s, affected by a history of exploitation, continued discriminatory policies, and a lack of political participation. Moreover, for black South Africans, the "political kingdom" moved farther and farther away. The decade opened with the Sharpeville Massacre in which nearly seventy people were killed by police. The apartheid government subsequently banned major black and radical political organizations, and the famous Rivonia trial of 1964 sent much of the ANC leadership to Robben Island to serve life sentences. State security forces gained more legal powers to take action against opposition and systematically used extralegal means to put down resistance, even torturing detainees to death. In addition to the new urban councils and homeland governments, the state also co-opted black leaders by creating representative councils for Coloured and Indian people. This gave people a sense of political participation but was not based on real democracy.

With the general silencing of black resistance in the 1960s, aboveground anti-apartheid activity on a national level continued with liberal, multiracial groups that carried out economic and social development activities. Engaging in less political activities deterred state repression. But these organizations also sought to affect politics by exposing the negative social and material impact of apartheid. Christian resistance to apartheid particularly gained momentum during this time. A larger Christian movement to focus more on the poor and oppressed was spreading worldwide. South American Catholic priests and theologians led in defining a new evangelism of building communities and promoting social justice, adopted by the Vatican II council, held between 1962 and 1965.[14] South African clergy and theology students engaged with liberation theology coming out of Latin America and Black Theology in the United States, both of which emphasized social justice.[15] They also responded to events within South Africa. The Cottesloe Consultation, held by the World Council of Churches after the 1960 Sharpeville Massacre, declared that South African society did not conform to Christian teachings on the equality and liberation of humanity. Beyers Naudé, an Afrikaner cleric, emerged from the Consultation as a radical voice. He broke with the mainstream Dutch Reformed Church and launched *Pro Veritate*, a journal that served as a forum for exposing the negative aspects of apartheid. In 1963, he helped form the multiracial ecumenical Christian Institute, which sought to unite all progressive Christians.

As the decade progressed, other ecumenical groups took a stronger stand against apartheid. In 1968, the South African Council of Churches published "A Message to the People of South Africa," which strongly rejected apartheid as against the gospel of Christ. The message called on Christians "to work for the expression of God's reconciliation here and now."[16] In 1969, the South African Council of Churches and the Christian Institute joined together to follow this admonition. They started by launching a study project designed to expose apartheid's evils through social science research. They named this initiative "Study Project on Christianity in Apartheid Society," or Spro-cas. Despite the focus on Christianity in its title, the study was comprised of six commissions: Economics, Social, Legal, Politics, Church, and Education. Over 100 people took part in Spro-cas's research and reports. Participants included church leaders such as Catholic archbishop Denis Hurley and liberal or radical university professors such as political scientist Richard Turner, economist Francis Wilson, and sociologists Lawrie Schlemmer and Frederick van Zyl Slabbert.

In publishing reports and conducting social science research, Spro-cas resembled the work of the long-running South African Institute of Race Relations (SAIRR). The SAIRR was a typical multiracial liberal nongovernmental organization (NGO) that aimed to "[further] inter-racial peace, harmony, and cooperation" by "[promoting] contact, discussion, and understanding."[17] Its membership was open to people of all races and various political leanings, though white people generally occupied leadership positions.[18] The primary way it sought to achieve racial harmony was to investigate the state of race relations in the country—or "[seek] the facts, and [make] them known."[19] To do so, the SAIRR produced its annual *Race Relations Survey* (or *A Survey of Race Relations in South Africa*). Starting in 1946, it reported on South African political, legal, social, and economic developments of the previous year. The institute also held various seminars, lectures, and workshops.

Spro-cas and the SAIRR's reports provided academic evidence for what was obvious to many: apartheid bred stark inequality. While churches and ecumenical organizations provided important space for anti-apartheid activity, in the early 1970s some people began to push the organizations to take more action. At the end of 1970 and the beginning of 1971, there was a stronger call for Spro-cas and churches to act on their pronouncements. In a letter written in November 1970, Archbishop Hurley stressed the importance of making the Spro-cas 1 findings significant beyond a group of academics. The problem was not a "lack for academic material on apartheid," he wrote. Instead, he was "convinced that the most important thing to do now is to plan on how the conclusions of the reports are to be communicated to non-academic people," and taken seriously enough "for an on-going program of action to develop."[20] Spro-cas director Peter Randall then moved to establish the second phase of the project, called the "Special Project on Christian Action in Society," or Spro-cas 2. It was under this second project that the BCP was initially established, directed by Bennie Khoapa, a Young Men's Christian Association (YMCA) social worker trained at the Jan Hofmeyer School of Social Work and friend of Black Consciousness activists.

The South African Council of Churches also supported many local initiatives led by white and black clergy to uplift black people. Regional councils provided financial and logistical support to social welfare efforts. For example, the Border Council of Churches operating in the Ciskei region ran a number of gardening and cottage industry projects as cooperatives to help small groups of people build their self-sufficiency. It also provided food and clothing relief programs and a Dependent's Conference to help relatives of political prisoners pay for their education and other needs.

Liberal and radical academics, along with student organizations, also engaged in action to address material inequality in South African society. University campuses provided some space for anti-apartheid activity in the late 1960s and early 1970s. Two major student organizations that emerged were the National Union of South African Students (NUSAS) and the University Christian Movement (UCM). Both of these organizations were multiracial, though made up mostly of white membership and more often than not led by white students. Both also attempted to run community outreach programs. The UCM's efforts centered on a literacy campaign. NUSAS organized educational assistance for political prisoners, ran community service projects, and even conducted research and action regarding worker conditions, inspired by Professor Richard Turner.[21]

While these multiracial organizations were most visible on the national stage, they were not the only groups working during this time to uplift black communities. Black-led nongovernmental self-help and cooperative groups with the goal of elevating black people economically have a long history in South Africa. Because of South Africa's history of combined political and economic oppression, those engaged in liberation politics often simultaneously addressed the economic and political aspects of black life. Others have been more apolitical. Many have been linked to Christian missions and Africanist religious movements, such as the Anglican Ethiopian movement. For example, some early economic programs were led by ANC men, Garveyite movements, or other African mission-educated elite.[22] In the 1930s and 1940s, less political small black trading and farming cooperatives sprang up throughout the country.[23] At the same time, a number of women's groups allowed for black female leadership. Like other initiatives, women's groups influenced by missionaries often followed Western social welfare models focusing on education, handicrafts, Western domesticity, or hygiene and sanitation. This focus made such organizations as the National Council of African Women generally politically conservative, similar to the segregated black Young Women Christian Associations (YWCAs) and YMCAs active in many urban areas.[24] Zenzele women's improvement clubs led by mission-educated African women in mostly rural areas had arisen in the 1920s and 1930s. Still active in the 1960s and 1970s, Zenzele groups also played a generally politically and socially conservative role with a focus on domestic skills.[25] Some individuals associated with these less political organizations and movements became involved in politics. For example, Charlotte Maxeke, a pioneering black social worker and founder of the National Council of African Women, was also a prominent ANC activist. From 1941 to 1960, the Jan Hofmeyer School of Social Work for black social workers also produced a number of politicized black people committed to uplifting their people, despite an apolitical education influenced by white liberal missionaries.[26]

Yet with the suppression of black political groups in the 1960s, many black-led welfare and development organizations working in the late 1960s and early 1970s shied away from overt politics. Many of their programs focused on improving access to education and economic self-reliance. For example, the Association for the Educational and Cultural Advancement of African people, founded in 1967 by former ANC Youth League members Philip Q. Vundla and Manasseh T. Moerane, sought to organize scholarships for black students. The Interdenominational African Ministers' Association also focused on educational assistance and even supported experimental farming in the early 1970s. Both organizations became involved in Black Consciousness initiatives at one stage, but feared the repercussions of appearing too political and eventually backed away. The Lay Ecumenical Center near Pietermaritzburg, a multiracial and multidenominational facility run by black people, was a little more daring. It offered space for leadership workshops run by political groups in addition to its women's craft and domestic skill groups and agricultural programs. The Wilgespruit Fellowship Center in Johannesburg played a similar role. Of course, black churches also continued to run welfare and relief programs, and many small black associations worked for the welfare of their group members or targeted specific disadvantaged populations. These smaller-scale programs could have had political implications, but for the most part, these groups did not coordinate their efforts on a large scale. Finally, many national councils that focused on the elderly, children, or people who were blind, for example, had black-led divisions; but many of these groups were also linked to the Department of Bantu Administration and Development, which imposed racial segregation or relegated welfare efforts to the homelands.[27] In short, while Africans elsewhere on the continent celebrated the political freedom to pursue economic development, social welfare and development efforts in South Africa generally tended to counter liberation.

Black students who joined SASO and formulated the Black Consciousness philosophy attended segregated black universities and encountered this sea of organizations and initiatives in the late 1960s. These students engaged the ideas and groups at work in South Africa and the rest of the continent as they brought their own experiences to bear on their interpretations of their society's problems and the necessary solutions. Painfully aware of the racial oppression in the country, they devised approaches to addressing the socioeconomic position of their people that promised to also address their political oppression. They did this in a way that boldly challenged the status quo.

COMMUNITY DEVELOPMENT AND BLACK CONSCIOUSNESS

As the government established segregated universities in the 1960s, it provided more educational opportunities for black students—and more politicization, despite the conservative Bantu Education curriculum. Black university student enrollment rose by 400 percent in the first half of the decade and doubled in the latter half. Black students attended the University of the North at Turfloop (for Sotho-Tswana speakers), the University of Zululand, the University of Fort Hare (reserved for Xhosa speakers), the University of Durban–Westville (for Indians), or the University of the Western Cape (for Coloured students). Many students who became involved in SASO and Black Consciousness also attended the University of Natal medical school Black Section (or UNB, as it became known during apartheid), which offered medical training for black students from all backgrounds. This brought black students to places where they could discuss ideas and share experiences.[28] Those among the growing number of black students who were interested in student politics found an outlet in NUSAS and the nascent UCM. However, as they became increasingly frustrated with the white leadership of these organizations, they decided to form an exclusively black organization. Led foremost by Biko and Pityana, they formed SASO in 1969. Membership grew (though not always easily) on black campuses throughout South Africa. From the beginning, SASO members engaged in community outreach work. As the students developed their Black Consciousness philosophy, they refined their ideas on the role and purpose of community work. These ideas became part of the BCP, though experience and Khoapa's training in social work added greater sophistication.

SASO community work began with a simple desire to help black people who lived in poverty. At its first training meeting in December 1969, Biko suggested that "work among the people" should be one of SASO's "primary occupations . . . designed to help alleviate the suffering so apparent amongst mainly the nonwhite people."[29] He termed this "field work." The rest of the students agreed. At the 1970 General Student's Council, SASO established a central committee on community development. Students at various campuses ran programs that addressed a range of pressing needs in neighboring settlements. The first were "physical projects" where students repaired schools or built houses during school holidays. Other projects included securing a clean-water supply or volunteering at local clinics. Students also proposed to teach home finance management and agricultural techniques to improve self-reliance and planned to run a national literacy campaign.

Engaging in outreach programs mirrored student activism in the late 1960s and early 1970s in already established organizations. Members of SASO may have been exposed to these projects through their involvement with NUSAS and the UCM prior to SASO's formation (even Biko at first proposed to collaborate with other groups to run projects).[30] Yet black students had many other influences and experiences prior to attending universities that made them sympathetic to the suffering majority. Service to one's community was not new among black people, and certainly many of the students had experienced poverty firsthand, either within their own families or in the urban and rural communities where they grew up. SASO students were both privileged and well acquainted with the plight of poor South Africans. While a number had parents who enjoyed some status through education or skilled jobs, many SASO students were first-generation university students. Furthermore, a black South African family's relatively high socioeconomic status did not mean they enjoyed great wealth and privilege. All black students were part of the lower class during apartheid. Many at the UNB were products of townships that had poor educational facilities. Their scholastic achievements opened doors for further education. For example, two fellow medical students of Biko's (whose Ginsberg community gave him a scholarship to attend Lovedale College), Siyolo Solombela and Mncedisi Jekwa, both grew up in the East London area and won coveted placement at UNB's medical school because of their outstanding grades. State scholarships in the form of loans guaranteed to black students if they promised to work in their particular province allowed many to attend the university.[31] Even students whose parents had above-average education and employment struggled financially.[32] Ramphele, whose parents were both teachers, arrived at the University of the North penniless. A state loan covered her tuition, and she lived on help from friends and "the hope that somehow the money problem would be resolved."[33]

The motivation to engage in community work for early SASO leaders initially came from their desire to improve the lives of the people they knew. As Mangcu has argued, Biko was compelled to community action as a response to the "lived experience" of people around him.[34] Peter Jones, a former student at the University of the Western Cape who grew up in a poor working-class family in Somerset West, stated that as the students met in study groups to discuss social and economic theories and methodologies, "it was almost a logical thing that when we [looked] at the world and when we [looked] at the people, that we would see people that we recognized, we knew and understood, and we knew we had to work with people."[35] Pityana explained that at Fort Hare, student political activity was revived in 1968 partly over the issue of the treatment of ordinary black workers at the university with whom the students could identify.[36] The 1971 May issue of the SASO newsletter reported the failed attempt of Student Representative Council members from the University of the Witwatersrand and Stellenbosch to meet with council members at the University of Zululand. The report of one of the Zululand members is evidence of the way black students identified closely with the poor working class. The member stated, "I asked one if he knew the surname of their servant at his home and he didn't; if they were really sincere about contact that's where they should start." He took this personally, concluding, "Moreover that servant could be my mother, you know."[37]

Some students' mothers and fathers had nurtured within them a desire to help those in need, giving their own limited resources to those who were impoverished. Jones believed he developed a sense of deep respect for people from his mother, "particularly, for example, people working obviously in situations of depravation."[38] Biko's family members often reminisce about his widowed mother's giving nature, even though her employment as a domestic worker and cook in King William's Town paid her barely enough to take care of her four children. Biko's younger sister, Nobandile Biko, recalled her mother feeding and housing people who otherwise would have slept at the train station near Ginsberg. She and her brother also regularly visited older Ginsberg residents on school holidays, providing tea and sugar (a valuable commodity) for those who did not have it. "Looking after people is something that we grew up with," she explained. When all of her siblings joined the workforce, "all of us in the family were connected somehow with working with people or for the community."[39]

Malusi Mpumlwana's parents influenced both him and his sister Vuyo in a way that led to their involvement in the Black Consciousness movement and its community work. They grew up in the rural Transkei as well as in Mthatha and East London, where their father and grandfather had taken part in the Ethiopian Anglican movement. Frustrated with racial discrimination, a number of African groups broke away from mainstream Christian churches in the late 1800s in order to practice Christianity under African leadership. Inspired by biblical references to Ethiopia's rise and the country's independence from European colonialism, these groups encouraged African cultural and spiritual expression within Christianity. As Malusi Mpumlwana (himself later a bishop of the Ethiopian Episcopal Church) explained it, the Anglican Ethiopian movement "championed the cultural identity of Africa before God and the political space for the recognition thereof." Having grown up in this tradition, he was attracted to SASO because it stressed "black self-reliance and taking care of your own business . . . and honoring what you are and what you have and taking responsibility for what you can do and can become."[40] As church leaders, his parents also constantly served poor communities. Vuyo Mpumlwana remembered her parents housing numerous poor students from surrounding villages who came to Mthatha to go to school. Her parents often told her not to wear her new shoes because these students needed them. Like the Biko children, she "grew up in that kind of culture where you put other people first and you have to look into the needs of other people and try and uplift them."[41] With this background, Malusi Mpumlwana became heavily involved in SASO community projects, and both he and his sister significantly contributed to BCP projects.

Interestingly, these activists' identification with poor black South Africans did not lead to an analysis based on class in Black Consciousness philosophy in the late 1960s and early 1970s. Whereas Tanzania and other African countries previously exploited by capitalistic colonial systems experimented with socialism, Biko made it clear that his interpretation of the major problem in South African society was racism. In response to those who said the struggle was a class struggle, Biko stated: "Let them go to van Tonder in the Free State and tell him this."[42] "It is not only capitalism that is involved," he noted, "it is also the whole gamut of white value systems . . . so your problems are not solved completely when you alter the economic pattern."[43] SASO students recognized and experienced the economic plight of their people, but education also promised to help them cross into a black middle class. In their view, racial barriers stopped them from reaching their full potential. Independent African countries to the north were proving that Africans were capable of ruling their own countries. And even though white students or other "white liberals" engaged in anti-apartheid politics, black students still experienced inequality in student organizations. Furthermore, these youths watched in frustration as their parents deferred to white people. They asked themselves why their parents did not speak out, but rather tolerated condescending or harsh treatment. They concluded that their parents believed in their own inferiority.

As SASO students read, debated, and wrote, they more clearly defined their Black Consciousness philosophy as addressing the mental state of black South Africans. In some ways, these sentiments echoed Africanists of earlier decades, but they also spoke to a different era, offering their own interpretations and redefinitions.[44] They examined philosophies of identity and liberation that spoke to their context, reading from leaders on the African continent and beyond. Franz Fanon and Zambia's president Kenneth K. Kaunda had a major influence on their discussions of race, oppression, and liberation. They read the writings of Leopold Senghor, the speeches of Malcolm X and Martin Luther King Jr., and the works of other black American writers. They also drew upon the ideas of Nyerere, attracted to his emphasis on self-reliance, developing people, and maintaining an "attitude of mind" focused on the welfare of one's community.[45] SASO students, as "autonomous shoppers in the marketplace of ideas," drew on the authors that made sense to them and combined their ideas with their own reading of their context.[46] At the heart of the philosophy of Black Consciousness that emerged was the idea that black people in South Africa needed a positive identity and self-affirmation to enable them to bring about a total transformation of society—to make the country reflect the majority of the people, culturally, politically, and economically and allow black people the freedom to "attain the envisioned self."[47] Proponents of Black Consciousness pointed to white racism with its psychological, structural, and material impact as the core problem in South Africa. On top of that, black South Africans helped perpetuate their own subjugation by believing in their own inferiority. The "most potent weapon in the hands of the oppressor [was] the mind of the oppressed," argued Biko, because if the oppressed believed they were inherently inferior and meant for subservience, they would not challenge white supremacy in any of its forms.[48] In a 1970 SASO newsletter, Biko wrote that the black man had become a "shell . . . completely defeated . . . an ox bearing the yoke of oppression with sheepish timidity." The first step to remedying this was to change the thinking of black people, to "make the black man come to himself; to pump back life into his empty shell; to infuse him with pride and dignity."[49]

SASO's interest in community work became tied to the Black Consciousness belief in the need for black self-affirmation. Students believed that improving their people's material conditions would build a sense of self-worth among them that could combat feelings of racial inferiority. Even with the Black Consciousness emphasis on race, SASO and BCP community work shows that activists did not discount economic exploitation as a reality that needed addressing.[50] Activists recognized the relationship between a sense of human dignity and one's material circumstances. They witnessed in their own lives and through their community work that those living in abject poverty and suffering from ill-health often became apathetic and hopeless.[51] A belief in one's own inferiority added to these poor conditions could be crippling. As Biko wrote, "Material want is bad enough, but coupled with spiritual poverty it kills."[52] Thus, activists saw cultivating black economic security as a way to restore people's dignity, a "prerequisite for emancipation and liberation."[53] Former SASO leader Pandelani Nefolovhodwe explained, "So [community work] was used as part of making sure that black people's identity, black people's self-esteem, black people's trust [in] themselves should all [come]. And then you are able to release a person in society who can compete with others."[54]

The last part of Nefolovhodwe's comment points to another important aspect of working in communities for black self-affirmation—an improved material condition and heightened sense of self-worth would help refashion black South Africans into confident agents who recognized they had the power ("although limited") to change their situation.[55] "These community development projects should be not seen only as another opportunity 'to do a good turn' in the charitable idiom of the Boy Scouts," Pityana told SASO members in 1971. Unlike apolitical organizations running welfare programs in the country at the time, SASO needed to engage "with the people in self-reliance" and "promote the awareness by black people of the forces that bog them down."[56] In his view, changing a people's situation could help them better understand those forces and thus better understand the need and possibility for change.[57] Ramphele explained that SASO students held "creative development work camps" during school vacations because they "became quite convinced that the only way we were going to have freedom in this country [was] to engage in restoring the dignity of people and encouraging people to be their own masters and mistresses, to be agents of history rather than its victims."[58] The BCP later articulated two of its main goals as helping the black community "become aware of its own identity" and "create a sense of its own power."[59] For these activists, human dignity, agency, and one's material circumstances were all tied together. In other words, the BCP explained, "DEVELOPMENT—in all its aspects" was necessary in order to change South African race relations.[60]

Development and liberation were thus inextricably linked to one another in the minds of Black Consciousness leaders. For them, liberation meant having the ability to imagine and reach one's full potential—to "attain the envisioned self" or become one's own master or mistress. Development meant giving people the tools to reach their full potential. This could be done first and foremost by giving them a new sense of human dignity and agency but also by improving their physical or material circumstances. In SASO's 1971 seminar on community development, it was suggested that development could even be defined as liberation. The report of the meeting read, "In South Africa the term 'development' has many negative connotations for blacks. This made the need for re-definition very important. In-depth discussion brought to light a more appropriate word—'Liberation'"—or the "realization of individuals' potentialities," an awareness of oppression, and "the need to work together for change."[61] In an era when political avenues for seeking freedom seemed closed and welfare and state initiatives did not generally emancipate, activists defined development as liberation and liberation as development to channel efforts in a preparatory and productive direction.

Black leadership in bringing about their envisioned transformation of society was essential for Black Consciousness activists. SASO's rejection of white liberals was a defining aspect of the organization and its philosophy—beginning with its break from the multiracial but white-led student organizations. Its rhetoric grouped all white people politically against apartheid as "white liberals," although this group of people held varying views and would have categorized themselves differently (some, such as Richard Turner, following a more radical philosophy).[62] Black Consciousness adherents believed these so-called white liberals, however well meaning, did not have the knowledge or commitment to articulate black grievances or act in support of black people's needs. Instead, white liberalism was viewed as an "obstacle to independent black initiative and organization." White leadership had the damaging effect of leading black people to believe they must depend on white people for ideas.[63] As Khoapa wrote, an "over-sized mental image of the white man and his abilities" stifled black "creative initiatives."[64] Black Consciousness activists also saw multiracial political or social welfare organizations led by white liberals as ineffective. Black people did not need all the studies these organizations produced to know the effects of apartheid. Activists not only believed black people had the ability to throw off their oppression but also that because black people truly understood the nature of their oppression, only black people knew what needed to change in society and how to make that change happen. SASO students taught that Black Consciousness was determined to build "a new culture and value orientation" that would "articulate the priorities and needs of the black people and act in terms of those needs."[65] Black people working in partnership with the black community would ensure organizations effectively addressed the "real rather than the imagined needs of the Black Community."[66] There was no room for white leadership who "[did] all the talking," exercised a "monopoly on intelligence and moral judgment," and "[made] all decisions."[67]

Black autonomy and unity were also integral to both SASO's and the BCP's definition of community development. SASO came to define community development as "making a community conscious of their need to undertake a venture jointly," resulting in people "undertaking [their] own schemes geared at corporate action, self-reliance and self-help."[68] Similarly, the BCP envisioned the outcome of its work as a self-reliant black community, unified in its development efforts. It listed two of its four main goals as "to enable the Black Community to organize itself, to analyze its own needs and problems and to mobilize its resources to meet its needs," and "to develop black leadership capable of guiding the development of the Black Community."[69] Activists viewed contemporary efforts to uplift black people as having opposite results. Apartheid had destroyed the "moral and spiritual" fiber of the black community. Black people had become apathetic. "Welfare and philanthropic" approaches had contributed to "the habit of letting someone else shape our lives for us." Activists believed if they could nurture "group awareness" and "corporate society," they could restore the vitality and creativity they believed naturally existed in black communities.[70] Khoapa wrote that a shift in methodology was required to achieve these goals. The BCP would need to "hook up" with those already working in the communities and to respond to the needs communities themselves disclosed. Instead of service to the poor that addressed symptoms, organizations should move to "working with and under" the poor to tackle causes. Instead of white people working in black communities, he wanted to see black people working together in their own communities. Activists acknowledged that this approach had limitations. It would take time, and action would not be controlled by the BCP or other organizations, so projects might not develop as they desired; but they stressed the importance of people learning to work together on what they themselves perceived as important.[71]

Similar to their vague political vision, in their discussions of development, activists emphasized principles and what happened to individuals in the process rather than offering detailed descriptions of what a developed society looked like.[72] It did not matter as much whether a project focused on improving health or helping matric students pass their exams. What mattered more was if the project cultivated self-reliance and collective action. Like Nyerere's Arusha Declaration, activists saw developing people as the core objective. Projects were thus viewed as both a means and an end in building a community's ability to work together to solve their problems on their own. Although the next chapter analyzes in depth what happened when activists put these ideas into practice, one example from SASO's experience is particularly instructive at this point. SASO students at the UNB ran a project in New Farm, an illegal squatter camp near the Phoenix settlement outside of Durban (an Indian area dating back to Gandhi's period in South Africa). Here they planned, among other things, to install a water pump. Students expressed frustration with the apparent lack of concern for others among the squatters. They thus counted it a victory when residents agreed to contribute R2 per household to finance the new pump. Ramphele wrote that matters "went awry" when a group of white university students from the University of Natal, led by lecturer Richard Turner, entered New Farm and offered to provide all the money for the new pump. Malusi Mpumlwana commented that this intervention "[killed] the initiative," and Ramphele wrote that it "[sapped] the community's motivation for self-help which activists had been at pains to nurture."[73] With sources only from the perspective of SASO, it is difficult to be sure that New Farm residents lost all their desire for self-help when the white students showed up. What this example does show is what SASO leaders saw as important. For them, the tragedy of this incident was not that a water pump could not be installed, but that the involvement of the white students threatened community cooperation for self-improvement.

SASO and the BCP worked from a political definition of "black" in addressing black unity and autonomy. In contrast to the apartheid government, which enforced a rigid racial hierarchy between Indians, Coloreds, and Africans, Black Consciousness activists sought to unify and uplift people of all groups of color discriminated against by the government. In political terms, this meant that young activists promoted cooperation between the major opposition organizations—the ANC; its rival, the PAC; and the Non-European Unity Movement (even though tensions and rivalries would later rise between Black Consciousness–aligned groups and these other organizations). In local community work, it meant that both SASO and the BCP worked in various black communities despite apartheid racial divisions. UNB played a particularly important role in the evolution of Black Consciousness with its multiracial student body of Indian, Coloured, and African students. Volunteering on the weekends at the Happy Valley clinic in Wentworth, the nearby Coloured community, became a part of student culture at UNB. Medical students also volunteered at a clinic in Inanda, an African township, and New Farm.[74] Students in SASO branches at all black universities—including the SASO Western Cape (Coloured) and Durban-Westville (Indian) branches—planned development projects in neighboring poor communities. In places where the BCP moved to the local level, it ended up working mostly with Africans since the majority of its employees were African and confined by banning orders to African communities. Yet the BCP and its Coloured and Indian employees simply viewed these as "black" communities. By working across geographically and racially defined groups of black people, both SASO and the BCP demonstrated the viability of an inclusive definition of black.

Although SASO and the BCP based their work on the same ideas about the importance of black unity, the organizations had different goals in this regard. For SASO leaders, community work was a way to "give students an opportunity to relate intimately with the community and locate mass solidarity."[75] In other words, it helped students stay in touch with their people. SASO leaders saw how many black people who obtained a higher level of education and economic status would distance themselves from the rest of the struggling population. In their view, black unity and expertise could uplift the entire black community if only black people had the commitment.[76] Pityana explained that "community development initiatives were an inherent part in our view of the ideology and thinking of Black Consciousness, in that the essence of Black Consciousness was to connect students with their roots and their communities and with the struggles—daily struggles—of their people." Blackness was "that inner sense of identification with black life, with black communities, black aspirations and struggles of the oppressed." By encouraging students to help build public facilities or work on literacy projects, SASO not only filled a need but also hoped to "address the problem that students become an elite that is disconnected from their communities."[77] Community work, on the other hand, would decrease the social gap between the students and the broader black community and make students more capable of effective leadership—to prepare them to act in terms of the priorities and needs of their people. This translated into "a fundamental commitment to plow back what you have" into one's community through outreach work. Malusi Mpumlwana explained that in general, "It didn't matter if you are a legal professional, that's where you contribute, if you are a health professional, that's where you contribute. If you are a social worker, if you're a psychologist, you give what you have. If you are a nurse, you are a community nurse."[78] For Pityana, who served as SASO's secretary general in 1971, the organization members' success in their "action program" served as a "barometer" of their "relevance" to their people.[79] Community work could also have the added effect of spreading Black Consciousness ideas beyond the university.

The BCP worked toward building unity in a more practical sense by coordinating among different groups working toward black development. The BCP recognized that "change agents" or other welfare, education, recreation, and church organizations already worked to uplift the black community economically and socially. It sought to make these efforts more effective by unifying them.[80] Whereas SASO worked in local communities on specific "physical projects," the BCP initially saw itself as an "enabling" agency for these organizations. Words such as "coordinate," "cooperate," and "encourage" were sprinkled throughout BCP reports and publications. It only planned to initiate local projects if necessary. Although it later took on such projects, it began by operating on a national basis in its efforts to strengthen and unify multiple black organizations and their diverse initiatives.

CONCLUSION

Black Consciousness activists came of age in an increasingly repressive South Africa, yet believed in their ability to bring about a complete transformation of society. For them, liberation and development went hand-in-hand, similar to newly independent African states of the time. In their particular circumstances, however, they engaged in liberation and development on a deeper, more individual level. In doing so, they hoped to prove the necessity and potential of black self-reliance and leadership. They believed if they could develop the whole black person—psychologically and materially— black communities would be capable of taking charge of their futures, and the political change they desired would come.

Many of these young activists felt a pressing responsibility to bring about the change they envisioned. They had the confidence of youth that they could do this much more effectively than the various other groups working for black development and liberation at the time. Students thus enthusiastically jumped into a number of projects. Peter Jones remembered, "It was always a constant question: 'What are the things that you are good at? What are the things that you are involved in your community?' and, 'Come and tell us what you're doing.'"[81] They learned, however, that putting their ideas into practice differed from thinking and talking about them. Both SASO and the BCP changed as they met the challenges and complexities of implementation. During this process, activists' practice informed their philosophy, just as their philosophy informed their practice.

CHAPTER 2

Creative Interactions

BLACK CONSCIOUSNESS ACTIVISTS DREW UPON A RANGE OF RESOURCES as they implemented their community development projects. One of the most valuable resources was the work of Brazil's educationalist Paulo Freire, most famous for his book *Pedagogy of the Oppressed*. Activists applied Freire's methods for teaching literacy to their work in a variety of ways. Experience also proved an effective teacher. Mosibudi Mangena, a member of SASO's branch on the Reef, recalled the lessons students learned from their difficulties in running a literacy program in Winterveld, a settlement 20 miles (32 km) outside of Pretoria in the Bophuthatswana homeland. He wrote, "No doubt [teaching literacy with Paulo Freire's methods] conscientized the Winterveld people, but they also conscientized us." He further explained: "There is a difference between knowing about oppression of our people on a theoretical level and actually getting involved with the community . . . and being prevented from making headway by a hostile wall of negative and anti-people structures."[1] Black Consciousness activists working elsewhere similarly faced practical challenges of working with people on the ground and obtaining resources to support projects. They learned that putting their ideas into action required more planning, research, and careful interaction than they initially thought. They also ran up against the "hostile wall" of a repressive state.

How SASO and the BCP responded to these challenges and took advantage of opportunities shaped their ideas and their work. Ultimately, the ways activists adapted strengthened their participatory methods and their connections with black communities. This chapter highlights three major ways activists refined their practices and mobilized resources in the early 1970s. First, it examines the way SASO students used Freire's methods to help them more effectively plan their projects and work with people. Second, the chapter analyzes the way SASO and the BCP drew upon various networks and financial resources to carry out their own initiatives. The formation of the BCP under Spro-cas 2 gave activists the opportunity to apply their refined ideas and methods on a more professional level. It also raises questions about how activists strategically worked with white liberals and accepted white corporate money while maintaining a commitment to black self-reliance. Finally, the chapter looks at how the BCP responded to state repression by expanding into local communities where it worked closely with local clergy and involved more youth and women.

SASO AND PAULO FREIRE

Motivated by their burgeoning Black Consciousness philosophy, a commitment to serve, and youthful enthusiasm, SASO students went out into communities to run projects near their campuses. As brash youth, they were uninhibited in embarking on these projects. Their youthful energy helped sustain them in their work, but their inexperience proved to be a hindrance. As Saleem Badat wrote, SASO's community outreach plans were initially too ambitious. The students had an abundance of ideas, but failed to prioritize their undertakings and lacked a practical understanding of what the projects entailed.[2] As they implemented projects, the students learned in concrete ways that black people were not intrinsically united. They also learned the importance of planning projects well and working *with*, not *for* people.

In 1970 and 1971, students launched projects repairing schools and building houses during school holidays in a number of locations. For many, this was a reality check. Students met frustrating results caused by poor planning, a lack of money, and a disconnection between the students and community members. In the Eastern Cape in 1971, for example, nearly fifty students from the University of Fort Hare worked for five days in July to make mud bricks and build a classroom in nearby Fort Beaufort. The students succeeded in laying the foundation and the walls, yet heavy rains subsequently destroyed their work. Rain and a shortage of funds for a corrugated iron roof delayed the project until the November school holidays. Students also reported that they struggled with poor planning and a lack of knowledge of working with the mud. In New Farm, SASO students from UNB attempted to repair houses destroyed by rain, distribute educational pamphlets on health, volunteer at the local clinic, and secure a better water supply. They reported that the residents greatly appreciated the help at the clinic because a doctor rarely visited. But when the students first arrived, New Farm residents were suspicious of the students' true motives and affiliations. The students recognized that before beginning their project, they did not attempt to involve the local people. With the help of an intermediary (referred to as an *Induna*—or headman), the students succeeded in holding a meeting to discuss obtaining a water tap and were encouraged by the people's increased confidence in the students because of their clinic work. Still, at the end of 1971 students were discouraged with the New Farm project. Their frustrations included a lack of funds, students who dropped out, widespread resignation and fear in the community, and friction between landlords.[3] In Ramphele's view, many of these problems were caused by the students' disorganization. They learned that planning and efficient operations helped them work better with residents and manage their resources well.[4]

Participating in community work also taught the students of their false assumptions about the natural harmony of the black community. SASO students had a romantic view of black unity. They believed that "our community is essentially a black one and there is no real geographical separation," and argued that "although situated in different places . . . circumstances are essentially the same."[5] Biko wrote in a 1970 *SASO Newsletter* that African values included "oneness of community" and easy communication. He claimed, "Africans develop a sense of belonging to the community within a short time of coming together."[6] Perhaps this view of black unity was influenced by the idealism of youth or Pan-Africanist sentiments. Biko's "oneness of community" also evokes an image of the Ginsberg Township where he grew up, where Coloured and African people had shared in a vibrant social life.[7] Biko may also have been referring to the African or Nguni notion of *ubuntu*, the concept of human unity and respect that has received more popular and scholarly attention in recent years. Students quickly learned through their outreach projects that in fact, black South Africans did not have an automatic bond, particularly in poor, transient places such as squatter camps. Some students ran into language barriers. Fort Hare students reported communication problems with the residents of Fort Beaufort. As the only university open to Africans for much of South Africa's history, some students who attended Fort Hare still came from various parts of the country. Many of the students who supported the SASO project came from the North and could not speak Xhosa, the local language. As a result, the residents did not understand the "real spirit" of the project. Fort Hare students who could speak Xhosa "were ashamed because of the 'up country' people's involvement."[8] In the local Fort Beaufort context, then, the realities of ethnic and linguistic differences posed a real challenge.

At times, general fear and suspicion bred by security police harassment and other forms of repression stifled projects. At other times, students were frustrated with the apathetic and resigned attitudes of poverty-stricken residents. In New Farm in 1971, UNB students reported that initial suspicion of the activists' motives came from the beliefs of residents that the "students were sent by the government," or that the student projects would draw unwanted police attention. The students also complained that among New Farm residents, "no concern was expressed for the next person." They cited one of the problems as being the nature of nonpermanent settlements and "inter group differences."[9] A similar problem existed in Winterveld. Ramphele headed a work camp there in December 1971. She remembered that her team of students became disillusioned by the deep feeling of powerlessness among the poor laborers in the settlement. She was also horrified at the extent to which the residents were exploited by black money lenders, landlords, and a "quack" posing as a healer.[10] For SASO students, this was evidence of the need for economic upliftment and psychological change if black people were going to work together to change their situations. In retrospect, however, Ramphele also wrote of the limits of SASO community development: "A serious and costly error of the [Black Consciousness movement] was its failure to recognize that not all black people are necessarily committed to liberation and that the poor are not inherently egalitarian." This comment reveals the idealistic view held by many SASO youth that all black people (but especially the humble poor) would adhere to their views, once awakened, and see the need to work together to uplift each other. Ramphele continued with a lesson for practitioners in general: "There are differentials of power along lines of class, gender, age and geographic location that need to be taken seriously in development strategies."[11]

Ramphele could have also included political differences, which affected the willingness of people to work with SASO. In New Farm, local authorities refused to cooperate because of SASO's politics. According to the students, over the 1971–72 school holidays, the neighboring Phoenix Settlement Committee, or Settlement Trust, "refused accommodation for a work camp during the summer vacation."[12] Later in 1973, even after it had been somewhat revived, the project was suspended because the Settlement Trust refused to "work hand in hand with SASO."[13] It is likely that the local authorities refused to work with SASO in New Farm because the Natal Indian Congress, which had strong ties to Phoenix, had a strained relationship with SASO and the Black People's Convention at the time. SASO members struggled to convert congress members to the Black Consciousness–defined black identity. In mid-1972, Strini Moodley and Sachs Cooper, who had built up the Durban Central branch of the congress, joined the newly formed Black People's Convention, taking many with them.[14]

By the end of 1971, SASO students had done enough community development work to know they needed more training to be successful. At a training meeting in December (held at the Edendale Lay Ecumenical Center), SASO students recognized their place as external agents and the need to focus on developing a sense of self-reliance before leaving. They further agreed that in order to sustain projects, community members must be included in the creation and implementation of the projects.[15] After all, SASO's definition of development was that a community would become self-reliant by working together to meet their material and social needs. For help in improving their community work, SASO students turned to the ideas of Paulo Freire circulating among student Christian networks in the late 1960s. Freire's writings about the dehumanized oppressed who could become agents of change if brought to a critical consciousness struck a chord with SASO students. He also offered concrete instructions on how to put their ideas into practice. For Peter Jones, this methodological component was crucial. He did not find the writings of European theorists especially attractive because "I couldn't understand what you *do*. I was very inquisitive about how do you *do*, how do you apply things, how do you live it." When they started reading more from writers within their world ("the African world, the Diaspora,") like Freire, "things became more simpler."[16]

In the decade preceding SASO's formation, Freire had developed his method of teaching people to read and write while debating societal problems in Brazil. The late 1940s and early 1950s in Brazil was a period of social and political change. The *Estado Novo* (New State) pushed for national economic development in order to raise the nation's status. Popular movements within the Catholic Church emphasized social justice and work for the poor.[17] Freire refined his literacy teaching methodologies while working in northeast Brazil. These vast interior backlands had not been adequately integrated into the rest of the country in the 1950s. The region thus had worrisome low rates of literacy among poor peasants and underemployed urban workers.[18] Freire also put his theories to the test in Chile from 1964 to 1969, where he worked with the Chilean national government on agricultural extension education and literacy programs. It was from Chile that Freire published his most well known and globally influential book,

Pedagogy of the Oppressed. Excerpts of Freire's writings in English made their way to South Africa in the late 1960s and early 1970s, at the same time that his full books were published in English.[19]

Freire's philosophy can be summarized as the belief that "man's ontological vocation is to be a subject who acts upon and transforms his world."[20] In *Pedagogy of the Oppressed*, Freire argued that every person was capable of critically engaging his or her world and changing it for the better. The oppressed had been dehumanized, crushed, and divided and thus did not realize their ability to create a strategy for liberation. He wrote that in order to realize the nature of their oppression and do something to eliminate it, the oppressed needed to critically discover their world. Furthermore, he argued that only the oppressed could bring about real change since they understood their oppression better than anyone else. Recognizing the potential of the oppressed required a fundamental change in approaches to education and training. For example, Freire argued that agricultural extension agents needed to change their methodology from extending technical information to people through lectures and pamphlets to engaging in dialogue, posing problems, and "conscientizing." Throughout his writings, Freire repeatedly stressed the importance of working *with* people and the need for constant evaluation.[21]

In his book *Education for Critical Consciousness*, Freire detailed his methodology for teaching literacy. Up until the military coup in Brazil in 1964, Freire worked with the Movement for Popular Culture (MCP) and the Cultural Extension Service (SEC) at the University of Recife.[22] There he ran "cultural circles" led by university students who conducted discussions about Brazilian society. Freire used this model of cultural circles to teach literacy. He and his trained "dialogue coordinators" (university students) first began with careful preliminary research. They learned the vocabulary of the local population through "informal encounters" and interviews in public places—in markets, in transit, or in neighborhoods.[23] Coordinators were to familiarize themselves with the community, begin meaningful relationships, and pay attention to the sentiments of the people expressed through their "typical sayings" and "expressions linked to [their] experience."[24] Coordinators then selected "generative" words (basic words to teach phonetics) and used visual representations of common situations to teach participants how to read and write while debating societal problems. The end goal was to have the participants learn to think more critically and become active citizens in democracy.[25] In Portuguese, this process of "awakening of consciousness" was termed *conscientização* ("to conscientize"). Although "to be conscientized" took on different meanings in South Africa in the 1970s, it was the one related to Freire's *conscientização*—developing a critical consciousness—that resonated with SASO activists who ran community projects and later worked for the BCP.[26]

After their evaluation meeting in 1971, SASO students sought training in Freire's methodology. SASO's connections to student and Christian networks led its leaders to Anne Hope. At the time, Hope was working with the Christian Institute and was closely connected to the radical student-Christian network that grew in the 1960s as part of the new evangelism and liberation theology sweeping the globe. She had finished her university degree as the National Party introduced apartheid, then moved to Europe, where she became involved with Grail, an international religious women's organization. This affiliation took her all over the world to various Grail education and training centers. After working in Uganda for four years, she ended up studying at Boston University at the same time that Freire was at Harvard, fresh in exile from Chile. Shortly after meeting with Freire, Hope returned to South Africa and started work at the Christian Institute. Biko approached her there at the end of 1971. She recalled, "Steve Biko came to me and he said, 'we believe you know "this Paulo Freire stuff"' and we want to learn.'" Hope told Biko that learning Freire's methods required a "whole process of adapting it." Biko replied, "Fine."[27] Hope and Biko arranged four weeklong workshops for groups of activists from five different regions in South Africa. Mosibudi Mangena remembered that the first group included himself, Deborah Matshoba, Barney Pityana, Welile Nhlapo, Steve Biko, Strini Moodley, Mthuli ka Shezi, Johnny Issel, Saths Cooper, Dumo Baqwa, Bokwe Mafuna, and Tebogo Mafole, among others.[28] Students practiced Freire's methods by going out into the communities to conduct research. They also held their own discussions on basic economic struggles, race relations in the church, and gender relations within SASO.

Hope reminisced fondly about working with a group with such a high level of commitment. Their discussions were "highly political," but she was impressed with the way they applied the methods to a variety of programs beyond literacy campaigns.[29] For example, SASO programs benefited from Freire's methods for conducting research in a community before embarking on projects. Preliminary research played an important role in the project in the Winterveld settlement, begun in 1972. Hosted by a local Catholic parish, students began work in a private prenatal and delivery clinic, run by a nursing sister in Mabopane. While working in the clinic, they surveyed the area. They noted "its geographic scope, population size, demographic details such as employment, education, and available amenities, common health problems, and quality and quantity of health-care facilities." They used unstructured interviews and observation, and visited shops, clinics, markets, and transport centers "to get a feel of life in Winterveld." At the end, they produced a detailed report on medical statistics and general conditions.[30] This process helped them better understand the needs of Winterveld residents and plan more effectively. The report read that it became clear that the root causes of ill-health in the community were ignorance, poverty, and "the fact that blacks are powerless . . . have no opportunities and the white man has the monopoly of wealth, power and privilege."[31] Once they pinned down the root causes behind Winterveld residents' ill-health, students reported that residents began to understand the goal of SASO's work and saw the need to work as a community to solve their problems. The project was later taken up by local students, and a group of university students from various schools succeeded in running a two-month-long literacy program in Winterveld.[32]

Hope's training sessions also helped SASO students refine their approach to nurturing relationships with community members. For young activists frustrated with their parents, who seemed to take discrimination as an unchangeable evil, this training helped them see the value of working with the older generation. Asha Moodley, then a member of the SASO Durban branch, explained that Freire helped her realize "how important it was for you not to take for granted older members of the community, that there was a lot of power in learning in these communities and that when you went into communities and you didn't go there with the idea of working for them, you worked with them and you learned from them." In other words, it taught Moodley, a young radical, to respectfully work with older people, whereas she had previously dismissed the older generation in her frustration at the way they catered to white people.[33]

Armed with new training, Malusi Mpumlwana and Siyolo Solombela, another UNB medical student, resuscitated the New Farm project in 1972. They applied Freire's teachings by modifying their strategy to include residents in identifying problems and devising solutions. They accompanied this with research, similar to those who worked in Winterveld. Their goal was to "make people know and feel that they [were] owning what they're doing." Malusi Mpumlwana described how he and Solombela worked to build relationships in the community and spark a more "indigenous" movement to obtain cleaner water. First, they "went into the Shebeens [small pubs], and all kinds of public places and just generally made ourselves friends." Then, they "started having conversations about water," which seemed to naturally emerge as a topic of concern. Eventually people in New Farm called a meeting to discuss how to obtain and pay for piping, resulting in the agreement for every household to pay R2 (before NUSAS students stepped in to pay for the project).[34] Aubrey Mokoape, a UNB medical student at the time, paraphrased the conversations wherein people themselves in New Farm defined the problem and came up with a solution. He explained to a court in 1976 that because medical students could diagnose the diseases, they started conversations by saying the residents' illnesses came from drinking bad water "or something of that nature." According to Mokoape, the people would then say:

> Yes, we drink bad water here because the water here is waste water from the sugar estates and it is stagnant water. So we say . . . what are you doing about it. They say well, we do not know what to do and so on. We say, you have got to do something about it because you are going to live in this area, the onus is on you. . . . And the people start saying, well, we wanted to dig a well and we did not have the resources. . . . We say, why can't you go ahead and so on[.] [I]t builds on until ultimately a solution is reached.[35]

Biko also explained to a judge: "we try to get blacks in conscientization to grapple realistically with their problems, to attempt to find solutions to their problems, to develop what one might call an awareness, a physical awareness of their situation, to be able to analyze it, and to provide answers for themselves."[36] Discussion leading to a critical evaluation of one's situation was exactly the kind of conscientization that Freire advocated in his writings. As SASO students and BCP employees applied Freire's methods to all of their programs, it helped them more effectively work with people and accomplish this kind of conscientization. They planned better, knew the communities better, and worked in dialogue with them about their problems and possible solutions. This helped them pursue their goals of building the capacity of communities to work together to solve their problems.

MOBILIZING RESOURCES AND MAINTAINING BLACK AUTONOMY

Despite the improved planning and research of the Winterveld program, the project was suspended in 1973 due to a lack of funds and volunteers. Other SASO projects met similar ends, challenged by financial strain and state repression. At first, SASO relied on its own resources to carry out its work. As Badat has pointed out, the volunteerism of SASO strengthened the

organization; but it also became a weakness when volunteers did not mate-
rialize or lacked motivation to sustain them in discouraging circumstances.
Badat saw SASO's overly ambitious community initiatives as unrealistic and
thus a particularly demanding part of SASO that attracted only the deeply
committed. With a naive belief in the inevitability of the success of their
ideas, SASO students failed at times to recognize their own limitations.[37]
SASO leaders expected students to have the same strong convictions as
Biko, Ramphele, and Jones about giving of their time and skills in community work, even when facing state repression or personal financial hardship
as poor university students. In 1974, the executive stated that the "lack of
funds cannot be used as an excuse, lack of initiative and dedication is our
strongest draw-back."[38] Yet to run its various projects, SASO had to be more
realistic. This posed challenges to its professed ideology.

In actuality, financial problems posed a major obstacle to sustaining
SASO projects. In 1970, the SASO budget reported internal funds of less
than R1,000. It estimated the cost of physical projects carried out during 1970 and 1971 at R13,200 (out of a total estimated expenditure of
R29,635).[39] In 1972, the New Farm project alone had an estimated total
cost of R13,910.[40] As the reputation of the student organization grew, it
attracted donations from sources within and without South Africa. This
helped the organization run its projects. SASO received much of its funds
from international organizations it had access to as a student group, such
as the International University Exchange Fund based in Geneva, and European and American churches (facilitated by UCM leaders Collin Collins
and Basil Moore and later the BCP).[41] SASO even accepted money from
the mining conglomerate Anglo American. In 1974, in an effort to be
more socially responsible, Anglo American created a Special Chairman's
Fund for contributions to community upliftment projects. Anglo American
also contributed big sums to the BCP. SASO accepted donations from the
Chairman's Fund, even though it had sent a strong message that it believed
foreign investments that supported the apartheid state should pull out of
South Africa. Jones explained why this "was a contentious issue in the movement" at the time:

> We were generally against any formal contact with what we considered
> imperialists—the American government, or back home, corporates and so on.
>
> LH: And there you have Anglo American . . .
>
> PJ: . . . which would be led by the biggest of course image by Anglo
> American—but Steve had very strong opinions about our responsibility to

manage things, that there should be ways in which one would be able to receive money for specific activities of a noncontentious nature, like community activities and so on.[42]

Like Nyerere, SASO leaders such as Pityana had said that black development should not rely on external aid because it usually came with strings attached. It would "compromise the meaning of Black Consciousness through self-help and self-reliance," especially if the aid was seen as coming from white sources.[43] At the same time, also similar to the Arusha Declaration, they recognized the need for money. According to Jones, for Biko, refusing the money was impractical as it could cripple their ability to run their programs. Other activists justified the contradictory use of funds from Anglo American by claiming the money came from the exploitation of black people and thus belonged to them in the first place. They also asserted that they would not let donors stipulate how they would spend the money.[44] Still others thought Anglo American had responded positively to SASO's call to stop contributing to an exploitative economic system, which was grounds enough for them to open a dialogue with the company and accept financial contributions.[45]

The need to finance their projects led Black Consciousness activists to accept money from those they outwardly rejected as organizations perpetuating white supremacy. Similarly, at the same time SASO took a strong stance against working with any so-called white liberals, SASO leaders sought training from Hope—someone who fell in that very category. For some SASO members, white participation at training meetings was difficult to accept. It seemed to go against the Black Consciousness declaration "Black man you are on your own." Under the surface of political rhetoric, however, things were different in Black Consciousness community work. White leadership and participation were bad when they sapped black abilities and misdirected action; but, when it came to practical and strategic questions of mobilizing resources, working with white people did not equal a transgression. In fact, Ramphele remembered Pityana threatening the participants of one meeting into grudgingly accepting that "there were truly good white people who were as passionately committed to liberation as we were." In her view, SASO students had to espouse a rigid policy against working with all whites to be clearly understood when they explained their position and recruited students.[46] In reality, working with people like Hope who could offer specialized training strengthened SASO in reaching its own goals, led by its own people. Ramphele later wrote of the importance of drawing a distinction "between self-reliance and insulating oneself from important sources of information and resources for the successful implementation of whatever task one has at hand." As activists mobilized resources to implement their ideas, they had to balance self-reliance and black leadership with these practical considerations. They thus "opted for creative interaction with a wide spectrum of people nationally and internationally, without regard to race, color, or creed."[47] As long as they maintained black leadership and autonomy, working with white people and accepting white corporate funds was okay.[48]

Along with the way SASO and the BCP pulled together financial resources, the history of the BCP's formation exemplifies this creative interaction. As mentioned, the BCP started as part of Spro-cas 2, a program led by white liberals. Yet circumstances and key individuals turned the BCP into a valuable opportunity to create a professional, relatively well resourced organization based on Black Consciousness principles. Spro-cas director Peter Randall was one of the key figures who helped create the space for the BCP in Spro-cas. He had a liberal background and experience in conducting research and publishing studies. After spending some time working for the Natal Education Department and teaching in South Africa and Britain, he was hired by the South African Institute of Race Relations (SAIRR). He worked there for four years until Spro-cas gave him a chance to leave what he viewed as an increasingly de-politicizing organization.[49] His experiences with Spro-cas led him to support black initiative. As Spro-cas director, Randall oversaw the research and writing of the various Spro-cas 1 reports. After analyzing the results, Randall argued that South Africa needed radical change: black people should share political power; workers should have the right to join trade unions; land, wealth, and income should be redistributed; people should have greater access to social security and education; and the government should overhaul the educational system. Furthermore, he predicted that black people would initiate these changes. They had begun to "taste of power," and white people could not indefinitely prevent them from enjoying the full meal.[50]

Randall's support for black leadership also grew as he associated with Black Consciousness activists who helped form the BCP. In mid-1971, Randall, Naudé, and others in the Christian Institute and Council of Churches began consulting organizations and people regarding the development of the second phase of Spro-cas. They met with the black-led Association for the Educational and Cultural Advancement of African People, the SAIRR, and white professors who had taken part in Spro-cas 1. Their goal was to establish an "enabling body" for existing programs, so as to "implement . . .

those immediately practicable recommendations for change" made by the Spro-cas 1 reports. Their broad aims were to concentrate on the areas that would be most effective in bringing about this change—or to "promote black initiative" (while still enabling white people to "respond creatively").[51] During this time, Randall also approached Khoapa to be the director of the then vaguely defined black initiatives. Born at the beginning of World War II to a chief in the Transkei, Khoapa had received his education at Adams College before attending the Jan Hofmeyer School of Social Work in Johannesburg. In 1971, he was working as the "Secretary for African Work" of the South African council of YMCAs.[52] His link to the church and his organizational skills made him attractive to Spro-cas. Little did Randall know that approaching Khoapa would also link Spro-cas to Black Consciousness activists.

By the time Spro-cas approached Khoapa to direct the BCP, Khoapa had already begun to associate closely with SASO, despite his nearly ten-year age difference. In 1968 and 1969, Khoapa received further training in the United States as part of his work with the YMCA. There he encountered the works of black American authors such as Lerone Bennet and tense race relations in the aftermath of Martin Luther King Jr.'s assassination.[53] Upon his return to South Africa, the SAIRR asked him to speak about his experiences in the United States at a seminar. Some SASO students attended this meeting, including female medical student Vuyelwa Mashalaba. Afterward, Mashalaba invited Khoapa to a debate on the meaning of blackness sponsored by SASO. Subsequently, Biko in particular began to "befriend" Khoapa.[54] Based in the YMCA office in Durban, Khoapa was accessible to the Durban SASO crowd. Throughout 1970 and 1971, he engaged in many discussions with Biko and his fellow SASO students, and they began to share the same views.

In September 1971, Spro-cas appointed Bennie Khoapa as the director of BCP. Joining an organization run by what SASO students would have named white liberals may have seemed contradictory to Black Consciousness. Yet Khoapa's assertiveness and Randall's belief in the need for black leadership ensured that the BCP enjoyed a great measure of autonomy. From the beginning, Khoapa demanded control over the BCP, and Randall was willing to give it. When Randall initially approached Khoapa about becoming a Spro-cas director, Khoapa agreed to take the position on one condition: that he be given the freedom to work on what he viewed as the real problems of black South Africans. He remembered telling Randall that he would only accept a position as sole director of a project, saying "quite bluntly":

I'm prepared to come in and work with Spro-cas 2 on condition that I work with what I consider to be the concerns of my people. Therefore, if I come in and work with you, I'm going to come in and work with you to address what I consider to be the core program of this country which is the way black people are treated. So, indeed, I'm prepared to be in Spro-cas . . . provided I [am] given a free hand to be able to think of things to be done.

He believed that they knew quite well what the problems were—"They were obvious to me, they were lying there, the faults and the difficulties and so on"—but he and others did not have the resources to address them.[55] Spro-cas gave him and other activists that opportunity, and they strategically took advantage of it.

The relationship that developed between Spro-cas, its sponsors, and Black Consciousness activists at times seemed paradoxical. For example, once Biko was hired by the BCP, he sat in at least one meeting with Neville Curtis, a Spro-cas employee and former president of NUSAS (1970–71) when SASO rejected it as a damaging white liberal organization.[56] For the most part, the initial arrangement with Spro-cas was acceptable because Khoapa was indeed given a "free hand" to shape the BCP.[57] He worked with Randall in structuring Spro-cas 2 and the BCP (bringing Biko into some of the meetings, during which Randall thought Khoapa and Biko were very patient in giving him a political education).[58] As director, Khoapa devised the "Suggestions for Action," hired staff, prepared budgets, organized conferences, and started work on a registry of black organizations. Randall continued with his Spro-cas 1 work by publishing the commission reports. Busy with their respective responsibilities, they worked largely independent of one another, holding occasional meetings. Khoapa sat with Randall on the Spro-cas Steering and Liaison Committees with the main sponsors, the Christian Institute and the South African Council of Churches, who put the final stamp of approval on budgets and hiring decisions. Khoapa received pay equal to that of the technical director, Reverend Danie van Zyl, of R6,000 per year, while Randall earned R6,600 per year.[59] Interviews and correspondence further suggest that Khoapa and Randall had a genuine friendship and respect for one another. For example, in a letter to Randall in December 1973, Khoapa updated Randall on his work and life as a banned person, writing, "Sorry to hear about your Bronchitis; you must be getting weak old boy. I think you could do with a 'BAN'—at least you can rest." He concluded with greetings to Randall's wife and family: "Say hello to Isabel and the children."[60]

Some Spro-cas sponsors had misgivings about the way the BCP shaped up, also indicating that Khoapa and the BCP exercised power to determine the BCP's direction. According to Randall, those in the South African Council of Churches particularly opposed having separate white and black programs as it seemed to conform to apartheid. It was not the kind of racially integrated arrangement that many white liberals preferred. Randall and Khoapa succeeded in convincing the South African Council of Churches that allowing black people to direct their own programs would be most effective. They allayed fears by pointing out that white community programs would help white people respond to those initiatives by educating them about their role in the current unjust system and their ability to change church, economic, or educational structures.[61] Biko's hire also raised concerns. Biko's expulsion from medical school at the beginning of 1972 (officially because of poor academic performance) made his employment by the BCP necessary. At the time, he had a young son, Nkosinathi, with his wife, Nontsikelelo (Ntsiki) Mashalaba. She had worked as a nurse until she lost her job because of her husband's political involvement. Khoapa had the means to offer Biko a job as a research officer in Durban, which allowed Biko to stay actively engaged in the Durban Black Consciousness hub.[62] A letter from John Rees, of the South African Council of Churches, reveals some apprehension about working with the new generation of black activists. Rees admitted that he did not know Biko very well but had been informed by others that Biko was "much stronger" than Khoapa. This was potentially a problem in his mind since Biko was not clearly connected to the church.[63] This second concern was not a surprise to Randall, whose own hire had invited criticism because he also did not have a strong religious affiliation.[64] More likely, Rees was uncomfortable with Biko's boldness and stance against white liberals.

Like the working environment at the multiracial South African Committee for Higher Education (Sached), described in Diana Wylie's biography of Thami Mnyele, white-black employee relationships did not always go very deep. Black staff found ways to assert their self-sufficiency.[65] Some older activists found it easier to work with white people, such as Khoapa and Oshadi Mangena, an employee of the Christian Institute and YWCA at the time who worked closely with SASO students. Mangena remembered incidents where younger black employees thought they had to assert themselves and, in her view, sometimes inappropriately gave white staff members a "hard time."[66] Khoapa also remembered, "Sometimes the black staff people felt that it was a major self-assertion to say we don't need to do any of these things with you." Still, even though Khoapa concluded that, for the most part, they had "very good relationships," records indicate that he also pushed back when black leadership seemed threatened.[67] He and other employees raised questions about the number of black versus white Spro-cas employees.[68] In a 1972 memo, he wrote that he believed the sponsors seemed to want to "program the action." For him, this went beyond the role of sponsors, who normally appoint a director and then leave the director to appoint "*his*" staff.[69]

Aside from Khoapa's leadership, the BCP sought to ensure it based its action on what black people needed by appealing to what it viewed as leaders of the black community. One of the BCP's first pamphlets explained: "The program operates on the principle that the source of authority for doing anything in the Black Community must be the Black Community itself."[70] Coordinating with different organizations in order to bring the core problems to the fore helped the BCP know what the "Black Community" requested. The BCP also formed a Black Advisory Panel. In 1972, Khoapa invited skilled and educated people he knew, and who were "sympathetic to our ideology and approach," to serve on the advisory board.[71] In the Transvaal, these people included one African woman (A. August, a community social worker); African men who had worked in social work, business, the church; and physicians (including Dr. Nthato Motlana, ANC Youth League member in the early 1950s and founding chairperson of the Soweto Committee of Ten in 1976). As such, the panels consisted of people who did not suffer the same plight as the majority. This would have been the same with Coloured and Indian members of the panels. The Cape Advisory Panel for a proposed BCP branch in Cape Town included Reverend McBride, Reverend Charles Albertyn, and Merwyn Kemp.[72] Still, the nature of their work as health practitioners, social workers, or clergy made the BCP believe they had valuable insights to offer. The composition of the advisory panels also reflected the BCP's view of the black community and national scope at the time. Black Consciousness activists defined the black community primarily politically, according to how one's skin color affected his or her political status. Thus, panel members were seen as members of the black community who could identify with their fellow oppressed, despite their socioeconomic status.

As 1972 came to a close, the BCP began to push for full autonomy as an organization. The main impetus for doing so rested on ensuring that black authority and leadership clearly directed the BCP.[73] Spro-cas 2 had originally only been planned through the end of 1973, so BCP independence was not contrary to its initial vision.[74] But questions did arise as to the relationship between the BCP and Spro-cas 2's white community programs post-Spro-cas. The Spro-cas Steering Committee proposed a joint trust headed by the members of the Steering Committee for both the white programs and the BCP to continue under one umbrella. The BCP staff opposed this on principle. Creating a separate trust for black programs would allow the BCP to act fully independent of white oversight—a more "logical and positive step in the creation of institutions and organizations for Blacks that are autonomous and are committed to developing a self-reliant, self-determining and self-respecting community."[75] The BCP also did not want to finance the white programs. Black programs were more successful than the white programs at attracting donors who wanted to contribute to South African liberation and alleviate the needs of those in dire circumstances. Khoapa did not want to be "harnessed" by a sister organization that could not finance itself, but would more likely take funds away from the BCP.[76] Randall and Naudé both expressed their support for the full independence of the BCP, and on September 24, 1973, the BCP officially became a registered nonprofit organization, a company limited by guarantee.[77]

After the BCP became independent from Spro-cas structures, it continued to successfully gain financial support from new and previous funders. Khoapa estimated that the BCP received more money than any other aboveground organization in South Africa at the time. While this may or may not be true, the BCP did operate with a substantial budget. The BCP had an estimated R200,000 in the bank alone when the government shut it down in October 1977.[78] Converted to 2014 equivalents, this roughly amounts to R6 million, or US$555,555.[79] As a nongovernmental and nonprofit organization, the BCP relied on funding from South African Spro-cas sponsors, foreign churches, and organizations such as the Dutch Interchurch Organization for Development Co-operation (ICCO).[80] Initially being part of Spro-cas helped the BCP tap into these funding networks. SASO's connections also proved fruitful—the World University Service based in Geneva donated money as well. International funders provided a large portion of the BCP's income. A police memo reported that the BCP received R154,150 in 1974 from mostly international sources; R161,680 in 1975; and R70,041 in 1976 (a year when the Soweto uprisings, the death of SASO leader Mapetla Mohapi, and detentions of many BCP staff members hindered BCP operations). From February to June 1977, the BCP reportedly received R217,843 from international sources, a sizable amount of the BCP's income.[81] Gathering resources from a number of international church and student organizations did not spark as much debate as the Anglo American funding. This money came from a sector of society that could play a relatively neutral role politically, and SASO and the BCP needed those resources. Still, the BCP was always uncomfortable with its dependence on outside funds. State repression often threatened to cut off SASO's and the

BCP's international financial links, making financial independence more urgent.[82] Police action against the BCP was always a major challenge. But as the BCP adapted to its circumstances, the effects of state action against the organization were not always negative.

THE BCP GOES LOCAL

In its first year-and-a-half of existence, the BCP focused on creating opportunities for black people and organizations to come together to analyze their circumstances and coordinate their efforts. For example, one of the first programs the BCP held in May 1972 was a black church leaders conference.[83] Khoapa's duties as BCP director included traveling around to organize and "maintain contact with points of development."[84] As a field officer, Biko assisted by collecting data and communicating with the different groups. In September 1972, Khoapa hired Bokwe Mafuna as a second field worker, which led the BCP to establish additional coordinating projects related to workers and publications. Born in Mafeking in 1937, Mafuna lived in Alexandra Township, north of Johannesburg. He worked as a reporter for the *Rand Daily Mail* until July 1972, when he resigned after the paper's sub-editors repeatedly changed the term he used to describe SASO students, "black," to "non-white."[85] When he was hired by the BCP, Mafuna brought with him SASO's Black Worker's Project, a coordinating and enabling project for workers denied the right to join or organize black trade unions at the time. He also helped found the Union of Black Journalists. Soon after the BCP hired him, he helped to start the BCP's yearbook, *Black Review*.

At the beginning of 1973, things changed profoundly for the BCP, forcing the organization to rethink its approach. During the previous year, student activists had begun to pose a greater threat to apartheid institutions. As Magaziner has argued, this moved Black Consciousness students into direct confrontation with the state. SASO students began to speak out more strongly against the homeland system. The Black People's Convention became the first aboveground black political organization formed since 1960. O. A. Tiro's scathing critique of the University of the North's administration led to his expulsion and widespread black student strikes in mid-1972. In February 1973, the apartheid government clamped down on Black Consciousness activists, banning nine SASO and Black People's Convention leaders. This included Biko and Mafuna. The state confined Mafuna to his home area in the Transvaal. It sent Biko 348 miles (560 km) away from Durban to the King William's Town District in the Eastern Cape.

Government banning orders were designed to render certain individuals politically ineffective. In addition to placing restrictions on their geographical movement, the state prohibited them from meeting with more than one person at a time, taking part in certain organizations, and being published or quoted. Ironically, however, Mafuna's and Biko's banning turned out to have positive implications for the BCP. As a result, the BCP expanded geographically and had a greater sense of purpose, activists increased their creativity, and the BCP involved more people in running its programs. After the banning orders, the BCP field officers became directors of regional branches. Since he was not "employed for [his] brawn," but his "brains," instead of letting Biko go, Khoapa told him, "Well, you continue doing what you were thinking anyway, and . . . we'll provide you with the support that you need."[86] At any rate, according to Khoapa, the staff knew they eventually wanted to work in the Eastern Cape, but had not yet acted on this idea.[87] Ready or not, Biko's banning took them there. Mafuna assumed official branch leadership in the Transvaal office. Two program assistants joined him: Tebogo Mafole and later Daphne Mahlangu. A few months later, in October 1973, Khoapa too was banned to Umlazi, a township southwest of Durban, where the BCP then established a Natal regional office.

The restrictions placed on its staff positioned the BCP to become an initiator of programs that more immediately addressed material conditions. Black leaders had expressed concern that the resources of the BCP should be more effectively applied in preventing and correcting the social circumstances that caused the "crisis in human and racial relationships in our country."[88] Aside from its publications, which could be worked on from any location, the BCP activists moved from facilitating and coordinating— approaches that had them traveling around the country—to doing this work themselves. Khoapa later felt that being confined in local areas kept activists from wasting time in meetings in white suburbs trying to get money and support, and allowed them to "apply a hundred percent of our energy to what mattered most, which was our own program."[89] Biko confided to Anglican priest Father Aelred Stubbs that he viewed bannings and police harassment as making the organization more stable because it unified the board of directors around this goal.[90]

All branches worked according to the issues and resources they found in their surrounding areas. Malusi Mpumlwana traveled to King William's Town to help Biko "settle down." He ended up working as a program assistant for four years and became part of the vibrant community of activists

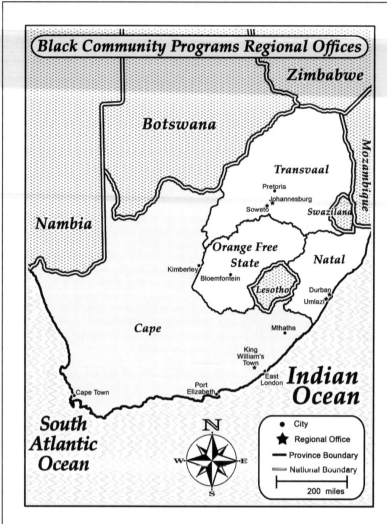

Map designed by Christopher Greenmun

that coalesced in King William's Town. From his perspective, those involved with BCP programs did not have a grand strategy for setting up projects, but were simply guided by the principles of Black Consciousness community development as refined in SASO. They sought to respond to the needs of the people as expressed by them and to nurture self-reliance and collective action, but with greater experience and financial resources. For example, just like the work on the New Farm project, Malusi Mpumlwana and Biko began by spending time listening and talking to people in local public places in Ginsberg. This led them to establish a grocery co-op.[91] Applying their principles generally as opportunities and needs presented themselves also meant that the BCP activists did not change their approach in urban versus rural areas. Khoapa explained, "We said that we were working with our people wherever we find them." They "could not possibly ignore people" living in extreme poverty in rural areas, he continued, but their approach to rural areas was "contained in our general philosophy."[92] Jones similarly commented that there was no distinction in his mind between urban and rural development. The important aspects were whether people were organized and if they felt they had control over the project.[93]

In answering the needs of surrounding communities, the BCP tended to implement health, education, and economic projects. The Transvaal office was comparatively weak, but the BCP managed to meet some of the health and economic needs of people in Soweto through its programs. Police harassment led Bokwe and Mafole to escape to Botswana in September 1973.[94] After they left, Aubrey Mokoena took charge of the office and oversaw a women's sewing group in Soweto, run by Mantuka "Tiny" Maisela (a former Fort Hare student involved with the BCP and Border Council of Churches). In the aftermath of the Soweto uprisings in 1976 and state detentions of nine BCP staff members, the BCP hired Ramsey Ramokgopa as branch manager. A Sowetan native (and brother-in-law to SASO member Deborah Matshoba), Ramokgopa was also a member of the Soweto Committee of Ten, which aimed to restore local educational and health facilities damaged in the violence during the Soweto student uprisings. Under his direction, the BCP established a mobile clinic staffed by volunteer doctors based at the Methodist Center in Jabavu.[95] After Khoapa's ban, the BCP secured office space in Umlazi, a township outside of Durban, where it developed an educational resource center as part of the Natal regional activities. The BCP Natal branch also eventually built the Solempilo Community Health Center at the Adams College Mission, where it improved on the work and experience of the Zanempilo clinic in the Eastern Cape.

Working within the confines of state repression and local black communities led the BCP activists to be more creative in drawing upon their personal contacts and local resources. The Eastern Cape branch emerged as the most successful BCP branch, in large part because of Biko's local connections and those recruited to help. King William's Town became a center of BCP and Black Consciousness activity. By the end of 1976, the BCP Eastern Cape branch had secured a staff of over thirty people.[96] Most of those who went to King William's Town were young male and female activists like Malusi Mpumlwana, who explained, "there [were] a number of people just coming in and learning what they can learn and imparting what they can impart." Like other regions, police harassment did not encourage local people to "easily step up to be associated" with them or "suddenly just be available to do this kind of thing."[97] The BCP relied heavily on willing and available young activists to cope with bannings and detentions at times when events sparked more police action than usual. Many brought in to help had to quickly learn new skills. For example, Ramphele became the head medical officer of the Zanempilo Community Health Center only one year after qualifying as a doctor. She later took over Biko's role as branch executive when the police restricted him from working with the BCP in 1975. Many who moved to King William's Town were also connected in intimate ways. Ramphele initially came to the area to be near Biko (with whom she had two children). She was later joined at Zanempilo by Solombela, Chapman Palweni, and Sydney Moletsane, all former UNB medical students. The BCP also recruited Malusi Mpumlwana's sister, Vuyo Mpumlwana, to head the Njwaxa project, and Biko's brother-in-law, Mxolisi Mvovo, served as sales manager. Nohle Mohapi, the wife of SASO leader Mapetla Mohapi, worked as the branch administrator. In addition to these activists, neighbors, friends, and employees also became integral to the projects and activists in their own right.

The BCP included both female activists and women in rural villages in its projects in the Eastern Cape. This differed from SASO. Pumla Gqola and Magaziner have both examined the masculine discourse and imagery of SASO that seemed to allow only men the possibility of attaining political and social adulthood.[98] Ramphele described how the young women who participated in SASO had to become "one of the guys" or "be outrageous" to earn the right to participate.[99] In order to show SASO men that they did not take part only as girlfriends or to perform domestic chores at meetings, she and other female students such as Vuyelwa Mashalaba and Deborah Matshoba became aggressive debaters. They learned to be "assertive," "tough, insistent, persistent and to hold our own in public" in order to enter "the world of political discourse which had been until then inaccessible to us."[100] These women also adopted a bold, defiant style: they stopped wearing wigs like many other black women at the time, and let their hair grow in Afros; they condemned the use of skin lightening creams; they smoked cigarettes and wore "hot pants." Yet, although they challenged gendered social conventions with their personal behavior and fashion, they did not generally push for women's political or social liberation. According to Ramphele, those women who won a voice in SASO in some ways saw themselves as honorary males, a privileged group of a select few who gained special status.[101] Those who tried to organize as women were not supported by SASO men.[102]

While SASO failed to address women's issues and SASO women struggled to have a voice, the BCP did better at including women in leadership positions and addressing women's issues. In part, this inclusion of women resulted from a concerted effort; however, it mostly came as the BCP recruited people to help according to their skills and availability, especially in the aftermath of detentions. In the regional offices, the BCP employed many women as office administrators as well as program assistants, researchers, and project managers. For example, Daphne Mahlangu and Sam Moodley (Indian SASO student and Strini Moodley's first wife) were professional research and program assistants in the Durban office. Thoko Mpumlwana and Asha (née Rambally) Moodley served as the head editors of *Black Review*. Ramphele was the only woman to have a level of employment within the BCP as high as branch executive, but other women in the Eastern Cape headed projects, such as Vuyo Mpumlwana in Njwaxa. Pumla Sangotsha, a social worker, managed the finances at Zanempilo. BCP employees later implied that this involvement indicated that what mattered was not a person's gender but what he or she contributed. In interviews, some male activists stated the BCP invited contributions from everyone and that activists would work with anyone, regardless of age or gender.[103] The BCP also attempted to form at least one program directed specifically to women. In a Spro-cas planning meeting in 1971, it acknowledged that women had particular concerns. Penciled in next to minutes that the Spro-cas methodologies should involve new people were the words, "including women."[104] The BCP subsequently created a women's division designed to build women's leadership, headed first by Daphne Mahlangu, then by Adina Nobantu Ndamse (who ran a sewing project in Mthatha). In the end, this division did not amount to much.[105] In general, BCP projects ended up addressing issues particularly affecting women almost unintentionally simply because of the demographics and the needs of the communities where it worked.

Finally, sympathetic and supportive clergy in each area provided significant moral support and safe spaces to run projects. The Soweto mobile clinic was based at the Methodist Center in Jabavu and often visited Winterveld on the weekends, where it coordinated with a Catholic parish. The Adam's Mission gave land to the BCP to build its health center, and the Congregationalist Church housed the Natal regional offices in Umlazi. Biko's links to the Anglican Church proved extremely helpful in establishing the BCP in King William's Town. Biko's mother was a devout Anglican and well known by the clergy in the area. When Biko landed in King William's Town in 1973,

Reverend David Russell was living behind an old, unused Anglican church on Leopold Street. Russell worked under black Reverend James Gawe and headed some of the Border Council of Churches welfare programs (while also bringing attention to the plight of victims of forced relocation in Dimbaza). Gawe gave the BCP use of the Leopold Street church and allowed SASO, headed by Mapetla Mohapi, to use an office there as well, turning 15 Leopold Street into a central meeting place for activists and community members.[106] The Anglican Church also gave the BCP land to build the Zanempilo clinic and the Njwaxa leatherwork factory. Without this church support, the BCP may never have succeeded in establishing programs in the Zinyoka and Njwaxa communities.

CONCLUSION

As activists responded to circumstances and sought resources to carry out their ideas, they adapted their practices and changed direction. They adhered to their guiding liberation philosophy, but creatively drew upon various networks for ideas, finances, and human resources. Generally, this made them more effective in reaching black communities. At times they deliberately sought ways to improve their strategies, while at other times they changed their approaches in response to their circumstances. SASO students consciously adopted Freire's methods to improve their interactions with people on the ground. On the other hand, circumstances forced the BCP to take up more concrete action in small geographic communities, such as those surrounding King William's Town. Thus, as the BCP moved forward in its independent work in 1973, it still carried on with its publications, conducting research and compiling different volumes in King William's Town and Durban. The combination of intellectual publications and local programs addressing immediate material needs in the same organization was the result of the BCP's response to its limitations and opportunities. Activists also saw both approaches as extremely important to achieving liberation and development from various angles. The next three chapters, with their in-depth analyses of the BCP's major programs, show how each program could have an impact on both the self-perception and material conditions of black communities, yet to different degrees and with different routes to conscientization.

CHAPTER 3

Black Review

EVEN AS THE ORGANIZATION UNDERWENT A NUMBER OF CHANGES, the BCP continued work on its yearbook *Black Review*. Considered by activists as one of the BCP's major development projects, *Black Review* is important to understanding the vision they had for their community work. From 1972 to 1976, the review provided coverage of "activity by and against the black community" from what the BCP deemed an authoritative black perspective.[1] For BCP employees and activists, these types of publications were crucial for bringing about the kind of conscientization they were initially aiming for. The BCP's production of knowledge was designed to cultivate the self-confidence and critical consciousness it saw as necessary for black-led development. In other words, through publications like *Black Review*, the BCP sought to create a liberated black community—defined according to activists' political definition of "black"—capable of collective action. It also served as a practical tool for development. The BCP continued work on *Black Review* while it engaged in projects in local communities because praxis on the ground needed to be accompanied by continuing debate, evaluation, and coordination.

Black Review is also important in comparing the effectiveness of the BCP's different approaches to development. The precise impact of the review is difficult to measure. Publications and educational materials had a more diffused and intangible influence than the BCP's health and economic programs. Yet reports and interviews indicate that a number of activists and local community members viewed the yearbook as a trusted source of information and an inspiration, showing that it had a psychological and practical impact in at least some black circles. For some, such as Reverend S. M. Mogoba, a lecturer at the Federal Theological Seminary in Alice, "*Black Review* [was] like the Bible."[2] But the value of this project is not only determined by its final product. The process of producing *Black Review* was just as significant as the product. The yearbook proved that black people could independently make a substantial publication and spurred the growth in black publishing in the 1970s. It also changed the people involved in its production, particularly young men and women who gained professional skills along with a heightened critical consciousness.

BCP RESEARCH AND PUBLICATIONS FOR DEVELOPMENT

Like black-led economic development efforts, black publishing has a long history in South Africa. While certainly not all black writing was politically motivated, more often than not black writers and presses fit within the categories of the resistance or alternative press—that is, the noncommercial press focused on the mission of their publications rather than earning a profit.[3] Resistance through the press ranged from the more subtle literature focused on African life (such as Sol Plaatje's poems and novels[4]) to alternative news reporting and calls to political action. Les Switzer's, Karin Barber's, and David Atwell's volumes have shown that these black writers and publishers played an important role in shaping communities and resisting colonial or apartheid hegemony. Through writing, reading, and publishing print media, black authors fashioned and reconstructed identities, created forums for debate, and gave voice to the marginalized.[5] Many of those engaged in writing and publishing came from the black educated elite. As Atwell argued, these authors grappled with their relationship with modernity or the dominant culture of their time. Early authors, for instance, often aspired to the type of civilization touted by Western missionaries and colonial governments while at the same time affirming the value of African culture. In other words, they created an alternative modernity.[6] Barber's volume expanded the scope of literary history to include less visible writers of letters and diaries and everyday readers who engaged in writing and reading to make a better future for themselves and their communities. South African literary figures of the early twentieth century such as D. D. T. Jabavu and H. I. E. Dhlomo similarly viewed reading as essential for advancing black economic and political interests. They thus promoted libraries as important for broad black development.[7]

BCP publishing fits within this history of black writing and reading for community building. While Black Consciousness inspired significant literary production, the BCP focused on news reporting and opinion pieces to accomplish its purposes. As Benedict Anderson has argued, newspapers have been particularly important to imagining communities, as they portray disparate groups of people unaware of each other as part of a greater whole and create a sense of commonality with a shared readership.[8] Furthermore, as Barber highlighted, newspapers have also created forums for debate in these communities.[9] This is evident in South Africa's history. Beginning with mission presses, black authors used African-language newspapers to spread information, link the black intelligentsia of the time, and carry out political debates. For example, the Lovedale mission in the Eastern Cape published *Isigidimi* (1873–88), the Xhosa periodical once edited by John T. Jabavu. Jabavu, also an early ANC leader, later launched the independent Xhosa-language newspaper *Imvo Zabantsundu* in 1884. Jabavu's paper was joined by other independent African-language papers, including first president of the ANC John Dube's Zulu *Ilanga Lase Natal* (1903). Other black papers with strong political ties included Gandhi's *Indian Opinion* and the ANC's *Abantu-Batho*.[10]

In the 1920s and 1930s, black literacy and publications spread. In 1930, nineteen independent African newspapers catered to this growing black readership. However, the economic depression of the 1930s started to curb the independent black press. Recognizing the potential of black readership, large white-owned corporations bought out many presses. Switzer reported that by 1954, only seven independent African newspapers had survived this increase in commercialization.[11] While black newspapers could be "distinctly subversive," white commercial ownership of newspapers and presses along with increased state repression had the effect of tempering the content of many publications in the 1950s and 1960s.[12] Some independent newspapers, such as *Imvo Zabantsundu* and *Ilanga Lase Natal*, survived the economic depression and commercial buyout of the 1930s. These papers persisted into the 1960s along with some organizational newsletters and student newspapers. However, by the 1970s four holding companies controlled the news media—the Argus Company and South African Associated Newspapers (English-language), and Perskor and Nasionale Pers (Afrikaans and multiple magazines). These companies generally shied away from politically controversial news. To appeal to black readers, they produced township inserts that focused on sensational or human-interest stories. The major commercial periodicals serving the black community, *Drum* magazine and the daily *Bantu World*, enjoyed relative freedom to speak against the government in the 1950s. Many black authors found a voice in *Drum* and *Bantu World*. However, state action against the papers and their writers also tamed much of their content in the 1960s. The more politically linked publications fell victim to state censorship and bannings, just like the socialist *Guardian* and the Communist Party's *Inkululeko* a decade earlier.

By the early 1970s, the black alternative and resistance press in South Africa was stifled. Ecumenical and white liberal organizations led in publishing studies and position papers exposing the evils of apartheid. For example, the Christian Institute produced *Pro-Veritate*, and the SAIRR continued to publish its annual *Survey*. Spro-cas contributed its six commission reports to this body of literature along with studies such as Turner's book on participatory democracy, *The Eye of the Needle*.[13] Turner added to the liberal and radical academic production of knowledge in the 1970s, which sought to inspire change by exposing the roots of the country's exploitative economic relations.[14]

The BCP stepped into this lull in black alternative news publishing. By publishing reports and position papers in the 1970s, it joined multiracial and white liberal organizations printing information in order to bring about change in South Africa. Yet, like earlier black publications, the BCP hoped to accomplish more than just disseminate facts. It sought to give voice to new black views, to mold public opinion, and to chart a new course for the future. As Magaziner argued, Black Consciousness activists viewed speaking, writing, and reading as crucial activities because they believed that these actions allowed the oppressed majority to reconstruct themselves in new, positive ways.[15] Black Consciousness activists also saw the production of knowledge as vital for equipping black people with information and ideas to help them reach their full potential. Unlike political tracts or community newspapers that arose in the 1980s, the BCP saw publishing and community resource centers as development tools, related to politics but not directly political.[16] It was part of a more subtle conscientization process. While Freire had used discussion and debate to teach people to read, the BCP sought to provide those who could already read with "relevant" information to spark discussion and debate, with the same purpose of cultivating a critical awareness that would lead black people to work together to change their situation.

Black Consciousness adherents often stressed how scholarship written by white people about black culture and history damaged black self-perceptions. For too long the history of black South Africans had been "written by white people who [tended] to give a completely destructive account of black lives and events."[17] Biko wrote in the first edition of *Black Viewpoint*, "We have felt and observed in the past, the existence of a great vacuum in our literary and newspaper world. So many things are said so often to us, about us and for us but very seldom by us."[18] Black people emerged from these writings as backward and inferior and—perhaps even worse—as hapless bystanders in a history driven by others. Ramphele, for example, later wrote that for her, scholarship in the late 1960s and early 1970s tended to portray black people only as objects of research and victims of racism. It did not include black people in formulating research questions and did not help them see themselves as active agents.[19] Similarly, Jones remarked, "I think, even though [*Black Review*] was very rudimentary, it was a very important project in terms of how we understood our responsibility within our communities to start recording things. We understood the issue of history, that we needed to re[-]create or create the proper sense [of] the people doing work."[20]

Activists had poignant experiences with newspapers, a favored source for the 50 to 60 percent literate adult black population in the late 1960s and early 1970s.[21] *Black Review 1972* read: "Sensitivity of the black community has been highest in respect to [white] 'biased reporting' of events within the black community."[22] This was a personal struggle for Mafuna, who had joined a growing number of black journalists hired by white-owned newspapers in the late 1960s. The *Rand Daily Mail* had employed him to work on the paper's township section. Like other liberal newspapers, the *Rand Daily Mail* challenged apartheid and practiced it at the same time. It kept all of its black staff on township duty while the white staff continued to report on national and international politics, economics, and social issues. As mentioned, Mafuna resigned in 1972 after the copy editors repeatedly changed the wording of his articles from SASO's newly adopted term, "black," to what he viewed as a negative, dehumanizing term, "non-white."[23] It was possibly Mafuna himself in *Black Review 1972* who wrote that "concern has been expressed by most groups that blacks will never communicate effectively until they control their own medium."[24]

For activists, the issue here was not the type of medium—SASO and the BCP used the written word and a similar format as other publishers at the time. The problem was control of the medium. If black people could control the medium, activists believed they could produce knowledge about themselves from their own perspective that would be liberating, rather than limiting. Biko urged his fellow SASO members: "We are aware of the terrible role played by our education and religion in creating amongst us a false understanding of ourselves. We must therefore work out schemes not only to correct this, but further to be our own authorities rather than wait to be interpreted by others."[25] One of the first steps the students took toward correcting false understandings of black people and acting as their own authorities was to establish the *SASO Newsletter*. Initiated by Biko as

SASO's publications officer in 1970, the newsletter played a significant role in spreading Black Consciousness among black students and giving voice to young black writers, particularly poets. The newsletter updated students on SASO activities, expressed views on current events, and gave special reports on various African countries. As Mbulelo Mzamane and David Howarth demonstrate, this was part of SASO's effort to reconfigure blackness—to re-create an identity and community through writing and reading. It also was part of "phase one" conscientization.[26] Similar to Lembede, who taught that a positive African history was essential in ultimately achieving political freedom, SASO and the BCP believed that black people would play a more active role in shaping the future if they had a positive portrayal of their past and culture.[27] As Biko pointed out to his fellow SASO members, "There is always an interplay between the history of a people . . . and their faith in themselves and hopes for their future."[28] Khoapa wrote a few years later that black people wanted to know, "and must know, more about who they were and who they are if they are seriously concerned about *whom* they intend to become."[29] Publications like *Black Review* were thus a direct way to effect a psychological liberation in preparation for further development and liberation.

The BCP also saw its research and publishing programs as having the practical outcome of giving the black community the knowledge and skills necessary to devise strategies for improving their future. A basic step in enabling people and organizations to organize, analyze their needs, and mobilize their resources to address those needs was acquiring relevant information. Similar to Jabavu and Dhlomo, who saw the importance of reading material to black economic and political development, the BCP saw research and publication programs as "particularly important" in helping the black community "learn the things they want to know more about and to develop the skills they wish to acquire."[30] The BCP promised to focus on issues directly affecting the black community, to give them information applicable to their lives and useful for future action. For example, Khoapa described *Black Review* as designed to "project present trends" to enable leaders to "assess these directions in the light of societal conditions predicted for the future, determine which trends should be changed and identify the kind of interventions necessary to effect such changes."[31] As it compiled its publications and stocked resource centers, the BCP determined which materials were relevant according to its view of what constituted the black community. In doing so, it also attempted to create this community.

PROVIDING A BLACK PERSPECTIVE
AND RELEVANT INFORMATION

The BCP produced a number of publications to reach its goals. Its smaller volumes included collections of position papers and essays. *Black Viewpoint* was one such collection that had a more explicitly political tone. Only four editions made it to print: "Black Viewpoint" (1972); "Détente" (1975); "Apartheid: Hope or Despair for Blacks?" (1976); and "Transkei Independence" (1976). The second and third editions were banned and thus had to be destroyed. Planned fifth and sixth editions to address apartheid in sports and the 1976 uprisings never made it to print.[32] *Black Perspectives* was intended to be a volume that included in-depth studies generated by conferences with black scholars on "major areas of national life" such as education, theology, culture, history, and literature.[33] The BCP kept hoping to publish these collections of essays—even preparing one issue after holding a conference by the same name as the publication—but, as Khoapa put it, "the manuscript fell among the thieves" when the police confiscated BCP materials.[34] Police repression and a lack of funds thus crippled the BCP's two smaller publication initiatives.

The BCP's publication directly geared toward the practical purpose of increasing cooperation between groups was the *Handbook of Black Organizations*, a directory of black voluntary organizations working in the black community, published in July 1973. Echoing Mweli Skota's 1930 *African Yearly Register*, through this book the BCP hoped to "introduce" these groups to each other and the public in order to help them understand what "each . . . is involved in doing" and draw out the common elements of "self-help, self-reliance and self-determination."[35] Nearly one hundred pages long, it covered organizations ranging from cultural to professional, political, educational, religious, and welfare agencies. Each entry included the organization's purpose, constituency, programs and activities, publications, affiliations, and contact information. The BCP hoped that, together with the *Handbook*, it could act as a "central registry" and assist "community leaders like clergymen, social workers, teachers, sociologists, businessmen and administrators in the course of their daily work."[36] Instead of taking on every aspect of development and forming numerous organizations, the BCP could build and strengthen existing efforts by linking these groups through the *Handbook*. The BCP planned to update the handbook annually, but only published one edition because of financial constraints. In any case, *Black Review* fulfilled this purpose by updating people each year on the activities of black organizations working within the black community.

Black Review was the most successful and substantial of the BCP's publications. Like its other programs, the BCP expanded on what SASO did, but with the benefit of greater professional and monetary resources. Khoapa explained, "What I really wanted to do was to broaden the area of influence by moving beyond students and their affairs, and in fact focus on community and national affairs."[37] As a publication with this broader purpose, *Black Review* was relatively politically benign compared to the poems and essays featured in the *SASO Newsletter*. Still, by espousing a black perspective, it challenged "biased reporting" by the white-controlled press. In particular, *Black Review* responded to the white alternative press as embodied in the SAIRR's *Survey*. As Khoapa remembered, "we were naturally offended by the fact that there seemed like only one publication that was really well resourced."[38] The SAIRR produced its annual *Survey*, starting in 1946, to make the facts known about South African political, legal, social, and economic developments of the previous year. In the 1970s, the *Survey* reported on pass laws, health and welfare, bannings and movements in exile, education, housing, and employment, among other topics. A team of academics and SAIRR staff compiled the information based on newspaper and government reports, particularly the parliamentary register, Hansard. Its style was empirical, with minimal analysis accompanying the presentation of statistics, new legislation, or journalistic accounts of events. Its coverage was extensive, with volumes almost always exceeding three hundred pages. As such, it appeared as the authority on the state of South Africa. But Khoapa, Biko, and Mafuna saw it as dangerously biased.

The BCP claimed that *Black Review* provided a "black" perspective as an alternative to the *Survey*. What was this black perspective, and how did the BCP know what its so-called black community needed to know? At one level, a "black perspective" meant what black people, defined in the Black Consciousness way, viewed and thought. Thus, *Black Review* focused on the various opinions and experiences of Africans, Coloureds, and Indians— those who merely fit the mold by being racially discriminated against in South Africa. The review included various political perspectives, highlighted artists and authors from these different groups, and reported on events across regions. It also highlighted the work various black organizations did to economically or educationally uplift black communities. At another level, a "black perspective" also meant the perspective of those who accepted the new cultural and political definition of black championed by Black Consciousness activists. Despite its empirical style and inclusion of opposing viewpoints, the review favored the opinions and progress of those who promoted black psychological liberation and rejected white liberals and homeland collaboration. In formatting *Black Review* in this way, activists engaged in creating a new consciousness and a new community. Khoapa wrote, "[The concept of *Black Review* came out of] the need to make the Black Community aware of her total experience."[39] Similar to black news publishers of the past, the BCP attempted to tie people together under its definition of black and bring them to a mental acceptance of their membership in this community. It did this by targeting them as readers and linking them to what was happening to black people throughout the country. Black Consciousness activists working for the BCP deemed this kind of national black news as "relevant" information for the unified black community they envisioned.

At first glance, the content of *Black Review* differed little from the *Survey*, using a similar format while focusing on black people in fewer pages. Each edition was around two hundred pages long and covered a specific set of topics. It reported on the happenings of aboveground organizations, followed political developments, presented statistics, and reported on events related to black education and workers. Yet *Black Review* diverged from the *Survey* significantly in what it did and did not cover and the terminology it used. The terms *Black Review* used and the layout of the chapters obviously distinguished it from the *Survey*. Using the inclusive Black Consciousness definition of "black," *Black Review* departed from the *Survey* by not separating sections for Africans, Indians, Coloureds, and whites. For example, while *Black Review*'s education sections mirrored the *Survey*'s emphasis on data presentation with little analysis, the former merged African, Indian, and Coloured together. *Black Review* separated the education chapters only by different levels of education and teacher training. *Black Review* also combined Indian and Coloured artists and poets with Africans in its reports on arts and entertainment. Instead of using the *Survey*'s section titles, "Attitudes of Members of the Coloured Community" or "Political and Constitutional Matters: The Coloured, Indian, and African Population Groups," *Black Review* reported on "Government-created Platforms" or "Government-created Political Bodies," grouping all African, Indian, and Coloured government bodies together.[40]

Black Review restricted itself to activities by black people and against black people, and to issues directly affecting black people—the things that the BCP thought mattered most to black people.[41] It "noted" that "the white-controlled press tends to give priority either to events that occur within the white world or to those aspects of black life that make good reading for the white readership of newspapers."[42] Thus, instead of starting with white political parties like the *Survey*, *Black Review 1972* began by discussing the status of the government-created Coloured People's Representative Council and the South African India Council, set up to provide a sense of political participation within those respective groups. When it reported on the happenings of aboveground political, cultural, religious, and welfare groups actively working in the black community, the review only reported on organizations run by black people. For example, it updated its readers on the activities of the revived Natal Indian Congress (covering its souring relationship with Black Consciousness activists in 1972), and on the status of the Interdenominational African Ministers' Association's scholarship programs and the Association of Self Help's literacy program. In the 1975/76 edition, it announced that the Institute for Black Research and Institute of Black Studies had been established at the Edendale Lay Ecumenical Centre. Like the *Survey*, the review gave updates on state repression, outlining security legislation and reporting on political trials. Yet, again, it paid more attention to the black experience. For example, one of the political trials *Black Review* followed was the ongoing trial of SASO and Black People's Convention leaders. As SASO became more political, it staged a number of rallies in 1974 to show its support for the victory of Mozambique's FRELIMO against Portuguese colonialism. SASO and the Black People's Convention held the rallies despite the fact that the government declared them illegal. The state then arrested activists and put nine of them on trial. *Black Review* covered the two-year-long trial (which resulted in relatively short prison sentences for the accused). Each edition of the review also listed those detained and killed in detention in the previous year, similar to the *Survey*; however, the 1973 *Black Review* differed by sharing individual experiences of the banned, such as Joseph Kesimolotse Morolong, a forty-six-year-old ANC member and father of five confined to the remote Ditshiping Reserve west of Johannesburg for ten years and counting.[43]

Topics received varying degrees of attention depending upon what had happened during the year under review and what BCP employees saw as important. For example, the 1972 edition gave an extensive report on the black student strikes sparked by O. A. Tiro's inflammatory speech as Student Representative Council president at the University of the North at Turfloop. The 1973 edition had thirty-six pages on the momentous worker strikes centered around Durban. *Black Review* reported on black worker organization, wage gaps, and the negative effects of migrant labor in each edition. In early 1973, a strike by brick workers who gained a wage increase sparked an unprecedented wave of illegal strikes around Durban. The 1973 edition of the review described a number of these individual industrial workers' strikes and reported on their outcomes, including police action against organizers.

Because of the push for "separate development" in the 1970s, the status of each homeland government and land consolidation also received considerable coverage. *Black Review* reported on local politics as the apartheid state set up new legislative assemblies in these homelands. Transkei independence in 1976 gained considerable attention and debate, with Black Consciousness activists calling for the homeland governments to unite against apartheid. The yearbook also reported on inadequate agricultural and economic conditions in the regions, the status of foreign investment, and Bantu Investment Corporation promises to create thousands of jobs by investing in homeland industries. *Black Review* included much less on the foreign affairs of the white South African government in favor of focusing on developments in Namibia. Each issue concluded with a chapter on the struggle for Namibian independence involving the South African government, Namibian liberation movements, and the United Nations. For example, the 1975/76 edition had a number of pages describing the United Nation's ultimatum that South Africa withdraw from Namibia in 1976 and South Africa's exclusion of the South West African People's Organization from a constitutional conference.[44] The BCP saw all of these topics as the most pertinent for black South Africans concerned with their own liberation.

Black Review also significantly reported more on black achievements than did the *Survey*. By constructing an alternative narrative to the one promoted by the mainstream media and the government, activists attempted to build a new positive black identity and consciousness. One of the more noticeable additions of *Black Review* to the *Survey*'s coverage was a longer section on arts and entertainment. While both the *Survey* and *Black Review* gave comparable space to sports (*Black Review* of course covering more black athletes than the *Survey*), in the 1970s the *Survey* only included a limited section with "some notes" on writers, artists, and the performing arts. *Black Review*, on the other hand, had more substantial sections on black poets such as Oswald Mtshali, Mongane Serote, and James Mathews. It highlighted the work of groups such as the Theater Council of Natal (TECON) and the Cape Flats Theater Group (under the direction of Adam Small in the Western Cape). It described the content of plays, such as Port Elizabeth playwright Khayalethu Mqhayisa's *Confused Mhlaba* about the trials of a rehabilitated Robben Island prisoner.[45] It also reported on musical festivals and noted the growth in popularity of soul music and jazz and the success of black South African musicians like Hugh Masekela, Letta Mbuli, and Miriam Makeba. Black Consciousness activists themselves had a great interest in theater and poetry, and thus thought that black people wanted to learn more about black artists. By calling attention to black artistic success, they also hoped to instill a sense of shared pride among the broader black community.

Furthermore, those who worked on *Black Review* provided different black perspectives by including more black voices than the *Survey*. Like the *Survey*, *Black Review* used newspapers and government reports as sources of information, but BCP employees and volunteers also conducted interviews. As they became more experienced at compiling *Black Review*, field officers became more sophisticated at researching, reporting, and presenting various opposing viewpoints. For example, they tried to present both the student perspective and the opinion of school administrators after the strikes in 1972. They recorded firsthand accounts through interviews with Eastern Cape miners sent home after strikes on the mines in 1974 and 1975, and obtained a different perspective by talking with Sam M. Motsuenyane, the president of an organization of black businessmen, the National African Chamber of Commerce (NAFCOC). BCP employees also provided more critiques of state-created black leadership than the *Survey*. The 1971 *Survey* had a fourteen-page section entitled "Constitutional Development of the African Homelands, and Attitudes of Leaders There." It reported on the perspectives of "Africans elsewhere in the Republic" on all other issues in the same edition in a mere eight pages. These eight pages included the results of a newspaper poll, a survey of Soweto matriculants, and a study of the elite in an unidentified township on the Rand. It curiously also presented the opinions of some white "observers" and Chief Gatsha Buthelezi, one of the more outspoken homeland leaders from KwaZulu and founder of the Zulu Inkatha Freedom Party. To the *Survey*'s credit, it at least summarized SASO's position and Black Theology at the end of this section.[46] On the other hand, *Black Review* reported more in-depth on opposing black viewpoints on particular issues. It included as a subheading in the chapter on homelands in 1972 "Groups and Individuals against Bantustans," and often included a similar subheading in regards to the Coloured People's Representative Council and the South African Indian Council.

At the same time, while it generally maintained a factual tone, the BCP's yearbook also paid special attention to the particular interests of its authors, such as the spread of Black Consciousness and youth activity. When presenting black opinions or reactions, *Black Review* always included the opinions of SASO and the Black People's Convention—and sometimes only those opinions. In the 1973 edition, for example, the state of black theater was assessed according to how plays or theater groups measured up to Black Consciousness principles and how they related to white theater groups. In the 1974/75 edition, the Interdenominational African Ministers'

Association's acceptance of Indian and Coloured members was marked as "growth." In these cases, the hand of Black Consciousness activists in creating *Black Review* was clearly evident. Yet the BCP was less concerned about trying to present an objective report than the SAIRR. Like the *SASO Newsletter*, activists also used *Black Review* as a place to claim a voice. The opportunity to speak for themselves was one of the purposes of the publication after all. And they viewed the *Survey* as having a natural bias itself in how it presented information and the kind of information it included. The *Survey* also did not always strictly present carefully chosen facts. For example, when describing the pivotal NUSAS conference in Grahamstown in 1967, where black students had begun to challenge white leadership prior to forming SASO, the *Survey* deviated from its factual tone with a sympathetic parenthetical comment: "The turning point came at a conference in 1967 when (through no fault of Nusas) the African delegates were accommodated separately from the rest, in the African township."[47] The authors of the *Survey* used this space to justify adherence to apartheid laws in reaction to Black Consciousness criticism. On the other hand, *Black Review 1972* related the events from the perspective of the black participants (Biko was the editor at the time), making its description more "authentic" in the eyes of some.[48] But through its publications, the BCP also hoped to convert others to its point of view. Paradoxically then, by reporting on opposing viewpoints, *Black Review* recorded tensions within the broader black community that the Black Consciousness philosophy itself failed to fully acknowledge.

CREATING *BLACK REVIEW* AND CONSCIENTIZED, PROFESSIONAL YOUTH

Perhaps the more powerful impact *Black Review* had came not in its content but in what the creation of the publication signified at the time. Its production by black people undermined racist white notions of black inferiority. This could have had an effect on people whether or not they agreed with the Black Consciousness perspective that shaped the review. Producing the yearbook also empowered participants—editors based first in Durban and then in King William's Town, and the team of people the BCP recruited to help in these places and around the country. Creating *Black Review* involved young men and women who developed a heightened awareness of issues affecting their people and who gained writing and researching skills. The repressive political climate dictated the publishing options open to the BCP and restricted who worked on this project. At the same time, it opened up opportunities for young men and women to get involved.

The fact that a black organization produced *Black Review*, a substantial publication comparable to the *Survey*, proved to various white interests, black readers, and even the BCP itself that black people could publish a serious research publication. Peter Randall suggested that "for many people [white and black] it was a revelation that this kind of [work] was being produced within the black community in South Africa."[49] Khoapa remembered that when the BCP members first floated the idea, they had difficulties obtaining funding because they competed with the SAIRR's established and professional work.[50] Some did not have faith in the BCP's black enterprise. Yet Khoapa and his staff thought they should push ahead:

> We knew that there wasn't very much money running around. So, we wrote to Ford Foundation (and we heard the Ford Foundation was supporting the Institute of Race Relations in producing their *Survey*). And they fronted us by saying, "Yeah, well, you know, you're the top two. We consider it's going to be between yourselves and the Institute of Race Relations *Survey*." Now, already [Institute of Race Relations] publications had four senior executives and an editor and so on; we had nothing. But we said that, I think we must challenge this thing and we will start it with our news resources.[51]

Despite their inexperience and lack of funding (the Ford Foundation never delivered), they proceeded with the project, in part to prove they could. Mafuna had experience as a journalist, Khoapa in preparing reports, and Biko in producing the *SASO Newsletter*, but no BCP employee had ever produced an extensive book like *Black Review*. Yet, after conversations about the *Survey* and the need for a black perspective, they said to each other, "Why can't we do it?" Their youthful energy and confidence urged them forward. Mafuna remembered, "We discussed and we did it. We just put together people and ideas, and we worked day and night."[52] Within a few months, the first edition was ready for printing.

Like other BCP initiatives, compiling *Black Review* was a collective project that involved available friends, fellow activists, and family members. Since the BCP did not receive grant money to do the project the first year, its members had to recruit help and put in long hours of work. Biko and Mafuna were "at the heart of it" for the first edition of *Black Review*, but amassed an army of fellow students and activists who helped collect and organize information at the Beatrice Street office.[53] Khoapa explained, "We would get hold of students that have got nothing to do, bring them down here [Durban] and we would start doing the basic research. . . . We got them during December [school holidays]. One time they sat around and cut [news]papers."[54] One editor, Thoko (née Mbanjwa) Mpumlwana, described the research process as involving "a lot of extraction of information" relating to black people, first from regular newspapers, then from secondary literature and interviews. Available activists and BCP employees who had an "interest and ability to write" carried out this research in libraries, by monitoring the news, and by speaking to key people and organizations.[55] Some had more training and formal positions than others. Every edition had a central editor with a team of people assigned to focus on certain topics. The identity of the authors of individual chapters is unclear, since *Black Review* only bore the editor's name. Khoapa's name appeared on the 1972 edition, Mafika Gwala in 1973, Thoko Mbanjwa in 1974/75, and Asha Rambally in 1975/76. After the 1973 edition and the Eastern Cape branch had been established, the editor was based in King William's Town. The small town had become a hive of Black Consciousness activity. Centering the production of the BCP's most significant publication added to the action there. Yet some activists conducted research in different parts of the country, where they lived and worked. Jones, for example, wrote a section while based in Cape Town. Like others, he would "go to the libraries, sketch out things, catalog it, record it, speak to people, [even] go around the country."[56] In the "midst of all [the research]" the editorial team often held "small discussion groups" and workshops "in order to tease out the issues."[57]

The continued success of *Black Review* provided further proof of the ability of black South Africans to publish a viable alternative to works such as the *Survey*. In the introduction to the 1974/75 edition, Thoko Mpumlwana wrote, "the knowledge that this is a Black effort at presenting goings-on in the Black Community; presented with a Black perspective which naturally comes out of Black experience should be more gratifying to us."[58] For Thoko Mpumlwana, *Black Review* became "a show-piece that we can do it. [It was] almost like saying, 'Here, listen to our story, this is who we are as black people. We are capable of taking our destiny in our own hands.'"[59] This encouraged black creativity in writing and publishing in general. By speaking out and publishing works such as *Black Review*, activists claimed the space and the right to sound their voice. This gave other black authors and publishers confidence to do the same and inspired black writers, poets, and playwrights who contributed to the cultural renaissance flourishing at the same time. Matthew Keaney, for example, has charted the Black Consciousness influence on writers in Sowetan literary magazines, such as *The Classic*, *New Classic*, and *Staffrider*. The last of these, begun in 1978, was run by Black Consciousness–oriented writers who promoted socially relevant material, more egalitarian editorial practices, and connecting to the broader black public.[60]

Activists also influenced the journalism sector. Mafuna founded the Union of Black Journalists at the end of 1972 to help black journalists navigate the world of white-owned newspaper agencies and raise awareness about their role in helping or hurting the cause of liberation.[61] Activists also won over the editors and staff of the paper with the largest black readership, *The World*, which helped spread Black Consciousness ideology (and resulted in the detention of the editor, Percy Qoboza, and the banning of the paper in October 1977).[62] Scholars such as Dick Cloete have pointed to Black Consciousness publications as a catalyst to the "surge in black publishing activity" that followed in the late 1970s and 1980s. The black-owned and -run Skotaville press serves as a prominent example.[63] Black writers from the newly formed African Writers Association and black employees who left the progressive Ravan Press (founded in part by Randall at the end of Spro-cas) banded together in 1982 to form this "truly independent Black printing and publishing house."[64] The founders, such as Mothobi Mutloatse and Jaki Seroke, symbolically named the press after former ANC general secretary and publisher T. D. Mweli Skota.

As the BCP drew young men and women into the work on *Black Review*, these youth gained an informal education on social issues and the skills needed for research and writing. One of the students Khoapa put to work in Durban was Keith Mokoape, a UNB medical student. Mokoape subsequently left South Africa in 1972 with three other SASO students to engage in the armed struggle as part of the ANC. He served in the Umkhonto we Sizwe command in Botswana and Swaziland and, after 1994, became a general in the South African Defence Force. Khoapa remembered how Mokoape thanked him for his personal political education:

> [Mokoape] said, "Go and tell them you taught me the first thing of politics." I said, "How did I do that?" He said, "We were sitting around doing nothing one time at the SASO offices and you said you were looking for students to go and interview for some social institute study that [you] were making, and [you] gave us some forms and we went out to Clermont" (which is not very far from [Durban], in Pinetown). He said, "It was the first time I had actually spoken to an African woman in a family and asked her questions about her life in [the township]. At the time to you it was just like, 'Have you finished that?' But to me," he says, "it opened my mind for the first time to the life of a black person in South Africa. And I believe that my political education started from that time on."[65]

Mokoape's experience was related by Khoapa, and that probably was not the first time Mokoape had spoken to an African woman; yet this anecdote symbolizes the lessons young activists learned when asked to intently listen to their fellow black people. Just as Mangena wrote about the Winterveld project, contributing to *Black Review* conscientized these youth further about the plight of other black communities.

In King William's Town, the BCP benefited significantly from the work of a young woman. Thoko Mpumlwana began to contribute to BCP publications after the student strikes at Fort Hare in 1972. She was among the SASO students expelled for their activism. A letter from Fort Hare's rector permitted her to study through UNISA from her home in Zwelitsha. Unintentionally, this decision allowed her to become more involved at the BCP/SASO offices in Leopold Street in King William's Town. She continued her studies, but was not required to attend lectures, giving her time to volunteer for the BCP. "And," she added, "anyway I was too angry to really focus on reading." The BCP put her to work doing research for *Black Review*. She credited her involvement with the project for heightening her political awareness and critical reading of the news. She found working on *Black Review* "so exciting" because of the way the staff read and analyzed the news:

> But when you read a newspaper, it was not about reading the entire newspaper. You would actually focus on what is happening in the black community. What does the newspaper say? When you listen to the news, you are listening in as far as, in what way does this impact on the black community? In what way are black people mobilizing themselves? What are black people saying on various topics?

She also gained writing and analytical skills. She "always [tells] people about Steve's intervention" when she first attempted to write a report. Looking back later in life, this stood out to her as a critical moment in her personal development. She recounted how Biko helped sharpen her abilities:

> Here I was coming from university, thinking that I know it all and I was asked to write an article to review something. So I sat and I wrote. I gave it to Steve, "How is this? Have I articulated things properly?" He looked at it and said, "This is absolute nonsense!" [*laughs*] He said, "You better get your act together." And I was so fed up. He said, "No, you've got to learn to do it right." . . . But he made me realize that I had a lot to learn. He was good at coaching so he coached and . . . I improved in my writing, in my analysis, and in my ability. [*chuckles*] I really got it there. I didn't get it at Fort Hare.

Thoko Mpumlwana continued to describe Biko as strict. But while he maintained a high standard of work, he "went with you"; he took the time to show her how she needed to work.[66] So, although she was at first "fed up" with his criticism, in the end she was grateful for the way Biko pushed her to produce better work.

Thoko Mpumlwana quickly improved her skills, and the BCP began to pay her a small stipend for "subsistence and travel." Soon she became intimately involved in *Black Review*. The detention of BCP staff sped up this process as it necessitated the involvement of others in the publication projects. This was another reason that a number of people worked on *Black Review*. Thoko Mpumlwana stated, "Of course, those days, the difficulty was that we had to learn fast because the turnover was very high with people . . . being banned all the time." When the top "layer" working on a project was detained or banned, those working underneath that top layer had to "immediately take over."[67] The BCP prepared for this. "In fact," she added, "as part of our training in our work, we were to be always ready to take over any aspect of work at BCP because it was anticipated that the 'system' would try to destroy our work by imprisoning or banning people."[68]

Black Review had a different editor every year because of state actions taken against the BCP. Biko served as the first editor, but the state banned him just as the publication headed to the printers. This delayed distribution for one month since Biko's banning orders prevented his words from appearing in print. Khoapa assumed the editorship to allow its publication. Shortly after *Black Review* was distributed, Khoapa himself received banning orders. Mafika Pascal Gwala, an aspiring black poet and writer who later contributed to *Staffrider* and edited a number of poetry volumes, then served as the editor for the 1973 edition. Khoapa explained that they chose Gwala because he had the skills but was not a high-profile person and thus was less likely to be banned. "People like Mafika were just people that we knew that had the interest and ability to write, but were still safe enough as far as the system was concerned," he said. But Gwala "wasn't very easy to get a hold of" because he frequently moved around in various literary circles. In 1975, the BCP moved the editorial team to the King William's Town office, where Biko could be "close by (editorially speaking)" to the people who were "still growing," and could give "ready advice."[69]

Thoko Mpumlwana then served as the editor until she was banned in 1976. Asha Rambally's name appears on the 1975/76 cover under a blackened line where Thoko Mpumlwana's unmarried name, Thoko Mbanjwa, had been printed. With yet another editor banned, the BCP had to search for a replacement. At the conclusion of the trial of SASO and Black People's

Convention leaders in Pretoria in 1976, Biko and Ramphele asked Asha (née Rambally) Moodley to move to King William's Town to take the position as editor. Moodley grew up in the small town of Colenso in the Natal Midlands and became active in student theater groups during her years at the university college reserved for Indian students at Salisbury Island (later known as the Durban-Westville campus). She and her fellow student activists came to know Biko, Ramphele, Vuyelwa Mashalaba, and other SASO members after Biko invited their theater group to perform at the medical school. They quickly formed alliances because of their shared experiences and readings of the world. Moodley's group addressed black oppression and liberation in their productions that included music, poetry, and satires with titles such as "Black on White" and "The Resurrection." Moodley saw these multimedia productions as avenues for "speaking out"—"trying to tell our fellow students that we need to discuss things" and "ask for greater student freedom."[70]

Moodley earned a teaching degree and taught English in Clairwood and Chatsworth near Durban until school authorities used her pregnancy as an excuse to fire this teacher of "relevant" black writers and poets. She had been discovering new black authors, such as poet Oswald Mtshali, and encouraging her own students to write about their observations. She saw *Black Review* as fulfilling a similar purpose. It allowed black people to "express how they saw things and how they experienced things" and challenged the "norm where your experiences were written about by people who were not really part of the experience." Moodley's unemployment, like that of other young activists in 1973, made her available to work for the BCP. After she gave birth to her son, she was asked to research and write the sections on black sports and bannings and detentions for *Black Review 1972*. Even though she already had writing and organizational skills, like others who worked on the review, "that instinct for doing research was nurtured" through her work on the publication.[71] Her background in English education, her previous work on *Black Review*, and her approach to reading and writing about the black experience made her a good candidate for editor of the yearbook when Thoko Mpumlwana was banned.

Moodley "didn't really find it strange" to move to King William's Town because she was "back with friends," doing work she enjoyed with people she respected. The police, on the other hand, often asked her what a "curry girl" was doing there among African people.[72] Indeed, Moodley's appointment as editor is further evidence of the significant involvement of black people of all historical origins in the movement. It is also another example of the central role women played in many BCP projects. As women,

Moodley and Thoko Mpumlwana were not editors in name only. Although the BCP appointed them to fill positions made vacant by state repression and they too learned research, writing, and editing on the job, they also had skills and knowledge that qualified them for those roles. Many interviewees deferred to Thoko Mpumlwana on interview questions about *Black Review* because of her intimate involvement in the process. Moodley's education and previous work also put her in regular meetings with Biko and Thami Zani, who sought her advice on a planned publication entitled "Ten Years of Black Consciousness."[73] Moreover, both did not remember feeling hindered by the fact that they were women, although both admitted that perhaps they and other women "were just not aware [of discrimination] because we focused on what we were seeking to achieve."[74] When exploring the male-centered literary cultural production of the 1970s black renaissance, Bhekizizwe Peterson asked where the black women were.[75] Two of them were working on more academic- and research-oriented projects (though Moodley was part of the theater group in Durban, she was not a main playwright). While Black Consciousness men played prominent roles in more political action, behind-the-scenes positions like editor seemed to be more acceptable for women in general at the time. The SAIRR also had women working on publications in similar positions. In 1971, Ellen Hellmann, the chair of the research committee, offered a special thanks to the research officer, Muriel Horrell, for preparing the *Survey* for the previous twenty-one years.

Police action against the BCP affected who was available to work on *Black Review* as well as who was willing to print it. For the first two editions, the BCP benefited from its relationship with Peter Randall and the Christian Institute. Ravan Press printed the first edition. Randall's name contributed to the "Ra" in Ravan Press. The "va" came from the name of Danie van Zyl and the "n" from Beyers Naudé. Randall, van Zyl, and Naudé formed Ravan Press at the end of 1972 to act as the printer for Spro-cas and the Christian Institute with the view of evolving into a full publishing house. Ravan Press was one of three independent presses, along with David Philip and Ad Donker, that published radical works and supported black authors beginning in the 1970s. Ravan went on to produce "arguably the most substantial body of anti-apartheid literature—poetry as well as prose—and radical, innovative research."[76] One of the press's first and more successful titles, *Cry Rage*, a collection of poems by James Mathews, sold out and was in a second round of printing when it was banned. Ravan also made possible various other popular, social, and historical works. The materials Ravan published are indicative of Randall's and Naudé's support of various anti-apartheid movements, but particularly the Black Consciousness movement.[77]

When Ravan Press stopped printing and focused on publishing, the BCP turned to printers with Christian ties. Zenith Printers, launched by the Christian Institute, printed the second edition of *Black Review*. Lovedale Press printed the third and fourth editions. Located in Alice, it was close to the BCP offices in King William's Town, where the editorial team was based during those years. This mission-based press also had a history of publishing black authors (albeit a complex one)[78] and was more prone to printing academic books—that is, when, as Jones put it, those books were not "too hot." Lovedale considered *Black Review* less political at first. Its factual presentation did not call directly for political action. However, after the 1976 student uprisings increased the possibility of political repercussions, Lovedale Press was reluctant to print a BCP publication. Printing anti-apartheid material could be expensive for presses forced to recall publications of a banned person, destroy works already printed, or spend hours blacking out passages by banned individuals. Lovedale thus declined to print the 1976/77 *Black Review* issue. Jones did not remember that the press did it in an "ugly way." The press managers just explained that they "always have attracted problems when we issue these things" and did not want to invite more police intervention.[79] Whereas Ravan and Zenith were willing to print *Black Review* because of its content and purpose, Lovedale would not. Ravan and Zenith supported the rising alternative press in the 1970s, but this mission press wanted to ensure its survival, so stuck to printing safe material.

DISTRIBUTION AND IMPACT

Once *Black Review* made it through the printers, the next step was to distribute it. The BCP's target audiences were black people in the townships and black organizations that could use the information in formulating strategies for the future. The challenges the BCP faced in printing, funding, and distributing *Black Review* limited its contributions to community development. The BCP had to rely on its funders to subsidize the publication and had to distribute it on its own. There was also a disconnect between the product and part of the intended readership. Yet despite its limitations, there is evidence that *Black Review* did provide information for a number of people, encourage black pride, and spark discussions. BCP resource centers in Umlazi and King William's Town helped the BCP reach a broader audience by making the raw materials and finished product of *Black Review* available along with other "relevant information."

Black Review "was never going to be a business proposition," Khoapa explained, since distribution was always a problem.[80] Bookshops would not sell it because of fear of attracting police attention and the lack of a market. Randall explained how Ravan Press itself "limped along" in its first years of existence because of the indirect restrictions the state placed on it through "the fear of the book sellers to stock its titles." Describing a familiar story for alternative and resistance presses at the time, he said, "Bookstores were actually visited by the security police and told, 'You don't stock that sort of stuff, otherwise there will be problems.'"[81] Moreover, at the time, few bookstores catered to black people, partly because of basic market concerns. As mentioned, Switzer estimated that adult African literacy rates in 1970s South Africa hovered from 50 to 60 percent.[82] This was an increase from 35 percent in the late 1950s, but with an estimated average income for African working men between R13 and R32 per week in 1973, and 61 percent of African female workers earning less than R10 per week (with only slightly higher figures for Coloured and Indian people), the black majority would have had little money to spend on nonessential books.[83] Khoapa further explained, "The population that we were aiming this thing at just could not afford even the purchase of a SASO newsletter" (sold for ten, then twenty and thirty cents). Even "very highly motivated" students with great interest in SASO's newsletter could not always afford to buy it.[84] *Black Review* sold for much more. The 1972 edition cost R2, and the price rose with subsequent editions, selling for R3 and R4. Selling a two-hundred-page English-language book in townships—where most readers and consumers of mass media lived—would have been difficult. Even in Ciskei urban areas, where people preferred reading English news sources and mission education had produced more people with formal education, *Black Review* had to compete with cheaper newspapers or essentials like food.[85] Some institutions and individuals bought the book. "But," Khoapa remembered, "otherwise the community itself, which was the one that we were much more concerned about, that people must actually read this in the townships and so on, they couldn't afford it."[86]

Because the publication was not going to make a profit, the BCP subsidized *Black Review* and distributed it on its own. The main goal was just to get the publication out to people. The first line of distribution of anywhere from eight hundred to two thousand copies printed was black institutions or organizations "of all kinds."[87] This would have included welfare organizations or those listed in *Black Review* such as the Association for the Educational and Cultural Advancement of African people and the Interdenominational African Ministers' Association. Free copies went to strategic institutions the BCP wanted to influence or inform about its philosophy, including university libraries and embassies.[88] Individuals who could afford it bought *Black Review* from the BCP directly at its offices, by mail, or at political meetings. Jones remembered selling it at Black Consciousness gatherings and meetings of sympathetic organizations.[89] In an effort to reach "the public at large" the BCP sent copies to the South African national library. At other times, university libraries or organizations such as the SAIRR bought copies.

Reaching a wider audience in the townships challenged the BCP. Assessing the impact on the "public at large" also poses problems. First, if the BCP kept track of distribution numbers, those records were confiscated by the security police. Both Ravan and Lovedale Press records have been difficult to locate as well.[90] On the other hand, distribution numbers do not always indicate how many people read or are influenced by a certain publication. One copy of *Black Review* could have been read by multiple people—the buyer's family, friends, and neighbors. Furthermore, government censorship often had the unintended consequence of raising the profile and interest in a publication. Banning a book prohibited its further circulation, but also often increased its readership as people would want to know what the government did not want them to read.[91] Then there is the question of measuring the publication's influence on those who read it. Unlike community newspapers in the 1980s or organizational newsletters such as *SASO Newsletter*, *Black Review* was not focused on politically mobilizing a narrowly defined audience. Rather, it sought to stimulate debate and dialogue and change black South Africans' perspectives. Gauging its influence on individual ways of thinking and acting is more difficult when the desired result is not linked to easily measurable outcomes such as membership or participation in particular events.

Even so, memories and some reports of BCP employees indicate that *Black Review* and other BCP publications did reach different audiences and had a fairly large readership. Khoapa characterized the first batch of the yearbook as "library copies" since libraries were the first to buy the review. Activists, academics, or other interested individuals followed. It is possible that these copies reached thousands of people. Khoapa estimated that Ravan Press printed just under one thousand copies of the first edition; however, Randall believed this may be a conservative number since Ravan Press had a usual print run of two thousand to three thousand copies at the time.[92] The BCP estimated that each copy would have circulated to between ten and fifteen people in libraries or through individuals.[93] If this indeed was an accurate number, even if five hundred copies of *Black Review 1972* were circulated in this way, it could have been read by between 5,000 and 7,500 people or more. Malusi Mpumlwana estimated that the BCP ordered almost double the number of copies of the 1972 edition for the second and third editions.[94] However, Khoapa thought that the first edition was the most popular. He speculated that *Black Review 1974/75* did not sell as well because of the fear of police harassment and the lower quality of the edition—the position of chief editor had been temporarily vacant before Thoko Mpumlwana stepped into it, which affected the end product.[95] Yet while state censorship may have limited circulation, the numbers of those who read later editions could have increased by over five thousand or more.

As it circulated through libraries and grew in popularity, *Black Review* became a trusted source of information on black activities in South Africa for some black academic circles. As a thick annual review, it is more likely that the book would have been read by people in this audience. The BCP itself claimed that the hundreds of copies of the 1972 edition had been used by "public libraries, educational and research institutions, students of race relations, and individuals interested" in black community development.[96] Thoko Mpumlwana stated that once they sent the book to libraries, "What they did with them, we don't know," but they heard that students and other groups used the book as a reference and the basis for discussion groups. She wrote of how she heard Reverend S. M. Mogoba, lecturer at the Federal Theological Seminary (and BCP board member), tell others that *Black Review* was "very useful whenever he and his colleagues had to talk about any field of black experience in any gathering," leading him to declare that the publication was "like the Bible."[97]

Mogoba appreciated *Black Review*'s content focused on black people and the amount of information it covered. As a BCP board member, Mogoba also adhered to the perspective it took. His opinion and use of the yearbook are indicative of how the publication reportedly also informed discussions of events, initiatives, and developments by organizations and activists in Black Consciousness circles. Roughly between 1972 and 1976, Jones was involved in various Black Consciousness organizations while living in Cape Town, where he ran projects in his own community and neighboring areas. When remembering how he was involved with SASO and other organizations at the national level, he described how they "were connected in ongoing discussions, and exchanging ideas." Many times, the material for these discussions came from *Black Review*.[98] Evidence does not reveal exactly how the publication informed debates or discussions, but Mogoba's and Jones's above comments imply that activists and academics turned to it for information when assessing the situation of black people in the country. Given the review's focus on the spread of Black Consciousness, activists very likely also turned to the publication to analyze the influence of their philosophy. Furthermore, the publication could have inspired some community action by reporting on the activities of educational, cultural, welfare, and religious groups working in black communities. If people knew that the Association for Self-Help planned to run a communal buying scheme, for example, or that the Edendale Lay Ecumenical Centre had expanded its hall to include women's craft groups and agricultural projects, they might borrow these ideas or make efforts to coordinate with these other groups. Among black academics and community organizations then, *Black Review*, available in libraries and at conferences, provided trusted information and inspired discussions and debates. In this sense, it reached its goal of contributing to development by helping those groups evaluate current events and efforts in order to determine the most appropriate future action to take. It also most likely helped build a sense of community among activists inclined toward Black Consciousness.

While *Black Review* was intended for a national audience, there is also a very local aspect to the BCP's research and publications programs. One of the BCP's goals falling loosely under these programs was to establish community resource centers. The BCP distributed and promoted its publications in these regional centers connected to its branch offices. This helped activists reach their most important audience—local community members. The BCP intended to train future leaders and "promote black creativity, self-reliance and a sense of purpose" by offering "facts and figures" and other information on "black life" at these centers.[99] This included collecting and displaying "black cultural artifacts" such as beadwork, woodwork, paintings, and sculpture, as well as developing a library of black poetry, music, speeches, talks, and papers (of course on what the BCP itself deemed as "relevant topics").[100] They also proposed to "collect for general readership all publications by black people in South Africa, the rest of Africa and other parts of the world."[101] The centers were open for people to "come and read, refer, borrow, and list materials of importance."[102] They were open for professionals for "informal tutoring" and served as after-school centers where high school and university students could study.[103]

BCP offices all acted as informational hubs, but the BCP opened official resource centers in Umlazi, in King William's Town, and later in Soweto. For interested community members, resource centers became libraries of information and places to "meet and talk."[104] The BCP employed a full-time supervisor to manage each of these centers, including women such as N. Made in Umlazi and Nomsa Williams in the Eastern Cape. The King

The interior of the King William's Town Resource Center. (*Source*: BCP Limited, "Projects and People," 1977, UNISA Archives, Documentation Centre for African Studies, ACC 20 Black Community Programmes.)

William's Town center occupied the main hall of the Leopold Street church that housed the BCP offices. In 1976, the BCP described this resource center as a focal point for educational activities and a library for the public. The Umlazi center offered the same services, but expanded to also provide space for conferences held by professional, self-help, church, social welfare, and cultural groups.[105] The BCP hoped that community members would utilize the centers to buy or read material like *Black Review*. The centers held printed copies of the publication as well as collections of newspapers employees had compiled during the research process. In addition, patrons could access other educational, literary, and musical materials. Similar to the libraries Jabavu and Dhlomo promoted decades earlier, the BCP hoped these kinds of centers of information would contribute to the overall development of the black community and the promotion of a black civil society.

Local people had an interest in the centers, which saw a fair amount of traffic. This went beyond just the easily visible intelligentsia. Again, as Barber has argued, more obscure writers and readers in Africa have long been engaged in widespread activities. Examples of "everyday literacy" in her volume prove that Africans across the continent have taken on "local, do-it-yourself archiving" like the BCP to open new spaces for promoting literacy for collective and individual betterment and the creation of new social beings.[106] If Switzer's study of Ciskei media in the 1970s is any indication of the interest the black community in South Africa had in alternative news sources, many people who lived near BCP offices were likewise hungry for a black perspective on current events and would have been attracted to its resource centers.[107] According to Jones, Malusi Mpumlwana, and Khoapa, youths (particularly high school and university students), teachers, and other people with the interest, time, and ability to read, visited the centers. Nohle Mohapi, then the branch administrator, described those who came to the resource center in King William's Town as "teachers, religious people, students, community members," even journalists. "So," she concluded, "it was a really community program [*sic*]."[108]

Black youths who hung around the resource centers and BCP and SASO offices became conscientized or politicized through their exposure or involvement there. They may not have had the money to purchase a copy of *Black Review*, but one copy held at a resource center could have easily passed through the hands of dozens of high school and university students. Other literature, materials, and discussions held at the center would have added to this informal education. One such youth who frequented BCP offices was Luyanda ka Msumza, a studious, politically active high school student and neighbor to the Biko family in Ginsberg. When interviewed in 2008, he still owned copies of *Black Review*. As a young man, "it was a piece of [available] work" that he could digest. For him, *Black Review*'s significance was twofold. He viewed it as "giving a new voice and a new dimension" to government reports and white media coverage so that one could have a "comprehensive picture of the happenings within the country." He also said it portrayed people as "champions of their own destiny." Whereas the *Survey* seemed to focus on "the suppression and the oppression," *Black Review* portrayed people like striking workers as proactively addressing their problems. Msumza acknowledged his bias in assessing the importance of *Black Review*. He knew the people who produced it and as a high school student who admired their views and work, "looked at them with some awe and envy."[109] Still, his comments suggest that hundreds of others who frequented BCP resource centers and read *Black Review* also valued its particular black perspective, found trusted information, and gained pride in their black community after reading about the activities and achievements of black South Africans.

CONCLUSION

Through both the product and process of publishing *Black Review*, the BCP challenged the apartheid paradigm. Completely directed and carried out by black people, the publication was powerfully symbolic of black success in the production of knowledge. It helped promote subsequent black publishing and empowered young students and women with new skills and professional experience. But the broader aims of the BCP's publication program—to provide relevant information for conscientization, evaluation, and development—were not widely achieved. *Black Review* directly targeted the formation of a critical consciousness and creating a black community more capable of coordinated action. This type of conscientization was less a part of local health and economic projects that addressed more immediate material needs. Yet these programs were arguably more successful in reaching the BCP's goals. Although those involved in these local initiatives may not have reached the kind of sophisticated political analysis the BCP sought to achieve with *Black Review*, the BCP had a deep impact on their self-perceptions and self-reliance by addressing their material challenges in a people-centered way.

CHAPTER 4

The Zanempilo Community
Health Center

WHEN MZWANDILE MANYELA'S WHITE EMPLOYER DROVE HIM HOME
to Zinyoka one day and saw the village's clinic, he exclaimed: "This isn't a
clinic, this is a hospital!" Manyela added: "*Tyhini*! That was the truth."[1] Other
Zinyoka residents interviewed in 2008, like Nosingile Sijama, expressed the
same opinion. Sijama explained: "It was like a hospital, you see, it was big.
It wasn't a clinic. It wouldn't close like a clinic. . . . It had everything. . . .
There were doctors—there were doctors, my child. The doctors were very
good and so were the medicines."[2] The high-quality health care offered at
the BCP's Zanempilo Community Health Center rapidly attracted patients
from Zinyoka and surrounding villages in the mid-1970s. In Xhosa, Zanempilo means "to bring health" or "bringing health." To the patients who attended
the clinic, this was a fitting name.[3] For others, the center brought more than
just physical health, but the other meaning of the word "*impilo*"—life. For
some Zinyoka residents, the clinic's importance lay in the economic opportunities it provided. As Dina Mjondo, a member of the clinic's women's craft
group, said, "We ate because of the clinic and our children were educated
because of the clinic."[4]

The BCP sought to bring much-needed health care to black South Africans through a comprehensive approach linked to its guiding philosophy of
liberatory development. Its human and financial resources helped it offer
a remarkable range of services to address the root causes of ill-health at
Zanempilo. As these shared memories indicate, this had a profound impact
on both the psychological state and material circumstances of Zinyoka residents. Empowering wage-earning opportunities, combined with health care

with a "more human face," bolstered the sense of self-worth of many villagers.[5] As with its other initiatives, the BCP's actions were also shaped by what it dealt with on the ground—the needs of the communities and political hostility. Not everyone in Zinyoka felt the same way about Zanempilo. For example, Sijama's husband tried to drive the BCP out of the village. The BCP responded to the needs of the Zinyoka community and the challenges it faced by drawing on its networks of fellow activists, neighbors, and well-connected friends, plus funding from an Afrikaner heiress and the Anglo American Corporation. Like the *Black Review*, the project also changed people unintentionally. Through the work of its employees, Zanempilo contributed to changing perceptions of the abilities of black women and the aspirations of educated, professional youth.

BLACK CONSCIOUSNESS, HEALTH, AND THE POLITICS OF HEALTH CARE

Most of SASO's community development projects involved medical students volunteering at clinics, and every regional branch of the BCP had a clinic or community health center. This relationship between health initiatives and Black Consciousness did not develop because of something within the philosophy that was specific to health or healing. It came from the broader goals of the activists, their approach to development, and the fact that Biko and many others were medical students. In the late 1960s and early 1970s, medical students often chose to be nurses or doctors because these were among the limited options for successful black students seeking a good profession.[6] SASO students, once converted to Black Consciousness, began to view their education as giving them needed skills to answer one of the glaring needs of their people. This carried over into the BCP. Malusi Mpumlwana explained, "It just so happened that in the case of Black Community Programs, which is where we were in King William's Town . . . Steve [Biko] himself had been a medical student. And there he was. And his girlfriend, Mamphela [Ramphele], was a medical graduate."[7] One of the BCP's first health projects thus focused on building a primary health care clinic run by black people.

Black Consciousness activists knew well the grim state of health and Western health care for black South Africans. This was directly tied to contemporary racist government policies, though not completely dominated by it.[8] At the same time South Africa could boast of the first successful open heart surgery performed at Groote Schuur Hospital in Cape Town in 1967, much of its population suffered from diseases of malnutrition or easily prevented diseases such as tuberculosis, made more communicable by poor living and working conditions.[9] Infant mortality rates, often used as an indicator of a society's health, are unreliable and spotty for black South Africans in the 1960s and 1970s (African births and deaths were not generally registered); yet estimates and statistics regarding the number of available doctors and health facilities indicate an extreme discrepancy between the health of white and black South Africans. For example, in the 1960s and 1970s the infant mortality rate for white South Africans decreased from 30 per 1,000 births, to 21.[10] In contrast, those classified as Africans suffered a rate six times higher than white South Africans. Estimates for Africans in the 1960s and 1970s ranged from 140 to 180 deaths per 1,000 births. It was much worse in the homelands, with an estimate of 250 in the rural Ciskei in the early 1980s.[11] Structural poverty led to high rates of malnutrition among rural black populations where few Western-trained doctors, black or white, worked. The World Health Organization (WHO) estimated that 58 percent of black deaths were caused by malnutrition and gastroenteritis and that only 2 percent of all doctors worked in the homelands in 1972.[12]

Black people often had to travel to seek Western medical care in clinics or urban hospitals, which did not have adequate space, equipment, and supplies for black patients. Malusi Mpumlwana remembered the serious lack of dental care for black people in Mthatha in the early 1960s. No African dentists worked in the Transkei homeland at the time. The white dentist only saw white patients, except for twice a week—on Mondays and Thursdays—when he would see a limit of fifteen black patients at the local hospital. It did not matter how many people waited or needed care, the dentist only saw fifteen. Malusi Mpumlwana described how people dealt with these circumstances:

> From across all the villages of Mthatha you knew that your chances—it's like a lotto. And if you were not there, if you're there as number sixteen, you [had lost]. Now, of course . . . people slept there the day before. This is Sunday—there is no public transport—you'll find a way anyway to get there and arrive late in Sunday afternoon to discover that you are number sixteen. You've got no way of going back to your village [at that time] . . . [so, you'll wake up] in the morning and go back and try to arrive on Thursday or come back on another day. That was the lot of black people at the time.[13]

Black people across South Africa had similar experiences, though conditions varied for Coloured, Indian, and African people, according to apartheid's racial hierarchy. Health practitioners were often restricted to serving people from their own apartheid racial category. With limited opportunities for Western medical education for black South Africans, this left black people severely disadvantaged. In 1972, the doctor-to-population ratio for white people was estimated at 1:400. It was more than double for Indians, at 1:900, while for those categorized as Coloured, it was 1:6,200. For Africans, the ratio was 1:44,400—that is 44,000 more people per doctor than the white population.[14] With 111 times more Africans than white people per doctor, access to care and opportunities for formal training were clearly weighted heavily in favor of the white population. "That section of the population which '[suffered] from the diseases of comfort and over-eating' enjoy the privilege of five medical schools," the BCP reported in 1974. But doctors from the black population that suffered from "malnutrition and poverty" could only train at UNB in the 1970s.[15] Black nurses, trained in greater numbers in the 1960s and 1970s, often served alone on the front line of health care in black communities, particularly in rural areas.[16]

As in many places across the African continent and the world, access to health care depended on a person's socioeconomic status and geographic location. Factors limiting one's access to adequate care included transportation, availability of personnel, the quality of equipment and medicine, as well as money needed to pay for services. Black South Africans in homelands grappled with these socioeconomic challenges more intensely than others did. Most homeland residents endured the effects of migrant labor, decreased agricultural sustainability, unequal economic development, and unemployment. Women and children suffered disproportionately. Wives, children, and the aged left behind by migrant workers relied on the wages of absent family members, meager pensions, or charity giving. There were virtually no wage-paying jobs in the villages, and most people could not support themselves through farming. These factors all contributed to a high incidence of tuberculosis, typhoid, and kwashiorkor and marasmus (diseases of malnutrition among children).[17]

If stark poverty was one strike against the health of homeland residents, state neglect was another. In the early 1940s, a radical movement in social medicine had emerged in South Africa and inspired government consideration. Drs. Sydney and Emily Kark, for example, headed the pioneering Pholela Health Center in southwestern Natal that de-emphasized medical specialization and technical hospital care, trained local black health assistants, and tried to cooperate with so-called traditional African healers.

For a moment, the medical profession and government seemed poised to significantly extend health care to rural and urban communities all over South Africa. Yet a lack of political will, hostility from certain medical practitioners, and the imposition of apartheid led to the abandonment of these initiatives.[18] In the late 1960s and 1970s, the South African government focused more on building the capacity of urban hospitals that offered curative medicine with high-tech equipment. Aside from a few hospitals like the famous Baragwanath (Soweto) and Groote Schuur, most served mainly white people.[19] In 1965, there were eighty-five hospitals in all of the homelands with a total of 13,600 beds, as opposed to 21,953 beds available for a much smaller white population. In 1972, the SAIRR reported the ratio of hospital beds as 10 beds per 1,000 white people and 5.57 beds per 1,000 people of color. The ratio of beds to population was worse in the homelands, with 3.48 beds per 1,000 people in 1973.[20] Rural clinics were few and far between and lacked supplies and personnel, particularly doctors. Mission stations (numbering eighty-five in the homelands in 1965 and increasing to ninety-three in 1973) provided hospitals in rural areas, but relied on government subsidies in the face of financial trouble and were for the most part taken over by the government beginning in 1973.[21]

In the Ciskei, conditions were as bad as in other homelands. Clinics were scattered ten to twenty miles from each other, requiring some patients to walk long distances for care. This would be a seemingly insurmountable feat for some, especially pregnant women about to give birth. Patients arriving at clinics would often find only two nurses (instead of the stipulated eight) and would rarely see a doctor.[22] In 1980 in the Ciskei, even after an initiative to build more clinics, there were only eighty-one clinics (ninety if mobile clinics and subclinics are included) and five hospitals for a population estimated at 55,306.[23] According to Switzer, the Ciskei had half of the minimum number of beds per Africans set by South Africa's Department of Health and a ratio of one doctor to every 8,707 individuals.[24] Mission hospitals that offered services in the rural Ciskei in the 1970s included Mount Coke, St. Matthews, and Lovedale. These hospitals struggled with funding, equipment, and a high volume of patients. The few ambulances in operation were difficult to maintain because of poor road conditions. The ambulance from St. Matthews reportedly was "so unreliable that it is not unusual to wait nine hours for it to arrive, and in bad weather it does not attempt the journey." The nursing sisters often had no vehicle, and "in urgent cases they [walked] to villages."[25]

A further burden was placed on homelands with a shift in policy by the apartheid state in the 1960s toward homeland self-governance. Health care

Clinics & Hospitals In The Ciskei by 1980

Thornhill
Sada
Cape
Seymour
St. Matthews
Keiskammahoek
Alice
Frankfort
Zanempilo
Middledrift
King William's Town
Njwaxa
Mdantsane
Mount Coke
Ciskei
Peddie
N
W E
S
Indian Ocean

Settlement
Clinic
Hospital
Highway
Land Outside Ciskei
25 miles

Map designed by Christopher Greenmun

(*Source:* Adapted from a map that originally appeared in Saldru, *Health and Health Services in the Ciskei*, 23.)

services that had previously fallen under the jurisdiction of the Department of Bantu Affairs were turned over to newly created homeland departments of health and welfare that relied on subsidies from Pretoria for funding. These health care services became increasingly inadequate as thousands of people were forcibly resettled in homelands within a few short years. Resettlement in the Ciskei resulted in areas still considered rural "because of their remote geographical location which is generally the countryside" becoming as densely populated as urban areas.[26] The existing health care system could not adequately serve its people, let alone absorb those dumped there beginning in the mid-1960s. As Switzer reported, although the Ciskei had increased the number of beds in hospitals and clinics in the 1970s, the proportion of those beds to the population virtually stayed the same, increasing only slightly from 2.1 per 1,000 in 1946 to 2.3 per 1,000 in 1980.[27]

To address these glaring problems, SASO and the BCP set out to provide primary and preventive community health care. This was of course not the first time black South Africans had experimented in community health care. Early, politically involved black doctors, such as Alfred Xuma, had committed to extend health care to their people in townships and rural areas from the late 1920s.[28] In the 1940s, the social medicine movement led to a change in medical education approaches. In 1949, Sydney Kark established the Institute of Family and Community Health at Clairwood to train community health workers. This merged in 1956 with the Department of Preventive Family and Community Medicine (established a few years earlier) at the University of Natal.[29] Yet by the time the first SASO generation of medical students arrived at UNB, the national social medicine movement of the 1940s and 1950s had dissipated. At that time, South African Western medical education focused on curative care in urban hospitals with little attention to community or social medicine.[30] Thus, a commitment to serve their people and their philosophy rather than the type of medical education they received led Black Consciousness activists to focus on primary and preventive community health care.

Aside from the lack of education in community primary care, activists and BCP employees had confidence in their training in so-called Western medicine or biomedicine. Despite the Black Consciousness call to embrace black or African values, doctors and nurses who worked for the BCP said they did not incorporate African healing practices in their work. Activists used general ideas about how to view patients in their "totality" from African medical practices, but otherwise "understood" that the medicine they learned in school "was the correct care."[31] This reflected their new black identity based more on a political and cosmopolitan definition of black rather than a strict adherence to local African culture.[32] It also reflected what they saw as most important in community development. As with their other projects, the BCP and SASO were not as concerned with the specific type of health care delivered, but more concerned with the end result—how it affected people. In running their health programs, they focused on ensuring people had access to care so as to enable people to exercise greater self-reliance.

Black Consciousness activists came to believe that as a "basic component of living," health was "a fundamental requirement for community development." Indicative of their goal to develop a person in his or her totality, they defined health as a "state of complete physical, mental and social well-being."[33] In line with their philosophy that emphasized self-reliance and Freirean methods of developing a critical consciousness, they sought to get at the root causes of ill-health and help people take charge of their own lives. Thus, they focused on primary and preventive health care instead of just curative care, and the BCP's health centers, Zanempilo and Solempilo, spawned additional economic, educational, and agricultural projects.

Yet Zanempilo, the BCP's first and most successful health initiative, did not start off as a full-fledged community health center designed to completely remake the village of Zinyoka. What the BCP encountered as it implemented its plans and interacted with Zinyoka residents shaped the clinic's activities. The Zanempilo experience proved crucial to the BCP's innovation in health care and development.

THE CHURCH, ACTIVISTS, NEIGHBORS, AND ANGELA MAI'S MONEY

According to Bennie Khoapa, Biko began thinking about a health project focused on primary and preventive health care about six months before he was banned in 1973. After the 1972 conference of black clergy held in Pietermaritzburg, "Steve had suggested that maybe there is something we [the BCP] needed to do about health" ("mainly because it was a primary need"). Khoapa believed in always having project proposals ready, "in case people wanted to help," so instructed Biko and Ramphele to do their basic research and "draft a plan." When they gave the plan to Khoapa, he remembered, "I liked it. . . . I thought it made sense and put it in a drawer." There it sat until "a certain Angela Mai" visited the office in 1973, after Biko's banning had sent him to the Eastern Cape. Mai was born in South Africa to the wealthy white Grinaker family. She had married a German doctor and in 1973 approached the BCP with a sum of inheritance money frozen within South Africa that she was interested in donating to an organization. After investigating other possibilities, Mai and her husband returned to Khoapa and told him they wanted to support the BCP, particularly if it had any health projects. At this point, Khoapa pulled out the plan Biko and Ramphele had devised. It did not matter that the money came from a wealthy Afrikaner family. As with other BCP and SASO sources of funding, the BCP saw this is a practical way to further its own agenda (and was indeed able to exercise its autonomy in using the funds). The Mais traveled to the Eastern Cape to meet with Biko and eventually gave the BCP up to R30,000 to cover the start-up costs.[34]

Biko's banning to the King William's Town District in 1973 meant that he put the BCP's primary health care plans into action near his hometown. The village of Zinyoka, 5.6 miles (9 km) from the town and within Biko's restricted area, became the chosen site. In the early 1970s, Zinyoka followed the larger socioeconomic trends of the Ciskei. A BCP brochure produced after the first year of Zanempilo's operation stated that the people served were "mainly rural people living on trust lands, freehold lands and white farms between King William's Town and Frankfort." Many of the women who made up the majority of the village population relied on wages from husbands who had gone to work in mines on the Rand. Other women worked for low wages as domestic workers in neighboring towns and farms. The BCP reported that most patients came from families of six, trying to live on R5–R10 per week, and included a high number of children, women, and men over fifty years of age.[35] Like the rest of the Ciskei, residents of Zinyoka and neighboring villages had very limited access to health care. Grey Hospital in King William's Town mainly served white people. Mission hospitals were far from Zinyoka and under resourced. The Mount Coke Mission Hospital, nearly 10 miles (16 km) east of King William's Town, reportedly had unsanitary and crowded nursery and maternity wards.[36] The next closest mission hospital was at St. Matthew's Mission in Keiskammahoek, more than 26 miles (42 km) from King William's Town.

Biko's connection to the Anglican Church and Benjamin Tyamzashe led the BCP to Zinyoka. Reverend James Gawe and David Russell had already provided office space for the BCP at 15 Leopold Street in King William's Town. In Zinyoka, the church owned a sizable piece of land adjacent to the Tyamzashe farm. A "dilapidated mud structure that passed as a church" stood on the plot.[37] Gawe decided to lease this plot to the BCP for the building of the clinic. Benjamin Tyamzashe (also known as "B ka T") owned a farm adjacent to this plot. A member of a progressive Xhosa mission-educated elite family, he was the grandson of a counselor in the King Sandile court (based at Mngqesha, the Great Place, or seat of the king of the Rharhabe Xhosa), and his father, Gwayi Tyamzashe, was a teacher, missionary, and intellectual. Like his father, Benjamin Tyamzashe studied at Lovedale and became a teacher. His musical training through formal schooling and from family members helped him become a respected composer. He wrote numerous songs and was asked by the

Map designed by Christopher Greenmun

Anglican and Catholic Churches to compose Xhosa adaptations of the liturgy.[38]

Tyamzashe spent most of his teaching career in Cala in the Transkei. When he retired in 1950, he became a revered elder of the Zinyoka village, where he bought the land of his brother, James.[39] In 1968, Deirdre D. Hansen described Benjamin Tyamzashe as a respected member of the community who, although not holding official judicial authority, "adjudicated on numerous occasions" and was called "the Peacemaker."[40] Zinyoka residents described the deference that Tyamzashe commanded from then Ciskei chief minister L. L. Sebe and Zinyoka headmen, claiming that no one could do anything in the village without Tyamzashe's support (the headmen or Biko).[41] Tyamzashe knew Biko's family through his participation in the musical life of Ginsberg.[42] His status and support—which included permitting the BCP to drill a well on his land and writing an article in the *Daily Dispatch*—allowed Biko and the BCP to bypass the barriers posed by local authorities.[43]

Biko and the BCP also drew upon their network of activists, friends, neighbors, and colleagues to build and run the clinic. Out of this group grew the community of activists that Ramphele and Reverend Stubbs fondly wrote about in their memoirs.[44] Ramphele herself was central to the establishment and operation of Zanempilo. She qualified as a medical doctor the year before the clinic was built and had moved to the King William's Town area to work at the Mount Coke hospital so she could be closer to Biko. She had also worked with Biko on devising plans for the BCP's clinic proposal. It made sense to appoint her as the head medical officer, though she had to learn much about how to run a health center.[45] Ramphele relied on fellow female health care givers to help her establish Zanempilo. She recruited two of the best nurses she worked with at Mount Coke: Nontobeko Moletsane and Beauty Nongauza. Mpumi Mcilongo and Leitisha Dubula were hired through their connections with the Federal Theological Seminary (where Mcilongo's husband studied) and the Border Council of Churches (where Dubula worked prior to Zanempilo). Other nurses such as Xoliswa Qodi Nqangweni and Yoliswa Ndzengu applied to work at Zanempilo after learning about the positions through advertisements.

When the workload at Zanempilo became too much for Ramphele, Biko and Ramphele brought in former classmates and SASO members Solombela and Sydney Moletsane as doctors. Biko asked Dr. Lawrence Menzeleli "Dubs" Msauli, a former UNB student a few years ahead of him, to serve on the board of the BCP's Eastern Cape branch. Msauli helped recruit other doctors in the area to volunteer periodically at Zanempilo such as Dr. Petheni from King William's Town and Dr. Kakaza. Biko asked a friend and Ginsberg neighbor working in the SABC Xhosa newsroom, Mziwoxolo Ndzengu, to be an assistant clerk and ambulance driver. Ndzengu later recruited Sido Hlaula, also from Ginsberg, to become the second driver. Biko hired Barney Flusk, an acquaintance of his from the King William's Town Coloured community, to construct the clinic and staff quarters. Some residents of Zinyoka, such as Siganyati Leleni, worked on Flusk's crew and thus gained carpentry and construction skills. Later, when state repression threatened to stall operations, the BCP called in other former classmates. After the Soweto uprisings in June 1976 and Mapetla Mohapi's death in detention shortly thereafter, the police detained many BCP personnel, including Ramphele, Solombela, and Msauli. In their absence, the BCP recruited another former UNB student and SASO member, Dr. Chapman Palweni, who ran Zanempilo for four months.[46]

Construction of Zanempilo was completed near the end of 1974. The building resembled the simple style of other four-room concrete community clinics in the region, but with more space—eventually including a reception area, waiting room, examination room, dispensary, lecture/staff room, kitchen, toilet, sluice, and incinerator room. The BCP also built living quarters for doctors and nurses. Ramphele and Nontobeko Moletsane (as the sister in charge) ordered medicines, bought beds and equipment from local suppliers, and even arranged for women to sew linens for the beds and patients. They also hired staff to cook and clean.[47] Clinic work began early in 1975, and on April 20 the BCP held an official opening ceremony. The dedication of the clinic was conducted by Bishop Lawrence B. Zulu and attended by an estimated 5,000 people "as far afield as Durban, Johannesburg, Port Elizabeth, and East London."[48] The program included speeches, choir numbers, and a meal. The BCP reported that the expenses for the occasion "were borne very enthusiastically by members of the public who contributed food and other refreshments."[49] A *Daily Dispatch* newspaper article mistakenly announced that the Ciskei interior minister, L. F. Siyo, had a place on the program.[50] If Siyo had attended the ceremony, it would have been a rare incident when Ciskei leaders responded positively to Zanempilo.

BRINGING AND RECEIVING HEALTH IN ZINYOKA

The BCP met a number of challenges in its attempts *ukuza nempilo*—to bring health to Zinyoka. Despite the desperate need for health care in the area, the headman of the village, Sidoko Sijama, opposed the clinic because of its political kinship to Black Consciousness. He tried to influence the community's reaction to Zanempilo, even calling it *Zanerattex*—"bringing Rattex," a brand of rat poison.[51] The BCP posed a real threat to the local headman and Ciskei homeland leaders whose own legitimacy was under question. At the time the Zanempilo clinic began officially operating in 1975, the

Zanempilo clinic and ambulance. (*Source*: BCP Brochure, "Zanempilo Community Health Centre," n.d., UNISA Archives, Documentation Centre for African Studies, ACC 20 Black Community Programmes.)

Ciskei government was just establishing a clear administrative authority. The Bantu Authority Acts of the 1950s and 1960s led to a "re-tribalization" of local authority in the homelands. In the Ciskei, the traditional ruling class had previously been replaced by appointed headmen under the direction of white magistrates. With new so-called Bantu or Tribal Authorities, government administration was channeled through chiefs overseeing newly defined districts. The chiefs formed part of a Legislative Assembly that had both elected and appointed members. Headmen governed villages on behalf of the chiefs, accountable both to the villagers and the chiefs. This meant that they had to strike a balance between implementing new government policies and answering to their own people. In many communities, people viewed those given power during this restructuring as puppets of the apartheid state. New chiefs were created "often on very dubious grounds," making them "a major focus of the critique of apartheid and especially of the homeland system."[52]

At the top, L. L. Sebe held an uncertain position as chief minister. He rose to power in 1973 as a self-proclaimed Rharhabe chief on a platform supporting separate development and faced political opposition from Mfengu chief Justice Mabandla and other Rharhabe chiefs in subsequent years.[53] Having Biko running community projects in the Ciskei threatened Sebe's political power. The year prior to Sebe's rise to power in the Ciskei, SASO ousted its own president, Temba Sono, for a speech suggesting SASO ought to cooperate with homeland leaders. From then on, Black Consciousness activists denounced the legitimacy of homeland politicians. In 1975, the Black People's Convention stated that homelands were "created for the continued oppression of the black man" and later, at a conference held in King William's Town, deemed Transkei's independence "a ploy to give apartheid credibility."[54] This kind of talk was dangerous for Sebe. He sought to drive Black Consciousness activists from the region, attempting to discredit the Black People's Convention and justify repeated expulsions of SASO students from Fort Hare. In newspapers, he accused SASO of disrupting education at the University of Fort Hare and the Black People's Convention of plotting to assassinate Ciskeian leaders.[55] Sebe also claimed the BCP vied for political control and that "Black Power" organizations did not "[express] the will of the people" but had been infiltrated with "communistic and imperialistic elements bent on achieving an end other than that chosen by responsible black people."[56] The Ciskei also drove the Federal Theological Seminary from Alice in 1973 for nurturing and harboring student activists.[57]

In Zinyoka, the headman Sijama likewise believed the BCP challenged his tenuous position of power. Issues of land-use exacerbated tensions between different factions in Zinyoka during this period of transition. Zinyoka was made up of both Freehold land (owned by Africans like Tyamzashe) and Bantu Trust land (administered by the state). The people of these two different areas did not always get along, particularly when the state enacted so-called betterment programs in the early 1960s. People in the Trust land—also known as Trustin—were required to reduce their livestock and consolidate their houses in one zone. Owners of Freehold land were exempt from following these policies. Those in Trustin resented the way landowners retained exclusive grazing rights, while they were forced to kill much if not all of their cattle. This led Trustin residents to demand that the headman for the village come from Trustin, resulting in the rise of Sijama in 1974, the same year the BCP started building Zanempilo.[58] With these underlying tensions, Sijama may have sensed that some residents had more respect for people such as Tyamzashe and viewed headmen as "toothless bulldogs" who could be intimidating but did not have a real bite.[59] Perhaps he feared that the services offered at Zanempilo would undermine his authority and spark a direct challenge to him as headman.

In an effort to offset the influence of the Zanempilo clinic in Zinyoka, the Ciskei government attempted to run a rival clinic. It employed a nurse to work from small wooden shacks in the village, a little over a mile away from Zanempilo. Journalist Leslie Xinwa pointed out the irony that "while many rural areas throughout South Africa are crying out for clinics," Zinyoka had two. This, he rightfully observed, "came as a result of politics."[60] Interestingly, although the headmen opposed Zanempilo, their family members went there for treatment. Unlike the clinic made up of shacks and staffed by one nurse, Zanempilo stood out as a strong concrete building on a compound with nurses' and doctors' quarters and a backyard garden. It had a full-time doctor, a lying-in ward (where patients ate meals prepared in part with food from the garden), and a dispensary stocked with numerous medicines. It also had new equipment and employed gardeners and cleaners to be sure patients attended a clean and inviting clinic. Without resources and a welcoming atmosphere like that of Zanempilo, the Ciskei government clinic did not last long.[61] The government used other tactics to undermine Zanempilo such as withholding an operation license and denying access to free immunizations.[62]

Until October 1977, the BCP was able to adapt and mitigate against state action by evading the police, using preventive measures, and replacing detained staff. Thenjiwe Nondalana, the domestic worker at the clinic, told of a time the police came to search for documents after the BCP held a branch meeting at the clinic. She recounted how she hid the documents in a bed sheet, placed it in a washing basin, then began to do her washing. The police never suspected that Nondalana was actually pretending to attend to the washing in order to hide the papers. She proudly recounted: "They searched and searched and all the while it is here [on my lap], and I am washing [*laughs*]."[63] On one occasion, when the police came to speak with Nontobeko Moletsane, she went into the labor room and locked the door. She was the only person in the room, but started making noises as if a woman was about to give birth. She screamed and yelled, "Push!"[64] At that time, it was enough to deter the police; however, Ramphele wrote that once the police overcame "their reverence for the medical profession and the respect they had for a place of healing" (which took "a while"), the police became "quite outrageous in walking around the health centre, and had to be physically restrained in some cases from entering the labor ward with a delivery in process." She recalled that they would have "fierce arguments" with the police about "their lack of respect for the dignity of the patients."[65]

Soon after the clinic began operating, the BCP employed watchmen and built a perimeter fence, partly to keep the security police out. Stanley Roji, a night watchman, remembered that police (both black and white) often raided the clinic at night.[66] Msauli described the time when visitors from the Anglo American Corporation came to the clinic to meet with BCP board members. During the night, as they relaxed after meetings, they discovered that the security police were lying in the grass outside of the fence. Emboldened by the Scottish whiskey brought by the Anglo American visitors, they stepped outside, loudly informed the police they were aware of their presence, and told them to leave.[67]

At a time when political activism was dangerous—someone attempted to bomb Roji's house because of his son's political activity—some Zinyoka residents initially viewed Zanempilo with suspicion. As Nondalana put it, they wondered why the church was mixing with "*izinto zeqindi*" (things of the fist).[68] Yet the community soon saw the tangible benefits brought by Zanempilo. As the nearest primary health care center for black people living in the area, it was easy for Zanempilo to make an immediate and significant improvement in the lives of people in Zinyoka and surrounding areas. The hostility of the headman in Zinyoka to the clinic showed village residents that the local authorities cared more about maintaining their power than the health of their people. The testimonies of the large number of patients who attended Zanempilo, including the family members of the headman, indicate that people at least temporarily lost their fear of state reprisal for attending the clinic, even though tensions between the BCP and the Ciskei government continued. Sijama may have maintained his position as headman and the Ciskei government may have counted the closure of the BCP in 1977 as a victory, but the legitimacy and authority of both declined in the eyes of many Zinyoka residents because of the BCP's work.[69]

Furthermore, Zanempilo did more than just provide health care. The Black Consciousness philosophy and previous experience of activists led clinic staff to investigate the root causes of health problems in Zinyoka and link the illness of patients to their environment. This pushed Zanempilo to take a holistic approach to community health. The clinic established a number of health and economic programs that not only improved the physical health of the people but also helped some Zinyoka residents feed their families and educate their children. This further built rapport between Zanempilo staff and villagers.

At first, Zanempilo was designed to focus on primary and preventive health care with one doctor and two nurses. The staff sent the more serious cases they could not treat at the clinic to the hospitals nearby, such as Mount Coke. As the clinic staff learned of the area's health needs, they realized more needed to be done to address the root causes of ill-health and extend the reach of the clinic to other villages. During its first years of operation, the medical staff at Zanempilo met with the BCP branch executive under Biko's direction each month to discuss the clinic's progress and service statistics. Nontobeko Moletsane remembered one month when, after she proudly made her presentation, Biko "was not impressed at all." Her presentation had included statistics showing a high rate of childhood deaths in the village. Biko told her, "The report you have given us . . . these are diseases that should be prevented, that are not supposed to be there. Therefore, yours is to go and find out why these people are suffering from these diseases." Although she was not trained in research, she chose one family who had recently brought children to the clinic with kwashiorkor as a sample. As Nontobeko Moletsane narrated:

> I went straight to this house after work—it was after five. And I just told them that I was their visitor, I've come to check on children, how they're doing and also the mother. What struck me there, they were sitting in this rondavel, all of them and there was fire and the three-legged pot was exaggeratedly big for them to be cooking a meal, but it was boiling and they were all sitting there. And the children started yawning and they fell asleep around this fire. And I said to the mother, "Ma, I've been here for more than three hours now"—(I think it was something to eight at the time)—"but why are you not dishing what you are cooking and so on?" and when I looked at her, the tears just went—rolled on the cheeks, and I could see the pain and anguish. I hugged her and I opened the pot. It was just water, just to keep the fires burning and also to . . . keep their pride. [70]

She learned from the woman that many husbands had gone to work in mines and had not come back or sent money. The women had lost hope and had become apathetic. They had even ceased gardening their plots of land. In order to address the poor health and economic conditions of Zinyoka residents, the clinic staff embarked on a program of relief and empowerment by providing food rations for children and then offering skill-building courses that taught women home budgeting, new farming techniques, and new crafts. Nontobeko Moletsane drew upon her own experience growing up in the rural Transkei to help the women use sisal to make baskets. She taught a deep trench gardening technique for growing plants in arid regions that she had learned on a nursing school field trip. [71]

Nonzwakazi Dl'ebusuku was one of the women whom Nontobeko Moletsane met during her home visits and invited to join the craft group. Dl'ebusuku had moved to Zinyoka with her husband in 1966. He had subsequently gone to work in the mines, but did not send home enough money. In 1975, Dl'ebusuku was working for the Tyamzashe family but struggling to make ends meet. She remembered that Nontobeko Moletsane visited her and asked her about what she was eating and when the money from her husband came:

She came to me first [because I lived near the clinic]. When she arrived, I was eating mealies. I was cooking it in the pots at home, in the black pot. She arrived. She said, "Mama, I've come to see you." "What do you want nurse?" She said I should explain my situation. I explained what I am eating, what I'm doing, how much money I was getting . . . how poor I was, that I was eating maize, that it was difficult to educate my children and so on. She said, "Mama, tomorrow morning, come to the clinic with others who are struggling here." I told [others]. . . . [The next morning they asked,] "Do you know how to work with your hands? . . . I am going to bring sisal." . . . Me, I made a basket [that day]. I finished it. Hey, it was beautiful, that basket! [72]

A group of about ten women began to meet at the clinic on weekdays, from 8:00 A.M. to 5:00 P.M. They made sisal baskets and mats, did beadwork, and eventually some helped with piecemeal work from the BCP's leatherwork factory in Njwaxa. Pumla Sangotsha, a social worker, and Mvovo, the BCP's marketing director, helped obtain raw materials and sell the goods in local markets to tourists. Dl'ebusuku claimed that because of her skilled work, she at one point earned R500 per month. This figure is high (Biko earned R400 then R500 per month as BCP branch executive, and a 1976 BCP

Women's group at Zanempilo. (*Source:* BCP Limited, "Projects and People," 1977, UNISA Archives, Documentation Centre for African Studies, ACC 20 Black Community Programmes.)

report states that the women who helped Njwaxa earned R20–R30 per month);[73] but Dl'ebusuku's exaggeration signifies that she felt her wages had an enormous impact on her life. Dl'ebusuku also measured the change in her life by what she ate. Before the clinic came to the community, she ate mealies. After she started the work at the clinic, she claimed that her family always had food in the house and that she was able to pay her children's school fees.[74] According to Nontobeko Moletsane, soon after Zanempilo instituted its extra programs, the death rate declined in Zinyoka, and the clinic stopped dealing with minute nutrition issues.[75]

Reflecting the perspective and purpose gained by experience, by the end of the first year of Zanempilo's operation the BCP wrote that its health programs were designed to meet the health needs of communities, taking into account the social and economic conditions of a community. It also emphasized the participation of the people, writing that the BCP could achieve its goals only through close cooperation with families (in most cases headed by women) and "if health services are properly integrated and decentralized so that they provide front-line services for the protection and promotion of the health of the rural community."[76] Dl'ebusuku's story as part of the sewing group is one example of the economic and skill-building programs run at the clinic. The staff also instigated a grocery bulk-buying scheme, a soup kitchen, and a chicken-raising cooperative to sell eggs locally, involving some village men as well. The garden behind the clinic provided food for patients and staff and a place to teach gardening techniques. When the BCP began constructing its Solempilo clinic in Natal at the Adam's mission station, it built upon the experience of its predecessor, Zanempilo, in the Eastern Cape. Taking advantage of the fertile land, the BCP established "experimental" or "demonstration" gardens for surrounding community members. Solempilo also included an animal husbandry section, a workshop, and a market stall for the extra programs the center would house in addition to the clinic.[77] Responding to the needs of the people led the BCP to a more comprehensive approach to community development that took into account the interconnected aspects of life in South African villages.

Zanempilo offered a high quality of care most black people did not have access to in the rest of South Africa. It was well equipped and fully staffed with black doctors and nurses. The clinic's infrastructure and equipment exceeded that of other rural Ciskei clinics and helped the BCP accommodate relatively large numbers of people. Along with the standard waiting and examination rooms, Zanempilo had various specialty rooms, including even a maternity ward and places for sterilizing equipment. The kitchen and gardens were used to provide full meals for in-patients.

The clinic expanded by adding beds and even obtained an incubator for premature babies. It was equipped with flushing toilets, electricity, a phone line, and a clean water supply (filtered with the clinic's own system), when most of the rural Ciskei did not enjoy these amenities. It had up to two full-time resident doctors, seven nurses, a community health worker, a social worker, two ambulance drivers, and six maintenance workers. Doctors and nurses were on call to treat those who came at all hours of the day and night, and Ndzengu and Hlaula lived in Zinyoka to drive the ambulance when needed. The clinic added its second doctor in January 1976, to help Ramphele deal with the workload. Solombela came to Zinyoka after finishing his internship at the Livingstone Hospital in Port Elizabeth. Ramphele did most of the work in Zinyoka (and in King William's Town when she became the director of the BCP branch office), while Solombela visited the satellite clinics. When Solombela left at the end of 1976, Dr. Sydney Moletsane took over his role. Msauli recruited other doctors in the area to volunteer their services on weekends, and medical students also came to learn from Zanempilo's programs.[78] Many of the nurses lived in Zinyoka, or nearby. Some of them, such as Nontobeko Moletsane, had training in midwifery (she had even received a gold medal in midwifery at King Edward VIII hospital).[79] Others, such as Dubula, were community health workers who focused on health education and distributing powdered milk for malnourished babies. For all this, patients would pay fifty cents or nothing at all, depending on their ability to pay (Zanempilo charged more for black "local civil servants" and those with medical aid).[80]

Word of the care offered by Zanempilo spread to neighboring villages and attracted patients from places over 30 miles (48 km) away, such as Peelton, Tyusha, and Stutterheim. For some, it would take over an hour to reach the clinic by car, while others came on foot.[81] Within its first six months, the clinic reportedly saw close to 2,500 patients (forty-one per day on average).[82] As it attracted patients from surrounding rural areas, the BCP staff decided to run a mobile clinic, something they also initiated in Soweto, when the 1976 uprisings disrupted health care services. The BCP procured vehicles for transporting patients and traveling to outstations, satellite clinics in other villages visited weekly by a doctor and nurses. On Mondays, Zanempilo staff might go to Tyolomnqa, 48 miles (78 km) away from Zinyoka; on Tuesdays, it could be Njwaxa; Wednesdays, Tyusha; Thursdays, a station near Stutterheim. They also visited Ngwenya, Ntsikizini, and Ginsberg. In some of these places people had petitioned for a satellite clinic. Zanempilo staff set up their clinic at rondavels, houses, or churches arranged by the village. Ndzengu or Hlaula, the ambulance drivers, would take names

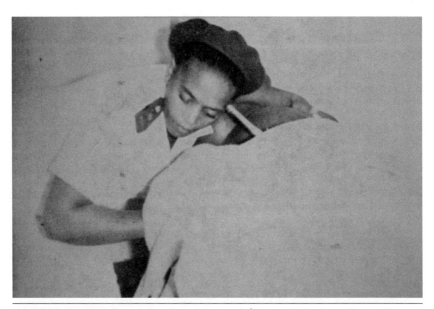

Sister Moletsane examining a patient in the labor ward. (*Source*: BCP Brochure, "Zanempilo Community Health Centre," n.d., UNISA Archives, Documentation Centre for African Studies, ACC 20 Black Community Programmes.)

and dispense medicine; the doctor and nurses would see maternity patients, children who might have kwashiorkor, or adults with tuberculosis or hypertension. They also would give immunizations. When Dr. Solombela began his work as the second doctor in January 1976, he remembered that most patients were undernourished babies.[83] Nurses such as Dubula or Yoliswa Ndzengu would make home visits and follow up on children and infants who had previously received milk powder supplements. In 1976, Zanempilo's mobile clinic reportedly saw nearly 3,000 patients at the outstations, evidence of the glaring need for accessible health care in these rural villages.[84]

The clinic had to rely on outside funding to support its work and expansion. This was a constant challenge. Ramphele remembered a continuously "stretched budget."[85] Yet the BCP was apparently able to manage its funds so that Nondalana and Roji claimed that they always received their monthly check on time. Khoapa described Zanempilo's funding as coming in an "ad-hocish way," first with Angela Mai's substantial donation, then from their usual South African sources (the Council of Churches and Christian Institute) as well as churches in Europe and America.[86] Msauli, the BCP Eastern Cape board member who oversaw fund-raising and health projects, said he did not find it very difficult to obtain donations because people were interested in funding health projects. He described Scandinavian countries, Germany, and Holland as his "happy hunting grounds."[87] Ndzengu and Hlaula remembered picking up visiting donors from places like Brussels at the East London airport. These countries offered financial support for many different anti-apartheid activities in South Africa. The BCP's health project also received substantial amounts from the Anglo American Corporation. The company's Special Chairman's Fund records indicate that Zanempilo received R15,120 in 1975 and R12,000 in 1976. The BCP received much larger amounts intended for the Solempilo clinic in Natal, starting with R910 in 1975 and jumping to R85,000 in 1976 and R91,173 in 1977 (about R2.7 million or US $250,292 when converted to 2014 equivalents).[88]

This funding allowed the BCP to bring health care to Zinyoka, but it also posed a contradiction. While the BCP stressed the importance of self-reliance, the clinic depended on outside funding. As suggested earlier, activists accepted funds from some controversial sources as long as the sources did not dictate how the money should be spent. SASO and the BCP needed these funds to help them start the process of building black self-reliance. The BCP also had plans to address its financial dependence on donors. But, as far as Zanempilo was concerned, the resolution of this funding issue was still far in the future. Theoretically the clinic could be more self-reliant financially once patients had enough money to pay for services. In the meantime, since it served those living in poverty, it more realistically needed funding from other sources—in other political circumstances, perhaps the government. Another question Zanempilo had yet to address was that of equipping community members with specialized medical skills. Aside from nutrition classes and consulting patients, Zanempilo staff employed by the BCP did not have plans to transfer these skills to local people. (It could have gone in this direction, though this would have raised more questions about how to effectively train and retain local people.)

Despite these unanswered questions, there is evidence that Zanempilo had some significant success in increasing black self-reliance and human dignity. Like *Black Review*, Zanempilo embodied the idea that black people could provide a specialized skill for their own people. As powerfully depicted in a political cartoon in East London's *Daily Dispatch*, the idea of a black hand extending this professional help challenged prevailing notions of black dependency and inferiority. In the community of Zinyoka, once villagers experienced the kind of care possible, they adopted higher standards for their village. Freehold land holders and a clinic community committee

Political cartoon in the *Daily Dispatch* on the day before Zanempilo's official opening. (*Source*: Don Kenyon, *Daily Dispatch*, April 19, 1975.)

formed in 1995 would later demand that the government provide services equal to that they received from Zanempilo's original owners.[89] Zanempilo also had a profound impact on the self-perception and self-reliance of individuals.

COMMUNITY AND STAFF RELATIONS

The clean, well-resourced clinic's extra programs and the type of medical care patients received at Zanempilo gave villagers a sense of human dignity and self-worth that their political, social, and material situation denied them. Having access to that kind of care meant a lot to those who were impoverished, so much so that many named their children variations of *impilo*, such as Nompilo and Philiswa. Nomalizo Felicia Madikane and her husband from nearby Zwelitsha were so impressed by the clean and welcoming conditions at the clinic that they named their son who was born there "Zanempilo."[90] Moreover, the way young black doctors and nurses respected their patients, the way activists adhered to cultural rules regarding age and communication, and the way BCP staff involved community members in their social events helped build good relations between young educated activists and older illiterate villagers. Zinyoka women and female BCP staff were often at the center of the clinic's activities. Female activists found space there to also challenge prevailing customs. Some activists and villagers resisted female authority and assertiveness, but BCP and village women found ways to connect, and the work of BCP women increased respect for women in professional positions and in some social relations.

Zanempilo attracted people from surrounding villages and urban townships in large part because of the black staff who recognized the humanity of their patients and treated them with respect. Zanempilo staff did not separate the body from its social context.[91] They took an interest in their patients' socioeconomic situations and respected their beliefs and culture. This meant that doctors and nurses discussed personal backgrounds and resources with patients, counseled patients about their diets and health, and explained the causes of their ill-health. Nongauza described how patients may have experienced this, highlighting the fact that doctors spoke directly to patients. In hospitals where white doctors could not speak the language of black patients, white health care workers often relied on interpreters and black nurses to facilitate communication. This further distanced white doctors and black patients already socially separated because of their race, class, and possibly gender. In contrast, as patients entered Zanempilo, the staff greeted them, asked them questions, and "we *listened* to them." Because they listened to their patients, "people had a way of opening to us . . . even the communication with the doctors—our doctors, they communicated with them directly. There was no interpreter. . . . So, each one would say all the things, 'I have this and that . . .' talking directly to a doctor and the doctor explaining directly to her, not through an interpreter."[92] Also, in contrast to dismissive white doctors, Hlaula remembered how Sydney Moletsane showed respect for patients by taking meticulous notes for each patient and insisting the staff keep their records well organized.[93]

Black doctors at Zanempilo who could not speak Xhosa well (Ramphele spoke Sotho, and Sydney Moletsane spoke Zulu) made efforts to speak to patients in Xhosa. Although this did not always go smoothly, patients appreciated it.[94] Ramphele wrote of how her efforts to speak Xhosa helped her draw closer to the women of Zinyoka who affectionately called her their *umSothokazi* (Sotho woman) or *iramram* (delicate one). She explained how

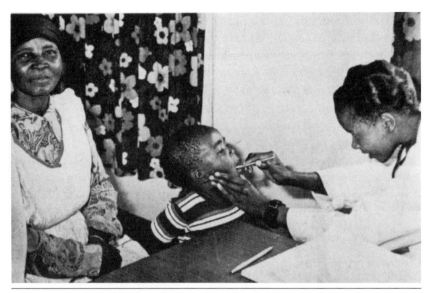

Dr. Ramphele examining Thenjiwe Nondalana's child while his grandmother looks on. Nondalana claimed this photo shows her mother, who had taken her son to the clinic on the day this photo was taken. (*Source*: BCP Limited, "Projects and People," UNISA Archives, Documentation Centre for African Studies, ACC 20 Black Community Programmes.)

becoming a student of the village women in learning their language put them "in a position of authority" over her, "being experts in something in which I was incompetent." This, she believed, broke down barriers between them as they saw that "doctors do not know everything" and her medical expertise was "seen in a less mystified light."[95] The connection Ramphele had with villagers and other staff was manifested in interviews. Aside from Biko, she was the most remembered and praised by villagers. Similar to Zinyoka women, Leleni remembered that Ramphele took the time to chat with men and women if she found them sitting on the veranda or clinic grounds.[96] Whether or not people had deep relationships with her, these sorts of gestures and memories of the care she provided made her seem less like an aloof doctor.

Zanempilo staff also showed they took a genuine interest in the people's health by making follow-up home visits. This was another way village women and female health care providers connected socially. Maria Nomutile Masiki, a Zinyoka resident, gave birth at Zanempilo in 1975. When asked to tell her memory of the clinic, she talked about how Biko improved the life of the village by giving people jobs doing handwork. But what was more important to her was the pre- and postnatal care the clinic offered. She described the care new mothers received: "After you had given birth, you would stay at the clinic for four days with your baby. Then, you would leave after four days with your baby and then a nurse from Zanempilo would come to your house to help you with the baby. She would wash the baby herself, at home, swaddle the baby at home." After ten days, the mothers were invited to visit the clinic for regular check-ups as part of what Zanempilo called its baby-clinic.[97]

Part of respecting a person and not separating the body from a person's beliefs and socioeconomic context was recognizing that Xhosa healing traditions were important to patients. Xhosa healers—diviners (*amagqira* or *isanuse*) and herbalists (*ixwele*)—treated both natural causes of ill-health and social or supernatural causes. People who consulted them would have acted under the belief that various causes of ill-health were linked to their interactions with other people or ancestors. While BCP staff believed that their training in Western health care was the most effective care (as Solombela remarked), unlike many other Western health care initiatives that failed in Africa, they constructively engaged Xhosa philosophies and traditions.[98] Sydney Moletsane and Nontobeko Moletsane both commented on how they shared with traditional healers the idea of looking at a patient as a social being and worked with some of these ideas to educate people about the causes and cures of their ill-health.[99]

At the same time that African health practitioners continued to thrive in many rural and urban communities, many Africans had also come to rely on Western medical care. They especially sought treatment from doctors trained in biomedicine for "European" or "white" diseases—new illnesses such as tuberculosis, influenza, cancer, and venereal diseases. They also increasingly used Western-trained doctors for surgery and childbirth. Catherine Burns estimated that 50 percent of patients from all of South Africa had shifted from home-based childbirth to hospitalized childbirth by 1950.[100] Indeed, maternity cases were most important for interviewees, both former BCP employees and the rural women Zanempilo served. Thus, while people continued to utilize Xhosa health practitioners in the Ciskei, they also believed in Western curative medicine. Often this care was symbolized by the stethoscope or injections. The stethoscope was a particularly powerful instrument as a technology of Western medicine that could help doctors "divine" what was happening inside a patient's body. As Nongauza commented, "You know, people wanted actually a stethoscope from the doctor. . . . They believed in the stethoscope."[101]

Many activists and Zinyoka residents commented on the solidarity and communalism prevalent at Zanempilo. Whether or not this was always the case, this remembered atmosphere influenced how villagers and staff felt about themselves and the clinic long after 1977. These positive memories also attest to what Jacob Dlamini and Simmone Horwitz have written: that despite the oppressive circumstances under apartheid, people still found ways to enjoy life and build relationships. They even found space to innovate and improve lives in various sectors of society such as health care.[102] Former Zanempilo employees remembered their high job satisfaction and staff camaraderie. Most said working at Zanempilo was like working with family, not least because they were all a similar age but also because of their commitment to serving the community and providing the highest quality care for people. As Ndzengu remarked, they were busy, but "never felt it" because they felt they were making their contribution to helping people.[103] The way these self-confident, empathetic, and welcoming activists interacted with Zinyoka residents changed the way patients and residents who worked at Zanempilo felt about themselves and their abilities as black people. Villagers did not engage in political discussions or join the Black People's Convention, yet the clinic's social and political messages were clear. Nondalana said Biko "wanted people to feel they were human." Biko used to say, "Black people and white people have the same blood."[104] Other community members and patients like Masiki talked of how the clinic showed black people they could do things on their own.[105] The BCP's efforts to help people do this were cut short when the state shut down the BCP, partly explaining why praise of individuals like Biko and Ramphele as saviors would be mixed with strong statements about the BCP's goals for building self-reliance. Still, the BCP staff sent a clear message about black human dignity. This went beyond racial classification to include socioeconomic differences between black people as well. Many villagers interviewed commented on the way the educated staff treated uneducated villagers as equals. It was important that these "intellectuals" did not look down on them. As Mjondo remarked, "At the clinic, you didn't have intellectuals and fools, there was just people."[106]

One fond memory for many was the *gumbas* (the activists' term for parties) or community *braais* held at Zanempilo after meetings or on weekends, when activists rejuvenated their energy. Solombela summed up the balance between work and recreation when he said, "When there was work," they worked hard, sometimes late into the night, "but at the same time there used to be fun at the clinic."[107] Activists had their own parties and meetings, but Nondalana talked about how Biko slaughtered sheep for *braais* where everyone was accepted and treated equally regardless of their socioeconomic or educational status. She even claimed that those who initially opposed the clinic came to these parties.[108] Dl'ebusuku remembered going to parties wearing traditional clothes and performing Xhosa dances. It was important to her that no one was asked to sit outside. She commented, "I was with them. There was no discrimination. It was as if there was no apartheid at that time."[109] This acceptance endeared the activists to the community, whose respect and admiration for these young people later translated into praise, elevating Biko and Ramphele as their father and mother, though they were at the time younger.

Zanempilo employees were generally in their mid-to-late twenties or early thirties and making the transition from youth status into adulthood, culturally and professionally. Few were married and had children, achievements required to reach full adulthood in Ciskei Xhosa society, along with economic self-reliance (or establishing a homestead). Their inferior status in Zinyoka as youth contributed to the opposition Zinyoka political leaders posed to BCP employees. Yet while BCP employees had challenged the status quo with bold styles and confrontational behavior as SASO students in major urban areas across the country, they showed they valued contemporary Xhosa customs by following cultural rules of respectful communication with villagers. In Xhosa society in Zinyoka, people were expected to address each other by their clan names, address their elders by their appropriate titles, and act toward a person according to his or her age status. For example, boys or girls would be required to address anyone their parents' age as *mama* and *tata* or *bawo* (a highly respectful term for father), and anyone their grandparents' age as *makhulu* and *tatomkhulu*.[110] By adhering to these rules and celebrating Xhosa culture at *gumbas*, activists challenged the apartheid status quo, which taught that all things African were inferior. Furthermore, as Mjondo's and Dl'ebusuku's remarks indicate, these actions were more poignant coming from university educated youth previously viewed as a detached elite. The transformations brought about by urbanization, labor migration, and homeland poverty had turned some village youth to violence, vandalism, and open defiance of their elders. Sijama even remembered her husband, the headman, disciplining gangsters and other young boys who had beaten their own mothers.[111] On the other hand, young BCP employees who worked at Zanempilo in the village not only brought high-quality health care to Zinyoka, they made it a point to address adults by their clan names and titles and treat them with respect as patients.

The way the government dealt with the clinic also influenced how Zinyoka residents viewed Black Consciousness activists. While they may not have joined in the politics of the activists, watching the government disapprove of the clinic and the police harass its staff indirectly raised the political consciousness of Zinyoka residents. Indeed, seeing how the government opposed those who provided them with high-quality service that made them feel like human beings may have been a large factor in the decline of legitimacy of the headman and homeland leaders in the eyes of Zinyoka residents, a sentiment freely expressed in 2008.

While Zinyoka residents and former clinic employees have overwhelmingly positive memories of staff camaraderie and community relations, tensions did surface, particularly in regards to Ramphele's position as doctor and the clinic's medical superintendent. Ramphele wrote of her frustrations when working with other activists who did not keep a rigid schedule as she did. She also resented the loss of privacy and the strain of feeding uninvited guests at the clinic. One former nurse alluded to personal differences that may have arisen from these frustrations when she said, "Mamphela had her faults." Ramphele also wrote that tensions surfaced between herself and Solombela regarding her position in the community and as his boss. Moreover, Ramphele also openly challenged cultural gender norms at gatherings of activists in Zinyoka. She and Deborah Matshoba both remembered disagreements with male activists about their participation in eating sheep heads after *braais*, a practice reserved for men in Xhosa tradition.[112] Ramphele also had some difficulties being taken seriously as a young, black, female doctor. Perceived as nurturers, women filling nursing and teaching roles did not meet as much resistance as did those like Ramphele serving in leadership roles or professional positions otherwise held by men. Malusi Mpumlwana indicated that "there were always jokes about whether she was up to it." It seems this also had to do with her age and appearance since "old folks [may have seen her as] a child."[113] Nontobeko Moletsane also remembered that at times they had to "talk sense" to men who did not want to be seen by a physically small (thin) and young woman doctor.[114]

Ramphele and other female BCP employees both intentionally and unintentionally challenged gender expectations in their work. The women in Ramphele's family had modeled ways to challenge male power by questioning certain cultural practices.[115] Through her education and aggressive debating style in SASO, Ramphele proved her willingness to go against the status quo as well. Yet, as discussed in the introduction, in her early years as an activist, she did not see herself as taking on a feminist cause. At times the mere presence of women in roles usually held by men had a more profound impact on Zinyoka villagers and those who worked at the clinic. While almost certainly the idea of a young, black, female doctor heading the clinic took some getting used to, both male and female Zinyoka residents interviewed would not acknowledge that as a problem in 2008, indicating that some perceptions of gender changed among villagers. Khoapa speculated that men who at first did not want to be examined by Ramphele complied when they saw her skill and the deference other staff paid her (including male doctors). Mjondo and Khoapa also believed that when men realized they had no other choice, they accepted it.[116] Others remarked that Ramphele's respectful and kind nature put patients at ease. This and Hlaula's comment that Ramphele was a mother more than a doctor also indicates that the gendered role of women as nurturers carried over into accepting Ramphele as a doctor in the eyes of some.[117] In contrast to those who remembered the challenges that she faced among villagers, in her own writings Ramphele has asserted that her novelty combined with her professional status gave her power and respect.[118] Similarly, Malusi Mpumlwana thought that having a black female doctor in the village was exciting because no one had any experience of a woman doctor in King William's Town, let alone a black woman doctor. He believed that Ramphele inspired Zinyoka women.[119] The fact that few villagers acknowledged a problem in interviews in 2008 shows that Ramphele's work and subsequent elevation in the eyes of the community meant they accepted that at least some young black women could reach professional adulthood.

In many ways, Zanempilo was a woman's world, greatly influencing the atmosphere and implicit messages of the clinic in regards to women. If not for the male doctors, two male ambulance drivers, and political visitors, Zanempilo would have been dominated by women. Ramphele served as head medical officer, Sangotsha as a secretary and social worker, and the clinic had up to seven female nurses. Most of the patients were women due to the demographics of the area and the community's health needs. Childbirth and maternity care were significant portions of the clinic's work. Sangotsha and the nurses taught nutrition and budgeting classes for Zinyoka women, and the main economic initiative of the clinic—the craft group—involved only women. Zanempilo is thus an example of how the BCP, although it did not make women's issues political, catered to and empowered women simply because women bore the brunt of rural homeland poverty. This is what led Mohapi to argue that through the clinic's programs, "women were mobilized as women to be able to come together and do something for themselves, instead of depending on their men."[120]

Dl'ebusuku most likely did not have gender relations in mind when she made her statement about the lack of discrimination at the clinic; but the people-centered nature of the work at Zanempilo and the number of women involved at professional levels had the natural effect of increasing respect for young black women and their abilities to perform work usually performed by men. Biko's multiple sexual relations outside of his marriage call into question whether his respect for women as colleagues extended to respecting women as sexual partners. Yet there are indications that professional interactions at the clinic between the staff, patients, and other villagers helped inspire greater respect for women in other men working there—both at work and at home. For example, Sydney Moletsane expressed that he believed the community took the clinic staff as a unit without differentiating between male and female.[121] More than reflecting what the community thought, this comment suggests how he himself worked in partnership with his fellow colleagues regardless of their gender (either because of his own personality and views or as a result of Zanempilo's atmosphere). Hlaula found it significant that Biko called female visitors to the clinic "Mama" despite their age. This, he said, taught him to display respect to all individuals.[122] Ndzengu looked to respectful communication modeled by BCP staff as contributing to greater respect between men and women at Zanempilo. When asked how his work at Zanempilo affected his life, he talked about how the staff had respect for each other and took time to sit down and explain things to patients. He commented that this culture of respect influenced his subsequent work with the Metropolitan Life insurance company and HIV/AIDS awareness in rural areas. It even affected "the way I'm running my family," he concluded. Along with making sure he did not fail when embarking on a project, his experience taught him "that you must treat a lady with respect."[123]

CONCLUSION

With the variety of services it offered, Zanempilo was a busy place, teeming with activity in the mid-1970s. It started by targeting one need—health care—and then expanded to take a more comprehensive approach and to serve surrounding communities. Local churches, activists and friends, and outside funding made this possible. Although they met resistance, women and youth played crucial roles at Zanempilo, changing the perceptions of the abilities of young black women and the motivations of black educated youth. Villagers came to view Black Consciousness activists as young, educated people driven by a deep commitment to improve the lives of black people. More important, Zanempilo had a physical and social impact on individuals. Village women gained economic opportunities and received a kind of health care they previously had not, elevating their economic self-reliance and sense of self-worth. It is unclear how Zanempilo would have functioned in the long term, and, unlike *Black Review*, the clinic's geographic reach was comparatively small. Yet this concrete example of the potential that black people had in carrying out their own development and establishing high-quality rural health services still deeply changed people in a way that met the BCP's goals of effecting a psychological liberation and improving material circumstances.[124]

CHAPTER 5

The Njwaxa Leather
Home Industry

On June 18, 2008, Lindani Ntenteni, Mark Mandita, and I drove into the village of Njwaxa to meet with Mandita's grandmother, Sarha Papu. She had worked at the BCP's Njwaxa leatherwork factory from its beginning in 1974 until it was shut down by the police in October 1977. Having never been interviewed before, Papu and five other residents who met with us that day eagerly shared their memories of the factory. They excitedly told us about their work, the factory's accomplishments, and the intrigues of a police informer, sometimes speaking all at once. The interest and energy with which residents talked about the factory indicates the significance the BCP had in the village. As its small leatherwork factory brought services into the heart of the homeland, it stood in contrast to misdirected apartheid separate development and other welfare programs that gave limited relief but did not empower. The BCP's emphasis on people-centered black management and black skills was central to the economic and psychological uplift it brought to factory employees and villagers. It was also key to the factory's growth. Female activists and village women played particularly important roles in the project as directors, essential village contacts, and the majority of its employees. The BCP thus especially changed the lives of village women. Yet state repression and contradictions within the BCP also posed challenges. The BCP creatively used its connections to recruit people and obtain resources, including local Christian networks. At the same time, the factory was never financially self-sufficient. This chapter grapples with the capitalistic-communal nature of the BCP and its financial dependency. Nevertheless, it argues that the BCP succeeded in giving many villagers means to support their families and, consequently, an improved sense of human dignity.

NJWAXA, SEPARATE DEVELOPMENT, AND HOME INDUSTRIES

In the early 1970s, Njwaxa was a typical Ciskei rural village secluded from urban areas, but significantly tied to them. Like the rest of the Ciskei and other homelands, its people were impoverished and dependent on wages from male migrant labor. Various state and civil society organizations had different approaches to addressing these conditions, ranging from welfare and charitable relief in the form of "schemes" (milk schemes, soup schemes, or ration distribution) to small-scale self-help projects. As discussed earlier, guided by apartheid ideology, South African government agricultural and industrial initiatives in the area at the time ultimately served white business and political interests. Local priests and the Border Council of Churches (BCC) attempted to build the self-sufficiency of poor villagers with home-industry projects, although their efforts could not transform the underlying structural inequalities plaguing homeland residents. These approaches related to the ideals of the BCP, which closely associated with the BCC and local priests.

Njwaxa lies nearly 30 miles (48 km) from King William's Town, past the town of Middledrift, off the main road toward Alice. The rolling hills that slope toward the Tyumie River hint that the Amathole Mountain range is not far away. Similar to today, Njwaxa was a small village with tenuous living conditions in the late 1960s and early 1970s. A 1965 "Reclamation and Settlement" report for Njwaxa estimated that 1,723 people lived in the area of 1,600 morgen (3,387 acres). According to the report, nearly 60 percent of 299 families in Njwaxa had land rights, while 35 percent owned neither land nor livestock. Those who had livestock kept cattle, sheep, and goats. Those who farmed produced maize, sorghum, and peas. A few successful farmers made a living off the land, but farming was not always reliable. The climate was arid to semiarid, receiving 18–20 inches of rainfall per year. The Tyumie River and one borehole with a hand pump provided the village with water. The soil was reportedly "fairly fertile," yet badly eroded in some parts, and the veld cover was "fair in parts" but "otherwise poor."[1] Droughts, which came often, could easily have devastating effects on Njwaxa residents. Many villagers did not have other means of employment and depended on their crops and stock or pensions and other villagers to survive if their crops and stock failed.[2]

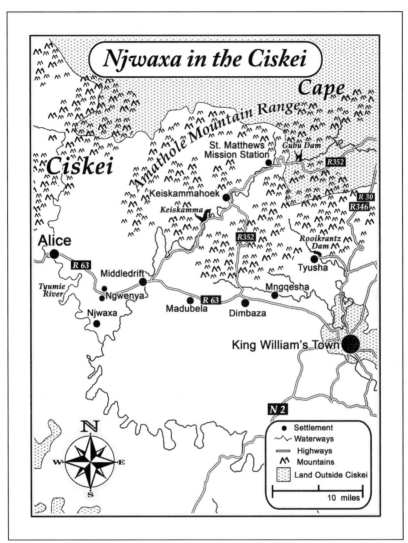

Njwaxa's economic and environmental pressures mirrored those of the rest of the region. A socioeconomic survey of the Middledrift District published in 1970 by the University of Fort Hare concluded that the villages in the district were "predominantly feminine" due to the high number of men migrating to urban centers for work. Unlike the neighboring Victoria East District, Middledrift did not have schools, white farms, or a well-developed trading center that could provide income-earning opportunities to supplement farming. In the early 1970s, Njwaxa residents needed wages to pay for goods they could not provide for themselves, which included food, clothes, and school fees. Cultivation had decreased, particularly because of drought, and men and some young women looked for work outside of the villages. Migrants found employment in the mines on the Rand or moved to Cape Town, Port Elizabeth, or East London for domestic, piecemeal, or factory jobs. Many Njwaxa residents struggled to meet their basic needs as they waited for promised cash from absent family members.[3]

In addition to environmental causes, the economic condition of Njwaxa was shaped by the view of the colonial and subsequent governments toward the development and relief of the region. Historically, the plight of the rural poor in the so-called Native Reserves had been a concern of the South African government only when it affected the labor pool and in times of catastrophic famine or drought. The government did not generally develop the infrastructure of rural reserves. Instead, missionaries had taken on the responsibility of establishing schools and providing health care (though they increasingly relied on government subsidies). With the implementation of apartheid, the government changed its policies in order to make the homelands viable as independent nations. This meant that the government retracted relief programs in the 1960s (as these were supposed to be the concern of new homeland governments) and focused on broader development.[4] The apartheid government knew that without some improvement of homeland agriculture and economies, it would not achieve its vision of white and black "separate development."[5]

In the 1960s and 1970s, the state promoted agricultural adjustment and development programs along with industrial growth near the homelands. Agricultural programs designed to improve the ability of the homelands to sustain a large African population first came in the form of so-called betterment policies. In the 1960s, the government (building on a program begun in the 1930s) sent agents to demarcate land into residential, arable, and grazing zones in villages. With a scientific modernization approach to agricultural development, government agents viewed African agricultural and livestock practices as backward and destructive. They believed their proposed changes would decrease soil erosion and increase the ability of people to live off the land. Yet betterment generally tended to reconfigure villages in a way that reduced the amount of arable land available for cultivation. It also threatened the economic and cultural basis of societies, particularly when the government required cattle culling. Because of these negative results and the nonconsultative nature of their implementation, betterment projects often caused social disruption and met resistance.[6] Like health services, betterment policies also could not accommodate the population growth of the Ciskei due to forced relocations. In the rural areas populations increased by as much as 54 percent in the 1970s. In the mid-1970s, the South African and Ciskei governments also began to promote larger commercial agricultural enterprises, such as dairy farming and pineapple plantations. But these only benefited a few, conspicuously including Ciskei National Independence Party members loyal to Sebe.[7]

The apartheid state's shift in economic policy in the 1960s involved encouraging economic decentralization in order to spread industrial and commercial growth outside of the Vaal triangle and in Cape Town, Durban, and Port Elizabeth. The government enticed investors and industrialists to underdeveloped white areas near homelands with promises of low wages, building subsidies, tax breaks, and soft loans. This led to the establishment of border industries located on the edge of homelands. Strategically placed industries could take advantage of cheap African labor residing in nearby homelands. White industrialists, investors, and businesses retained control over decision making. The Bantu Investment Corporation and its local subsidiaries took the lead role in investing in border and homeland industries and commercial ventures. The Bantu Trust (founded in 1936 to direct land acquisition and consolidation in the reserves) formed the Bantu Investment Corporation in 1959 to promote investment near the homelands. This took the form of industrial, agricultural, and commercial ventures. The corporation and its subsidiaries embodied the ideology behind the government's economic policies. Different divisions were formed to correspond with the homelands designated by the government. Leadership and ownership remained in the hands of white people and co-opted black people. For example, the Xhosa Development Corporation (XDC) was formed in 1968 to serve the Xhosa homelands of the Ciskei and the Transkei. White businessmen, government officials, and later Ciskei and Transkei officials ran the XDC from East London, though they claimed they would eventually turn the corporation over to black people. The Bantu Investment Corporation leadership operated in a similar way in the Bophutatswana and KwaZulu homelands. White oversight and the corporation's close supervision caused some ire among Tswana and Zulu leaders like Lucas Mangope and Buthelezi until they were granted local investment subsidiaries with more African input.[8]

By the early 1970s, it was clear that industries set up near East London and King William's Town, like other border industries, only attracted more unwanted urban migration. This increased African urbanization, along with calls by homeland leaders for investment and international pressure (applied after the plight of people forcibly relocated to the Ciskei had been exposed), served to motivate the apartheid government to open up the homelands for industrial development.[9] In 1969, the government allowed investment within the homelands—provided that government investment agencies directed these initiatives. After it obtained "self-governing" status in 1972, this applied to the Ciskei. The settlement of Dimbaza, southeast of Njwaxa, was designated as a primary growth point. A paint factory built there in 1975 serves as an example of the nature of XDC initiatives. At the opening ceremonies on March 11, the XDC's general manager, a Mr. Meisenholl, praised the factory for creating opportunities for black scientists, twenty-two black workers, and, in the future, twelve matriculated black staff members. "'The only white who will be employed here will be the managing director,' Mr. Meisenholl added." He also announced that they had "signed agreements with seven other industrialists involving an investment of R1.3 million for further development in Dimbaza."[10]

The developmental legacy of the government investment corporations and homeland leaders like Sebe is complex. Ciskei's chief minister, Sebe, welcomed the XDC's work as progressive (while Mangope and Buthelezi initially demanded more autonomy from the Bantu Investment Corporation). Sebe promised that the creation of an independent Ciskei would provide an opportunity to elevate the Xhosa people economically. He defined development as stable government and more job opportunities and farming cooperatives, the stated goals of the XDC.[11] Residents of Njwaxa, King William's Town, and surrounding areas often point to the Dimbaza factories, tarred roads, Ciskei government jobs, and the small city of Bhisho as fulfillment of Sebe's promises. Yet Sebe's political authority and monetary resources largely came from the apartheid government, which built up homelands for the ultimate purpose of privileging white South Africans. Industrial development under the direction of XDC white-managed agencies created only a small number of jobs in proportion to the entire growing population.[12] The XDC also kept control over decision making in the hands of white people and benefited only a few small businesses or large capital-intensive (as opposed to labor-intensive) enterprises, often run by Sebe's political supporters. The XDC was criticized for giving "too few loans at too high interest rates." Loans favored initiatives with white managers since they required "severe conditions pertaining to the management abilities of prospective borrowers."[13] In the end, commercial development still concentrated in areas outside of the Ciskei, and a downturn in the economy in the mid-1970s rendered any gains insignificant.

Of course, long before the XDC and new apartheid government policies, many nongovernmental and black-led groups had initiated programs to uplift black communities in the Eastern Cape. As discussed in chapter 1, black people led a number of economic programs and small-scale cooperatives before the 1960s and 1970s. Zenzele women's improvement clubs active in the Ciskei in the 1970s demonstrate that African self-reliance initiatives in the Eastern Cape involving women were not entirely new. These groups sought to create unity among Xhosa women and focused on helping the women grow gardens and improve home sanitation and other domestic practices. Other small, black-led programs targeted specific disadvantaged groups, including a settlement for the aged and people with disabilities near Peddie, handicraft centers, a reform school, and a children's home.[14] For the most part, however, these groups did not make an impact large enough to rival XDC or Sebe-endorsed enterprises and were generally politically and socially conservative.

Other approaches to addressing glaring poverty in the 1960s and 1970s by the state, civic, and religious organizations in the Ciskei often reflected a mentality of charity giving or paternalism. Many organizations provided relief by distributing rations. In times of drought and famine, the government distributed food or soup powder from clinics. They particularly targeted schoolchildren and, in their mistrust or stinginess, instructed the distributors to restrict supplies to those deemed truly needy. At times the government offered fruit or other market foods at lower prices.[15] In some places, it combined infrastructure and environmental projects with material compensation for work. For example, the government paid Njwaxa residents to eradicate a thistle weed and build retaining walls to prevent soil erosion.[16] These programs were only temporary, however, and not designed for lasting change, such as long-term job creation. White "do-gooders" enjoyed both the benefits of a society that privileged them and the satisfaction of doing charity work when they received publicity in newspapers like King William's Town's *Kei Mercury*. The paper praised the generous donations of King William's Town residents to the Red Cross and local schools, and reported on the activities of groups such as the Cripple Care society.[17]

Clergy had firsthand knowledge of the debilitating poverty in the rural Ciskei as they witnessed the plight of their congregations. These churchmen of different races sought to provide immediate relief and to improve economic opportunities for Ciskeian residents. They did much of their social welfare work on a local basis. Specific emergencies or crises often dictated their responses. For example, they distributed food rations, clothing, and other needed items to victims of forced removals who were dumped like refugees in Dimbaza. Priests and ministers also began to address structural poverty through cottage- or home-industry projects—small cooperatives where congregation and community members produced an item to sell in surrounding villages or ecumenical organizations' offices. Like some Zenzele projects, many of these home industries centered around sewing and involved women, the majority of the residents in rural villages. These projects made school uniforms, "African" attire, and religious uniforms. Some did beadwork. The goal was to give people an alternative to living on relief or welfare by developing skills, promoting "black collective entrepreneurship," and encouraging them to "exploit their natural resources."[18]

Individual priests led most of these projects, but the BCC supported many of them. The BCC was a regional ecumenical council, organized and run by local black and white church leaders. Like its affiliate, the national South African Council of Churches, the council provided financial and logistical support to social welfare efforts. For example, David Russell helped manage some BCC projects from the old Anglican church where he was staying on Leopold Street in King William's Town. One of these projects was the BCC's Dependence Conference, which provided a small stipend for families of political prisoners. When Russell left King William's Town for Lesotho at the end of 1973, Reverend Temba Sibeko became the office manager. Sibeko had started to run self-reliance gardening and cooperative projects among his own congregations before joining the BCC. He was drawn into the organization as he worked more frequently with Russell. He continued to run his gardening projects from the BCC offices.[19] Even though the larger structural aspects leading to rural homeland poverty needed to be changed for real development, home industries at least could provide longer-term solutions. And, they promoted a different mind-set than government and most charity groups.

The shared belief in building self-reliance between BCC people like Sibeko and the BCP facilitated the development of a relationship between the two organizations and contributed to the growth of the local network of Black Consciousness and Christian activists between Alice and King William's Town. Radical students from the Federal Theological Seminary and the University of Fort Hare in Alice often joined the groups of religious and Black Consciousness activists working in the Middledrift, King William's Town, and Alice Districts. Theology students fulfilled a practical requirement by helping priests minister to congregations and work on BCC projects.[20] Black Consciousness activists had become friends with these white and black priests and students. The UCM had brought them together as students in the late 1960s. Activists and theologians had also engaged each other as they formulated and promoted Black Theology. The seminary frequently served as a haven for Fort Hare students escaping the security police. What's more, they all shared offices at Leopold Street in King William's Town. In 1974, the BCP reported that they had acted as a sort of sales agency by helping the BCC with supplying and marketing their home industries in Dimbaza, Alice, and at the St. Mathews Mission in Keiskammahoek. Mvovo, who had joined the BCP staff in 1974, headed the sales and promotion for the BCP and BCC home industries. Biko also at times discussed project management issues with Sibeko.[21] In the case of the Njwaxa home industry, a single priest began the project with his congregation. Then, on the suggestion of a colleague at the seminary, he asked the BCP to take over the whole operation.

THE LEATHERWORK HOME INDUSTRY TURNED FACTORY

In the early 1970s, Father Timothy Stanton, a member of the Anglican Community of the Resurrection, served as the rector of St. Bartholomew's Church in Alice. He was also on the faculty of St. Peter's College, the Anglican section of the Federal Theological Seminary. As the rector of St. Bartholomew's, he and his colleagues looked after three congregations in villages close to Alice. The largest congregation was in Njwaxa, where the desperate poverty he encountered moved him to start a home-industry project. Stanton wrote, "Except for a few who had work locally, and due to the migrant labor system, most of the able-bodied men were away. The population consisted of the elderly, women and many children. I was appalled at their extreme poverty. In various ways I tried to help."[22] Stanton reportedly sold food such as milk, soup, and sweets at a low price and helped the community build a dam. He also knew of a tannery in King William's Town where one could get the unwanted off-cuts of leather for free. He decided to take advantage of this resource and introduce a leatherwork project in Njwaxa. He set up shop in the mud house in the churchyard and recruited a small number of women who made purses, belts, and shopping bags. Nothemba Sinxo, the wife of prominent community member and Xhosa author Guybon Sinxo (jailed at one point because of his political views), had a small crocheting and sewing group with some Njwaxa women who met at her house. Stanton was familiar with this group and coordinated with Sinxo when he brought the leather and started the work at the church.[23]

As the project grew, "Keeping [the women] supplied with materials and coping with marketing problems" became "too much" for Stanton.[24] His letters and applications failed to gain financial support for the Njwaxa women from the South African Council of Churches networks.[25] Stanton discussed his difficulties with his colleague Lawrence Zulu, a fellow Anglican priest at the seminary. After listening to his challenges, Zulu suggested that Stanton talk to Biko about the possibility of the BCP taking over the project. Stanton did so, and Biko agreed to take it on. Under BCP management, the home industry expanded into a thriving, though small, factory with skilled craftsmanship and proper equipment.

Since Njwaxa fell outside of the King William's Town District, the confines of Biko's banning area, Malusi Mpumlwana took charge of the project. When he first went to Njwaxa he was unsure of what the BCP could really do, but he thought that working with leather made sense. Other home industries such as sewing projects did not end up making a profit because people sold among themselves, saturating the market with their goods. In his view, leather, a unique product, had greater market potential. The BCP thus began to increase the materials and marketing power of the project through its connections. Malusi Mpumlwana secured a greater supply of leather with the help of Biko, who was a friend of the son of the owner of the tannery in King William's Town. They easily worked out a deal to purchase proper leather pieces. BCP employees then quickly taught themselves how to work with leather. In the process of taking over the project, Malusi Mpumlwana "actually had to learn something about how the hides are organized, the different tans, and which parts of the hide are good for what kind of thing . . . treatment, dyeing." He returned to Njwaxa to "lecture" about what he learned.[26] Mvovo, as BCP marketing director, tapped into tourist markets beyond Njwaxa and its neighboring villages and thus increased the demand for their products. The BCP's broader structure and networks allowed it to offer these human resources to this small, remote project.

Soon after taking over the project, Malusi Mpumlwana recruited a young female SASO member to serve as manager. This activist happened to be his younger sister, Vuyo Mpumlwana. She became available to work at Njwaxa at the beginning of 1974, when she completed her nursing certificate at King Edward VIII Hospital in Durban. Before moving to Njwaxa, Vuyo Mpumlwana had never worked with leather. Once she took over as manager, her brother continued to help her, and the villagers "put their thoughts together" to identify feasible designs. For the most part, however, this young woman managed the factory by herself and learned by doing. At times this was a lonely job, made more difficult by the lack of electricity, public transportation, and phone lines in the rural area. But, like others working in the area who "[had] their hands on the plow," she jumped in and took over the focused production work. Her older brother's charismatic friend whom she had looked up to as a student leader was able to persuade her to take the position. Vuyo Mpumlwana reminisced that Biko had "such an authority" and a "way with words," so that after talking to her about the idea, she thought, "Yeah, I can do that. There's nothing wrong with that. Come on!" It probably also helped that she came from a family of community workers and had a youthful "zeal and passion" for what she was doing. Her zeal and passion were fueled by the satisfaction she gained from watching Mvovo and her brother pack up and drive away with completed orders.[27]

Having a young woman manage the Njwaxa project had its benefits. In many ways, as in Zinyoka, Njwaxa women were at the center of the project. Women constituted the majority of the population in the village and had little means of income to support their families while their husbands worked far away. Women thus became the majority of the factory's employees—the BCP's main beneficiaries. Stanton had started his project primarily with women for the same reasons. Women employees were also responsible for the quality of the factory's products. Sinxo, who had liaisoned with Stanton, continued to play an important role as a key elder in Njwaxa by working with Malusi and Vuyo Mpumlwana to organize villagers to work in the small mud building next to the Anglican church. A picture of the first Njwaxa home-industry group published in the BCP's 1974 report shows Vuyo Mpumlwana with five women and three men, each holding a finished product. Sinxo recruited all of these women to the project.[28] Papu remembered that Sinxo, "a woman at the church," came to her and told her about the leatherwork project. Papu was interested in the prospect of a wage-earning opportunity and went to the church to sign up. She remembered that Vuyo Mpumlwana wrote their names down and started to teach them how to cut and sew leather. She started by making purses, then added belts and Bible and hymnbook covers.[29]

Sinxo and project managers recruited women in need like Papu, relatives of workers, and, in some cases, women known to have specific craft expertise. All of the women who worked at the factory over the years gained leatherworking skills and valuable wages to feed their families and send their children to school. Unlike Zenzele groups, the BCP's small industrial project focused on providing goods to sell to earn wages rather than domestic instruction. Papu's story and those of two other women who worked at the factory and were still living in 2008 represent the dramatic impact factory employment had on the lives of many Njwaxa women. Papu seized the opportunity to earn wages by doing leatherwork because in the early 1970s,

The humble beginnings of Njwaxa Leather Home Industry. From left to right: unidentified man, Nomust Mpupha, unidentified man, Sarha Papu, Vuyo Mpumlwana, unidentified man, Niniwe Mamase, Esther Mpupha, and Nothemba Sinxo. (*Source*: BCP, "1974 Report," 14, UNISA Archives, Documentation Centre for African Studies, ACC 20 Black Community Programmes.)

she had seven children to help feed and send to school. Her husband worked as a deliveryman in Cape Town and did piecemeal construction work. She stayed in Njwaxa and sold pork in cities to earn some cash. She did some farming, but "couldn't only depend on farming because farming can be so unreliable." Together, Papu's and her husband's incomes paid their children's school fees, but she had to "scrimp and save" to buy them clothes. What's more, once her children reached Standard Four, they had to leave the village to continue their schooling.[30] Others remembered Papu struggling to support her seven children, even surviving on handouts at times.[31] "It was difficult," Papu remembered, but her life changed when she started working at the factory because "you could get things with those wages," like food and shoes and school jerseys.[32]

Nontozande Nofence James's husband was not working at the time she was recruited to the factory because of his poor health. James had moved to Njwaxa as a young girl to live with her uncle after her parents both passed away. She married her husband in 1942, and subsequently she and her children depended on him to provide wages to meet their material needs. He worked for the railway in the area, traveling to and from places such as East

London, Adelaide, and Uitenhage. When he got sick, their economic situation became very bad. She herself did not have a job, but attempted to look after her husband and children. "We were hungry," she recalled. "A person who is sick needs to be helped all the time with everything that is needed. *Yho!*" James grew up working with beads and was known in the village for her beadwork. About a year after the BCP had taken over the leatherwork project, it needed someone who could place beads on bags and purses. The factory sent Nolize Papu, another employee, to ask James to come and work for them because of her reputation for beadwork. Despite her previously acquired talents, James remembered being "afraid" and "anxious" at first about being able to duplicate the samples she was given. "But," she said, "the Lord helped me so that I was able to. I was fine after that." Obtaining work within the village near her husband and children changed James's life. Her wages enabled her to nurse and feed her husband, and clothe and educate her children. She later testified that this economic security gave her peace.[33]

When James began working at the factory, there were few other employees (she remembered working with nine other people). Yet orders continued to come in, and James could not keep up with all of her work. She even took work home. "I didn't sleep at home, I was working with the beads," she explained.[34] Seeing how James struggled to cope with the amount of work she was given, the manager (at this time, Voti Samela) decided to hire another person to help with the beadwork. James recruited Nontombomhlaba Mamase, a village woman who had also grown up working with beads and had acquired a reputation because of her skills. Mamase was born in Njwaxa and had recently returned to the village in 1974 or 1975 to live with her father's family after working on a pineapple farm in Ngqushwa (Peddie). James brought Mamase to the factory, where Samela asked her to produce a sample by threading beads on a garment. Mamase claimed he was so impressed with what she made that he wore the garment himself.[35] Indeed, Mamase was a great asset to the factory—James praised her in 2008 as a hard worker whose skills surpassed her own. Eventually the factory stopped producing beaded work because it was not worth the time and money. James and Mamase then both joined other workers in marking, cutting, dyeing, and sewing purses, bags, belts, and shoes. In return for her work, Mamase's wages allowed her to build a rondavel and relocate her elderly mother to Njwaxa, where Mamase paid for all of her groceries and other needs.[36]

Fond memories shared thirty years after the factory's operations had ceased reflected the economic frustration villagers experienced in the early 2000s. Aside from problems caused by an assistant manager suspected

Esther Mpupha with Nontombomhlaba Mamase (*right*) putting glue in the purses. (*Source*: BCP, "Projects and People," UNISA Archives, Documentation Centre for African Studies, ACC 20 Black Community Programmes.)

of being a police informer (discussed further below), any recollections of tensions between workers were eclipsed by memories of a time when the women could earn wages within their village. These wages offered them economic security and hope at a time when both seemed scarce. Yet the way Papu, James, and Mamase remembered working at the factory also indicates that associations between Njwaxa women contributed not only to the recruitment of employees but to the smooth operations of the factory as well. Although all of the women said they were constantly busy and did not have time to chat (even if orders came in randomly), they recalled enjoying working with each other. Furthermore, Njwaxa women interviewed about the factory in 2008 remembered the names of the women who worked with them, but had difficulty remembering the men, even when presented with pictures of some of them. This may have been due to the fact that there were not as many male employees, but also because the women had a closer association with each other. Women who worked at the factory included sisters and relatives such as Pinkie James, Niniwe Mamase, Nothemba and Nozukile Sinxo, and Esther and Nomust Mpupha (relatives of Papu, born in the Mpupha family). Certainly, tensions between villagers and among relatives did exist in

Njwaxa, but working with close relatives on a project that focused on elevating the well-being of individuals and their community apparently helped create a positive work environment in the BCP factory.[37]

The women also did not remember anyone being fired for poor performance or creating friction between employees. For example, according to Mamase, another woman had initially assisted James with the beadwork, but this woman's inadequate work had to be undone at night (most likely the work that James took home). Even so, this woman was not fired, only shifted to a different task.[38] Each worker learned to perform the different tasks and thus could help when a certain stage of production needed extra hands to move it along more quickly. James likened the atmosphere at the factory to a classroom, "like the work of school children . . . training . . . like school children that are being taught, let them do it like this: writing, reading." Like students, the employees learned and worked together. The difference was they got paid.[39] Although factory managers themselves had not been trained in Freire's methodologies, the classroom atmosphere James described suggests that SASO's earlier training on cooperative learning informed by Freire had filtered down to Njwaxa. Some interviewees indicated that learning to work by the clock was more of a transition for some than others.[40] Yet most employees were eager to go to work. James maintained that they arrived early every day and that she herself was never late and never sick.[41] It is possible that James was correct in relating her prefect attendance. As Dina Mjondo, a member of the women's craft group in Zinyoka, remarked, "A person who is hungry" learns quickly and "works well" because "you don't want to get fired."[42]

As an employer of many village women, the factory had the potential to change the economic power of women and gender relations in Njwaxa. For Papu, James, and Mamase, this was indeed true. Though it is unclear how much of Papu's salary made up the total family income, at least James and Mamase became sole economic providers for their family members. Mamase even built her mother a house, seemingly unrestrained by any patriarchal control over land and other resources. Yet evidence does not suggest that these developments changed gender relations in Njwaxa in a significant way. In fact, it was not uncommon at the time for factories in the area to employ a large number of women. According to Switzer, women made up almost 70 percent of the workforce in Dimbaza factories. Njwaxa residents said jobs and money were so scarce that women took work in factories and did hard labor that had previously been seen as unfeminine.[43] Thus, a woman taking on industrial jobs previously seen as men's work was either accepted as a necessity or as increasingly normal. Moreover, the factory only operated for four years. Many of the men continued to work outside of Njwaxa during this time, even if they planned to obtain work at the village factory. Certainly, as Mager demonstrated, gender relations in the Ciskei had been undergoing changes caused by urbanization and the implementation of homeland policies, but the BCP factory did not have a particularly noteworthy influence on these changes.[44]

The factory did employ a number of men in particular need of work because of their political involvement or physical condition. For example, the factory hired a young man who could not walk and used a wheelchair. The BCP had also hoped to help ex–Robben Island prisoners and their families living near Njwaxa by creating jobs for them at the factory. Tainted by their political imprisonment, these men found it difficult to obtain work, and their families suffered during their imprisonment. The factory helped a few of these men, but Biko shifted the focus on political prisoners to a different project when he created the Zimele Trust Fund that offered grants to ex-prisoners for starting their own ventures.[45] As it happened, most able-bodied Njwaxa men lived and worked outside of the village and thus did not compete with women for employment within Njwaxa. Moreover, the promise of a second shift that would provide more jobs lessened tensions between employees and those who wanted to work at the factory but did not, including village men. As the factory grew, the BCP planned to extend operations to include a shoe-making section that would require an evening shift. The names of men and women hoping to obtain work when the second shift opened were placed on a waiting list. The promise of a job in the near future reportedly prevented anyone from becoming jealous of those who already worked there.[46]

A particular feature that made the Njwaxa factory especially stand out from other factories in the region was that at one point it had a young, black, female manager. A second picture of Vuyo Mpumlwana with her employees in a BCP report shows her teaching two men how to use what appears to be a punching tool. General gender expectations and her age could have elicited negative responses to her leadership from villagers; but at least Vuyo Mpumlwana did not feel inhibited by the fact that she was a young woman managing a factory and teaching older men and women to work with leather (often seen as a Xhosa man's craft). She pointed out that her role as the manager showed that Biko, her brother, and other Black Consciousness men trusted her and recognized her abilities. Moreover, she believed that her youth and gender worked to her advantage. Although she was in a position of authority over them, Vuyo Mpumlwana felt the employees saw her as a daughter of the community. She lived and ate with them like

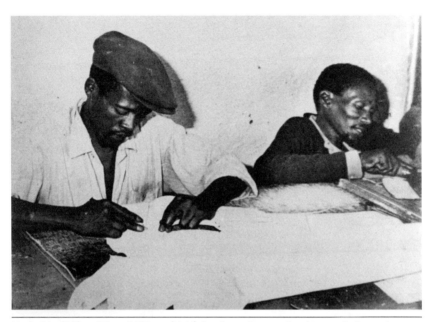

Mr. Socisha (*left*) and Mncedisi Xhape (*right*) drawing patterns and making marks for sewing. (*Source*: BCP, "Projects and People," UNISA Archives, Documentation Centre for African Studies, ACC 20 Black Community Programmes.)

a family member, and village men and women protected her when police came looking for her.[47] She represented the young activists working for the BCP who were committed to improving the economic position of Njwaxa. And, although they worked with leather alongside a few male employees, having another Xhosa-speaking woman join them would not have differed much for the village women who had previously worked together in informal or formal sewing and craft groups.

Vuyo Mpumlwana did not stay long enough in Njwaxa for her presence to have a noticeable influence on village gender relations. As with the Zanempilo clinic, the security police often went to the factory in search of activists and to uncover "subversive" acts. As soon as Vuyo Mpumlwana began managing the factory she became a "very interesting attraction" to the Special Branch of the security police. Perhaps they paid particular attention to her because she was an anomalous young, black, female manager in a rural village and seemingly easy to intimidate. The police frequented Njwaxa to question or detain her, but were often frustrated in their attempts. The men who worked with her devised a system with other villagers to help her evade the security police. The Anglican church building stands on a flat hilltop, deep in the village, well-positioned for spotting anyone entering Njwaxa. As Vuyo Mpumlwana related it:

> The beauty of it was that because it was a village, we could see the cars coming from way, way, way far away . . . and you know that that is not a village car. There is no village car here. So, already we knew and immediately the people I worked with would take me through the back window and someone else would go on the other side with a blanket and they would throw me through the window into the blanket and carry me and hide me somewhere.

When the police realized that driving into Njwaxa tipped off the villagers, they started parking their car outside the village and walking in. Still, "they were not that smart." Njwaxa residents knew each other and the BCP staff, so when black policemen walked into Njwaxa, villagers quickly recognized them as strangers.[48]

Despite the community's help, police harassment became "so uncomfortable" and such a distraction that Vuyo Mpumlwana thought she had to leave. Near the end of 1975, she left the Eastern Cape. After a brief sojourn in the Transvaal (where she completed ANC underground assignments in Alexandra Township), she reportedly walked over the mountains into Swaziland and then made her way to Tanzania via Mozambique.[49] In the absence of a manager at Njwaxa, the BCP recruited the temporary help of another young woman, Mantuka "Tiny" Maisela, a Fort Hare student who had become active in SASO with fellow female students Thenjiwe Mtintso and Thoko Mpumlwana. Because of her sewing skills, Maisela had helped with many of the home-industry projects run by Fort Hare and Federal Theological Seminary students and eventually became a field worker for the BCC. In 1975, she moved to the Johannesburg area, where she established a sewing project for the BCP's Transvaal branch.[50]

The BCP was set back, but not deterred by police harassment and the loss of Vuyo Mpumlwana. Just as the banning of Biko and Mafuna had led the BCP in more productive directions, the BCP found a way to move forward and build up the Njwaxa project. In this, it was aided again by local church connections. At the beginning of 1975, the BCP was fortunate to find a new manager named Voti Samela, a skilled craftsman in leatherwork. Samela came from Sterkspruit, in the Herschel District. An older woman who traveled to different churches as part of a women's prayer group (remembered only as Mrs. Maisela) knew of Samela and suggested to the BCP that it invite him to work in Njwaxa. Mvovo made the 200-mile (322-km) trip to Sterkspruit to make Samela an offer. He found that Samela had formal training in leatherwork, but had trouble getting work in the cities (he had been kicked out of Port Elizabeth for not carrying a pass or work permit). When Mvovo found him, Samela was making shoes with tools his father had helped him buy to set up shop near their village. Samela agreed to work with the BCP, and Mvovo helped him pack up his tools and move to Njwaxa.[51]

The BCP wrote about its project at Njwaxa as a "Home Industry," but Njwaxa residents and Samela all referred to the project as a factory. Indeed, thanks to Samela's steady management, machinery, and technical skills, the project evolved from a small cottage industry that involved a few people to a budding factory that acquired electricity and planned to add a second shift. Samela brought his specialized machines and knowledge of leather to improve production, and the project quickly expanded during the course of 1975, taking on more employees like James and Mamase. Workers continued to make purses and wallets, using punching machines and foot-powered sewing machines. They also began to produce seat cushions and moccasins and to tan sheepskins.[52] People from neighboring villages came to Njwaxa to purchase some of the finished products, while Mvovo and Malusi Mpumlwana continued to solicit orders from other markets. Nail bags were reportedly particularly popular in local hardware stores. Unlike small home industries, the factory had a broader market and bigger demand, with Mvovo and Malusi Mpumlwana fostering markets beyond local areas to Knysna and other tourist hotspots in the Western Cape and near Durban.[53]

In 1976, the BCP felt the impact of the Soweto uprisings even out in the "bundus" as the state clamped down on Black Consciousness leadership.[54] Police detentions of staff at the branch office slowed down the factory's work. Malusi Mpumlwana and Mvovo were two of the many BCP staff members detained for about four months around the same time fellow activist Mapetla Mohapi was killed in prison. (Other BCP staff detained included Ramphele, Solombela, Msauli, Sangotsha, Thoko Mpumlwana, and later Biko, though the state had restricted him from official BCP employment earlier in the year.) The detentions of BCP staff delayed the factory's plans to expand its building and also affected the ability of the BCP to raise funds and obtain materials. Still, production continued, and the factory experimented with making saddles and shoes. The BCP even organized women in Zinyoka to do the finishing work on some of the nail bags to help Njwaxa cope with its orders. Near the end of 1976, progress was made on a new wood and corrugated-iron structure in the churchyard intended to provide space for new machinery and more workers.[55]

In 1977, production began to pick up with the BCP staff back at the office, new machinery, and recruited skilled help. The growing number of workers (which would reach fifty near the end of 1977 according to Samela) started using the new building, and the factory planned to open its additional shoe-making section. Within the first three months of 1977, the BCP proudly reported that 160 pairs of shoes had already been made. It hoped to soon purchase a generator "for heating and attaching sole to shoes," and a "toe lasting machine" so that "the industry [would] have the capacity to produce up to 100 pairs [of shoes] per day."[56] Njwaxa residents bought these products, so did not have to go to the shops in towns and cities to buy what they needed. The BCP began to market school shoes among black communities with the slogan "buy black" and the argument that the factory would sell high-quality leather shoes for a lower price than those made out of man-made material marketed by PEP clothing stores.[57] Instead of paying big corporations, the BCP encouraged people to support black initiatives that provided local economic opportunities. To help with the expansion into shoe manufacturing, Samela recruited another young man from the Herschel District with skills in leatherwork, known simply as S'buku, or *umHerschelana* (in Xhosa, the diminutive of *umHerschela*—the nickname Njwaxa residents gave to Samela—because S'buku was younger and came after Samela).

BCP BLACK MANAGEMENT AND CAPITALISTIC COOPERATIVES

In the middle of 1977, the factory had enough money to "electrify the place." Samela approached an electrician based nearby in Alice to do the job. When he came to survey the factory building, the white electrician could hardly believe that black people ran the factory. Samela recounted:

> We went to an electrician in town, in Alice. . . . He asked me where this place is. I told him, it's at Njwaxa. "Can I go and see it?" I said, "Yes, you can follow me." We went there. When he came in there, he was surprised to see the set-up there and then he asked: "Is there any white man here to lead you?" I said, "No." But then he said, "But who am I going to talk to?" I said, "You are going to talk to us." [*laughs*] Because we used not to say, "this is mine," "this is his"—it's ours, you know. I said, "You'll talk to us." "But, will you have the money?" I said, "Yes. There's no problem. We will give you the money."

Samela assured the electrician that if he wanted to check on their finances, he could call the head office in King William's Town. A few days later, the white electrician came again, looked around, said he would come back, then left. After a week or so of waiting for his return, Samela went looking for the electrician in Alice. He did not find the man in his shop, but met a black shop worker. The worker asked Samela, "Who are you? . . . What type of people are you?" After listening to Samela's answers, he warned him that the police had listened to his white manager's conversation with the BCP's Leopold Street office and that the manager had been in contact with the police. Afraid of negative repercussions from working with this man, the BCP decided to hire an electrician from East London to do the job.[58]

Samela's retelling of this incident is significant not only because it highlights the reach of the security police. It also vividly illustrates the significance of the factory's black management in contrast to apartheid separate development. The white electrician's surprise at the factory's accomplishments independent of white leadership mirrors the shock of many white people at Black Consciousness assertions of black intelligence and capabilities. Working autonomously of the government and white business threatened the political and economic goals of grand apartheid. The Njwaxa factory stood in stark contrast to the paint factory opened by Sebe and the XDC in Dimbaza in 1975. Establishing a factory in the Ciskei was not a radical idea, since the government and businessmen implemented plans to use the Ciskei for industrial projects with low-wage homeland labor. As a home-industry project, the Njwaxa project also did not differ much from the work of churchmen in the area. What was unique about Njwaxa was its black management and substantial growth under that management. The XDC boasted of the twenty-two jobs that the paint factory offered Dimbaza residents. The Njwaxa factory had an estimated fifty employees when the police destroyed it in 1977 and over one hundred names on a waiting list to begin work when the shoe section expanded and the factory began two shifts. Moreover, the Njwaxa factory grew without a subsidized building from the state, the XDC, or a white managing director.

Samela's response to the Alice electrician is also indicative of BCP efforts to cultivate local black leadership and a sense of confidence and ownership among its employees. A successful black-run factory (or clinic or publication) proved assertions of black capabilities to be true to white and black people alike. In addition to white people, it must have made an impression on the Njwaxa villagers to see how the project continued and flourished under young black management after Stanton left. For Vuyo Mpumlwana, the leatherwork project proved to the villagers that black people could make "those things"—in other words, to change their mind-set from being "receivers of ideas" and expecting whites to run production to black self-confidence that "I can actually establish my own thing. I am creative. I can do this and do that. Belt doesn't have to come from a white person and be sold in a departmental store. . . . I can actually have my own factory which is business orientated and develop a business idea and implement it."[59] This is the perception of a manager, but there is evidence that the BCP did inspire confidence in the villagers in their own abilities to run such projects and that it did cultivate local management among Njwaxa residents. For example, Papu at one point thought that she would like to start her own factory.[60] In 1975 and 1976 BCP reports, Mrs. N. Papu, a Njwaxa resident, is listed as a production and clerical assistant under the staff section, evidence of the BCP's efforts to develop local management. The ideological purposes of the factory—fostering black self-reliance and conscientizing people of their ability to change their place in society—also contributed to a feeling of unity and self-confidence at the factory, another reason why interviewees may have forgotten or not experienced interpersonal conflicts between workers.

Samela's insistence on calling the factory "ours" was a way he attempted to build a sense of ownership among his employees. This was an extension of the unity he felt with his own managers. Vuyo Mpumlwana and Samela both emphasized the cooperative management style of Biko and the rest of the BCP that encouraged leadership development. At BCP meetings, each project manager prepared a report and distributed it to all the project managers. Each manager then had time to explain the progress he or she had made or challenges he or she faced and would receive input from others. Samela praised the way that Biko required everyone to prepare and present reports. He said he learned from Njwaxa "how people are united—how people can be united and do one thing with one voice."[61] Samela's description of BCP management echoes statements by former Zanempilo employees that working at the clinic was like working with family. Working with fellow activists and nostalgic memories may explain this assessment of employee relations. The BCP management style Samela described may also have contributed to cooperative relations among BCP employees (although the conflict between Samela and S'buku discussed below suggests that individual egos may have also caused tensions at times). Vuyo Mpumlwana further claimed that Biko brought out the best in people because he expected everyone to be a leader, work hard, accomplish what they had been mandated to, and report back.[62] In his individual, personal interactions with staff, Biko reportedly respected his employees as individuals and gave people the benefit of the doubt, part of the philoso-phy practiced by the BCP generally.[63] If the project managers' memories indeed reflect their sentiments of the 1970s, this influenced the way they interacted with workers at Njwaxa.

Yet the factory did not survive long enough to buttress local leadership enough. Nor did it resolve the contradiction between its financial depen-dence and promotion of self-reliance. Even if it did not rely on government subsidies or white management to succeed, it did rely on outside funding because it never made enough profit to be self-sustaining. It was difficult to create a home industry that was commercially competitive. Russell said that he himself did not expect much success from BCC home-industry programs. He pointed out the complexity of creating a viable factory: "It was hard . . . when you've got the economics of scale and PEP stores can produce all these things and then you try to get some materials and [you've] got to market it. How do you market it? Where do you market? What's the transport?"[64] The BCP had addressed some of these challenges by hiring Mvovo full time to supply the factory, find markets, and transport goods to the markets. Still, the BCP relied on its sponsors for capital to increase the factory's competi-tiveness. The BCP was good at harnessing capital from donors. One of the reasons the factory grew beyond a typical home-industry project was its ability to tap into financial sources. The South African Council of Churches supported the factory's growth along with European churches and orga-nizations such as the Dutch Interchurch Organization for Development Co-operation (or ICCO, which donated a substantial amount to finance the new factory building). This support was linked to the BCP's creativity and professionalism. At the same time, the politically hostile situation posed dif-ficulties in securing that funding. The possibility of state restrictions always hung in the air. Jones explained that the BCP deliberately limited the scale of its commercial ventures for that very reason. Greater investments would have meant greater loss if the government stopped the cash flow.[65] The BCP was thus never financially secure.

The way the BCP attempted to address its dependence on donors led to an ironic mixture of capitalistic ventures with ideas of black communal-ism by Black Consciousness activists. As a move to remedy its financial dependence, the BCP began to invest in property and businesses. Just before Biko's and Jones's imprisonment in August 1977, it bought a cloth-ing factory in Cape Town. It did this in part to convert its funds into assets so the government could not freeze or confiscate its money. But it also wanted to bring in a profit.[66] Ramphele also wrote that one strategy to address cash-flow problems was to organize the Njwaxa factory into a joint-share company where the BCP held 51 percent of the shares and the workers held 49 percent. According to Ramphele, this "capital injection" would have "[hastened] attainment of a break-even point," and eventually would have helped build the capacity of local factory employees, who could then help finance other projects.[67] In light of these ideas and initiatives, the BCP looks very much like an entrepreneurial organization. And yet while the BCP invested in manufacturing, Black Consciousness activists discussed the idea of black communalism. This term, though not fully fleshed out in the mid-1970s, referred to a social, political, and economic system based on notions of egalitarian African democratic practice and communal economic activities, similar to Nyerere's socialist *ujamaa* (which activists drew on as they debated black communalism).[68] Thus, while activists talked about creating a society where people worked together to ensure all maintained a comfortable standard of living, they also sought to participate in a capitalistic economy that focused on gaining wealth. Home industries like the Njwaxa factory embodied both of these aspects and can be viewed as capitalistic cooperatives—small economic ventures designed to earn a profit for a group of people working together to share in that profit.

The BCP did not live long enough to necessitate any resolution of this seeming contradiction. The tension between the BCP's entrepreneurial activities and black communalism may have even prevented the full development and adoption of black communalism by activists at the time.[69] It is also possible that BCP business initiatives reflected the influence of black middle-class sensibilities (people looking to investment and business to obtain better socioeconomic circumstances).[70] But the BCP was also in survival mode. Not so unlike postapartheid ANC economic policies that scholars have described as neoliberal, the BCP worked within the existing broader economic system to sustain its activities and hopefully redirect some economic growth.[71] At the time, activists did not have a concrete vision of what a restructured society would look like economically. Instead, the BCP's business ventures were small scale and local. Furthermore, what was more important to activists at the time was what happened to people involved in the projects.

The Njwaxa factory remained a project owned by the BCP (thus factory employees were BCP employees). Thirty years later, some Njwaxa residents looked to the Steve Biko Foundation to revive the factory. Giving the sense that the BCP's work was unfinished, they said they needed leadership and capital from outside to help their struggling village. The BCP, with its activists who came from outside of the village, had linked the village to financial and market networks and provided skilled leadership. Despite its efforts, the goal to cultivate local leadership remained largely unfulfilled. Still, the demonstration of black abilities to manage a factory was a significant aspect of the project—possibly the most significant, considering the BCP's ultimate community development goals. In the time that the BCP had, it worked with the opportunities and resources open to it. Government and police intervention often determined what those opportunities and resources were, and eventually eliminated them.

A SYMBOL OF SELF-RELIANCE AND A BEACON OF HOPE FOR A BETTER FUTURE

The key to measuring the impact of the factory lies in the memories of Njwaxa community members. Interviews conducted in 2008 revealed that the BCP's goals in Njwaxa were at least temporarily met. Initially, the BCP hoped to alleviate poverty, encourage self-sufficiency, and provide economic opportunities for ex–political prisoners and their families. Though ex–political prisoners did not end up featuring as prominently at the factory, oral histories revealed the importance of cash wages to Njwaxa women and the dramatic impact the factory had upon their economic situation. As discussed above, the ability to significantly contribute to the family income and gain marketable skills enabled them to provide a better future for themselves and their families. When asked about her favorite memory of the factory, Papu hesitated, then replied: "*Imali* [The money]." She explained, "It was the money there that helped me." Thanks to the BCP factory, she was able to feed and send all of her seven children to school. In 2008, all of Papu's children were alive and economically secure, in large part because of the education their mother helped pay for. One daughter was a teacher, two worked at banks, one worked at the local municipality, another was a nurse, and her sons worked as carpenters or builders.[72] Mamase built a new life for her and her mother in Njwaxa with her earnings. James's wages enabled her to buy food, purchase her husband's medicines, and pay for her children's school fees. "They paid, and I had work," she stated, "That is what makes me like [Biko] so much."[73] The long waiting list for positions at the factory is further evidence of the valued role the factory promised to play as a provider of local employment opportunities for other villagers.

In Malusi Mpumlwana's view, however, an increased belief in one's ability to do something for oneself was the more important aspect of the Njwaxa factory. He saw the factory not as a solution to the inequalities of South African apartheid economics, but a symbol for saying to people: "stand up for yourselves."[74] Evidence suggests that while debates about black communalism or Black Consciousness politics did not take place among most villagers, an affirmation of black capabilities did come across to factory employees in various degrees. Vuyo Mpumlwana remembered discussing with workers the reasons for their economic status and how they might change that (similar to SASO students using Freire's methodology).[75] She saw a change in the mind-set of workers during the factory's first year of operation as they came to believe in the ability of black people to run a business-orientated, industrial project. Therefore, while Njwaxa residents did not take part in the Black Consciousness movement for political reasons and later expressed the need for outside help, they did gain a new understanding of themselves and their world as they associated with Black Consciousness activists. In addition to wages, working at the factory gave Papu the intangible benefits of marketable skills and confidence in her manufacturing abilities. After the factory closed, Papu worked at a BCC sandal factory in Alice. After this sandal factory declined, she thought about starting her own factory. She did not have the money to do so, but again, the fact that she thought she could shows that she believed in her ability as a black woman to run an industrial project.[76] Other workers expressed the pride they felt and the human dignity they gained when they saw the factory grow because of the value of their finished products. Mamase said, "We were very proud. . . . We knew we were happy because we were going to start going in shifts."[77] As James pointed out, "[Njwaxa] was valued by the other villages in the area. . . . [People from those villages] would come buy purses, belts, and shoes."[78] Others noted how self-sufficient the Njwaxa residents were—they did not have to go to shops to buy these goods.[79]

Similar to Zanempilo, community-staff relations helped improve the villagers' sense of human dignity, and police action against the BCP politicized residents. It was clear to the residents that the BCP had different goals from the apartheid state and that those goals included working for the best interest of the village residents. The BCP enjoyed community support in Njwaxa because of the economic opportunities it brought to the village, as opposed to XDC initiatives established closer to the homeland borders. The positive, communal style of BCP leadership also showed the residents that the BCP worked on their behalf rather than for its own profit. This translated into subtle politicization and solidarity between BCP and Njwaxa residents in the face of police harassment. Unlike in Zinyoka, the headmen in Njwaxa did not oppose the BCP's work. Rather, they welcomed it (evidence that not all headmen in the Ciskei worked closely with Sebe or consistently opposed Black Consciousness). Samela told how the headman of Njwaxa at the time, Paige Ngono, came to him and told him that the police had directed him to expel the factory from the village. When Samela asked him if he would allow the factory to stay, the headman told Samela, "Well . . . I see no other way because you are creating work for people here."[80]

The way the police treated BCP employees and the factory confirmed to villagers that the apartheid government was only interested in maintaining its own power and that the BCP was interested in their welfare. A group of villagers conjectured that the government destroyed the factory because it thought the factory was part of the liberation movements. To this, they replied that they did not care if it was part of a political party because they were able to survive and live decent lives because of the factory.[81] When asked why the police destroyed the factory, James replied, "They didn't want us to work." When asked what was so wrong with working, she replied, "Well, we still ask ourselves that question today."[82] Others agreed that the government did not want black people to stand on their own feet or speculated that the authorities were jealous of the success of the factory. BCP managers, on the other hand, were genuinely interested in the welfare of Njwaxa. Samela always told police when they asked him if he owned the factory, "This is *our* factory," not just to evade police questions, but because he believed it. In 2008, villagers contrasted this approach to a government initiative carried out years after the factory was destroyed. The government constructed three white buildings on the Njwaxa community hall grounds, with the intention that residents would use them for community projects. Some people did try using this space for small sewing and beadwork projects. Then, they discovered they were required to pay rent. Residents accused those who built these structures of only wanting money, declaring, "They are not smart people, they are money people."[83] Mamase threatened to use the building without paying, telling government representatives, "It's our factory; it's ours, [you politicians]."[84] The three white government buildings stood empty and unused in 2008, a reminder of the frustrations that came with disingenuous government initiatives.

While the BCP did not encounter opposition from headmen as in Zinyoka, state action against the BCP did find its way into the factory. Interviewees pointed to S'buku as a suspected police informer and source of conflict. Samela had recruited S'buku from Sterkspruit to manage the shoe section of the factory because of his leatherworking skills. S'buku excelled at making footwear and reportedly brought more machinery with him. S'buku claimed that he had received his training in leatherwork in England and held a certificate of "general training." In hindsight, Samela thought this strange certificate should have made the BCP suspicious of S'buku. He should have also taken the fact that S'buku often went to Alice as a sign that he worked with the police.

Yet it was the incident when Samela and S'buku argued at the factory that heightened concerns about S'buku's possible role as a police spy. Apparently, S'buku was a heavy drinker and smoker (evidence to some of the Njwaxa residents of his bad character). One day, shortly before the police shut down the factory, Samela caught S'buku drinking on the job. Samela confronted S'buku about this in front of the other employees, which led to a heated argument. This may not have been the first time they argued (some villagers said the fact that S'buku owned some of the new machinery and had better skills, yet was paid less than Samela, was a source of contention between Samela and S'buku).[85] But some pointed to this as the spark of what later ensued. At the next BCP staff meeting, which Samela and S'buku attended together in Zinyoka, Samela said S'buku was still visibly irritated with him. When it came time for Samela and S'buku to report on the factory, S'buku complained that Samela had reprimanded him in front of the staff, interfering with his job and undermining his position. Samela remembered that Biko affirmed that S'buku was wrong to drink at work, but also instructed Samela to speak to S'buku alone or come to BCP management to deal with such incidents. Samela recounted that after the meeting ended, Biko took him aside and told him that he suspected S'buku because he had not been arrested with another man when crossing the border into South Africa from Mozambique after supposedly carrying out an ANC mission. Biko had seen this in the paper and told Samela to keep an eye on S'buku.

On the day the factory was shut down, S'buku's relationship with the security police was confirmed. While Samela was held in police custody at the factory site, S'buku was left alone. When the police allowed Samela to go to his house for food and to relieve himself, he and the black policeman escorting him saw S'buku dumping water outside his door. The policeman accompanying Samela referred to S'buku and said: "That man has finished you." He then told how S'buku had frequented the police offices in Alice.[86] Njwaxa residents later reported that S'buku had also taken his machinery before the police came to close the factory. They saw this as further proof that he had cooperated with the security police.[87] It is uncertain just how dangerous S'buku was. Nonetheless, speculations by Samela and Njwaxa residents of the damage he could have caused to the BCP or Biko highlight the severely repressive political environment the BCP worked in and the lengths the security police would go to gain information.[88]

October 19, 1977, the day the police came to shut down and destroy the factory (a month after Biko's death) stood out clearly in the memories of the people in Njwaxa. Factory employees and other residents were suddenly stripped of their jobs, a devastating blow given the dearth of economic opportunities in the area. It was also dramatic because the police confiscated all of the factory's leather materials, finished goods, machinery, and Samela's personal tools, then proceeded to demolish the new factory building. They left the concrete slab foundation, as Ramphele wrote, "as a monument to the destruction wrought by a repressive state bent on the elimination of symbols of self-reliance and beacons of hope for a better future."[89]

CONCLUSION

The Njwaxa leatherwork factory was short-lived and only partially successful. It operated for only four years, and the few attempts to continue with similar projects after 1977 failed. Despite its premature end, however,

The factory foundation in the churchyard as it appeared in 2008. (*Source*: Photo by the author.)

the Njwaxa factory did achieve some success. By addressing basic material needs, Black Consciousness activists helped to temporarily alleviate the suffering of poor communities and offered a poignant example of competent and autonomous black management. This transformed the way some black South Africans thought about their abilities to change their socioeconomic conditions. The factory quickly grew as activists capitalized on local skills and their social connections with local priests and international funding groups. Throughout, village and BCP women critically shaped the factory's work. They brought management and craft skills to the project, and the associations of the factory's majority female employees contributed to its smooth operations. Although Njwaxa residents were not conscientized at an explicit political level or engaged in debates sparked by *Black Review*, they recognized the difference in ideology and approach between the BCP and top-down separate development. Instead of holding out on the sidelines and reserving profits for a few, the Njwaxa project leadership relocated to bring economic opportunities into the heart of a Ciskei village. Njwaxa residents later fondly remembered the factory in the context of their present struggles. They repeatedly expressed concern about their unemployed youth and frustration with the lack of jobs in the village. They longed for the BCP factory and marveled at the thought of where it could have taken them had it continued to operate. In their view, it exemplified how services can be brought to people in a way that improves their self-reliance.[90]

Conclusion

In August 1977, Steve Biko and Peter Jones took a trip in Ramsey Ramokgopa's station wagon out of Biko's banning area to hold meetings with leaders of the Black People's Convention and the Unity Movement in Cape Town. The meetings never materialized. Biko and Jones turned back and were stopped by the police at a roadblock outside of Grahamstown, on August 18. When they learned they had some of the most politically influential people in the country in their custody, the police detained them under Section 6 of the 1967 Terrorism Act and sent them to the Special Branch in Port Elizabeth. In the following weeks, security police interrogated the two men at their headquarters in the Sanlam Building about their alleged involvement in distributing "subversive" pamphlets. Jones was released 533 days later, in February 1979, after solitary confinement and torture. Biko died in a prison hospital in Pretoria on September 12, 1977, after suffering brain damage sustained by police interrogation, inadequate medical care, and inhumane treatment.[1]

Biko's death sparked national and international protest and was a prelude to the end of 1970s Black Consciousness organizations. For Khoapa, "from a personal angle it was absolutely devastating," and "from an organization point of view," it was "very confusing."[2] The BCP indeed had suffered a great loss. Biko had been integral to the organization. He and Mafuna had started *Black Review* with Khoapa in 1972. He had served as the yearbook's first editor and took an advisory role in subsequent editions. After his banning in 1973, Biko built up the BCP's most successful programs in the Eastern Cape along with people like Malusi Mpumlwana, Ramphele, and others who worked in Zinyoka and Njwaxa. The tragedy of Biko's death was deepened by the subsequent banning of all Black Consciousness organizations and related groups and individuals (the Christian Institute; youth organizations; the *World* newspaper and its editor, Percy Qoboza; and East London's *Daily Dispatch* editor, Donald Woods). James Kruger, then minister of justice, signed the order declaring these organizations illegal just two weeks after Biko's funeral in King William's Town. On the morning of October 19, the government shut down the BCP and all of its projects in one coordinated sweep. Police closed all BCP offices and confiscated the organization's documents, assets, machinery, and goods. The state never returned these materials to anyone associated with the BCP. Most BCP employees were sent home without jobs.

The closing of the Zanempilo clinic and the destruction of the factory building at Njwaxa were particularly dramatic for BCP employees and village residents. At Zanempilo, Sydney Moletsane, the lone doctor in charge, was awakened in the dark hours of the morning. Two armed soldiers came to his room in the doctors' quarters next to the clinic. Police searched his room before going to the clinic to take stock of supplies. They ordered him to continue with his normal clinic work throughout the day, but when he instructed the nurses to refuse to help the police, they took him to a local station, where they detained him until late that night.[3] While he was detained, the police locked the gates to the clinic to keep the others inside while they sorted through the clinic's assets. Hlaula managed to hide "important dockets" in the ceiling of the doctors' quarters, but the police took most everything else, including the cutlery.[4] They even cut the telephone lines. When he was released from police custody at the end of the day, Sydney Moletsane was informed that he no longer had a job and that the BCP had been shut down.

While Sydney Moletsane and Sangotsha, the clinic's social worker, lost their jobs at the clinic, a few of the nurses and the ambulance drivers retained theirs (the state health department of South Africa took over the clinic until 1981, when it handed it over to the "independent" Ciskei government).[5] Despite his dismissal, Sydney Moletsane stayed in Zinyoka for a month, trying to keep the clinic and its outstations going. Eventually, he felt too threatened by the police and was urged by others to leave, so he left the Eastern Cape. Subsequently, the government lacked the means, commitment, and inclination to continue the same level of care that the clinic offered under the management of the BCP. The clinic was no longer open twenty-four hours a day during the week or on weekends; it no longer had resident doctors or an abundant supply of medication. Staff salaries were reduced so that Ndzengu and Hlaula both left for other jobs, and the ambulance service ceased. Out of fear and a lack of resources and direction, community members and the remaining staff did not resume the craft group or other cooperatives. Without the traffic of regular visitors, financial resources, and a large staff, Zanempilo and Zinyoka changed drastically. Nondalana said,

"We waited, and there were no meetings. . . . There was nothing, we just waited."[6]

In Njwaxa, Samela was also awakened by the police pounding on his door in the early morning of October 19. The police took him to the factory building in the churchyard, where they kept him in a guarded car. They then proceeded to remove all of the factory's equipment and goods. By the time workers arrived to start a normal day of work, the commotion at the factory had attracted other villagers, who gathered outside the locked gate. A few individuals saw Samela and called to him to ask what was happening. The police ordered Samela to tell them to go home because they no longer had work. Afraid and confused, some workers went home. Others watched in fear and horror as police finished emptying the factory, dismantled the walls and roof, then cut the frame pillars. Still recovering from the news of Biko's death, villagers watched as their livelihoods and their hopes for a better future were destroyed. Like Sydney Moletsane, Samela tried to continue the efforts of the BCP for Njwaxa residents. Soon after the factory closed in Njwaxa, the Border Council of Churches attempted to establish a sandal factory in Alice and asked Samela to manage it. Some of the Njwaxa residents went there to work. They made sandals that reportedly became popular in Cape Town. However, police harassment resumed, and Border Council of Churches resources could not keep the sandal factory working at the same pace and scale as in Njwaxa, so Samela returned to Sterkspruit.[7]

Looking back thirty years later, Samela was disappointed that activists and BCP employees did not put forth a greater effort to continue with their work. There is little evidence in the villages that community members became political activists as a result of BCP projects (or even knew about Black Consciousness publications like *Black Review*). Nor did they oppose the police as they shut down the BCP programs. Few attempted to revive the projects after 1977. Some may view this as proof that the BCP in fact had failed to instill a sense of self-determination or that villagers never did own the projects as activists hoped. Yet the BCP did promote self-reliance and black human dignity. Despite its contradictions and challenges, it found some success in improving the material and social development of black South Africans in both village-based projects and national-level publications.

First, there is evidence that the BCP had a major impact on the material situation and self-perception of a number of individuals. After the end of the Njwaxa factory, Papu used the skills she gained at the BCP project to work in another factory. In Zinyoka, Dl'ebusuku proudly displayed her yard in 2008, where she continued to employ the dry-land gardening methods she learned at the clinic. Women in both villages spoke of the education their children received (either through wages or grants from the clinic), which eventually raised the self-reliance and socioeconomic status of their families. Others talked of the impact these projects had on their sense of self-worth and dignity. These assessments may have been exaggerated by nostalgia. Villagers' descriptions of Biko's attributes and kind deeds could be seen as a reliance on Biko for cultivating a belief in the worth of black people. Still, the testimonies demonstrate that many individuals felt a greater sense of self-worth as a result of the BCP's work, despite the BCP's unfinished business and an oppressive apartheid environment. By extension, the BCP's impact on individuals left a memory in the communities of what is possible if resources and leadership exist. The fact that some women in Njwaxa formed sewing groups after 1977 and the demands of the Zinyoka clinic committee on the government to restore the clinic to its initial state indicate that the BCP's work inspired some collective action, even if small. Limited evidence also points to the influence of BCP publications like *Black Review* on both individuals' self-perception and the ability of communities of academics and activists to further black development (though the impact was more diffused).

In assessing the achievements of the BCP, it is also important to consider the power of state repression and related loss of resources. After viewing interview clips where interviewees like Samela laughed about police harassment, one Njwaxa villager urged others not to forget the political danger and fear prevalent in South Africa in the 1970s. Indeed, the state was a powerful force that delivered a heavy blow to the BCP in 1977. When police dismantled BCP projects, Biko had just been killed in police detention. Villagers knew other victims of state repression, and some had been on the receiving end themselves. The unexpected nature of the attack on the BCP and fear and emotional grief were strong deterrents to resistance for many, even if they were conscientized. The state also scattered BCP employees. Some, like Moodley and Jones, were detained for long periods of time and only learned long after the fact that Biko had died. Others were banned or believed it was too dangerous for them to remain in the country, such as Khoapa who left South Africa via Lesotho with his family in 1978. The impact of state repression on the BCP included decimating its material resources as well. The police confiscated all of the assets the BCP had worked to accumulate, including all the machinery and leather materials in Njwaxa. The government took over Zanempilo, and police completely destroyed the factory building in Njwaxa. Taking away these material and human resources plunged the BCP projects back to square one. Attempts to continue BCP initiatives by villagers would have been plagued by the lack of funding and networks the BCP had provided. Not having connected villagers to these resources was part of the unfinished work of the BCP, leading some Njwaxa women to emphasize the benefits of outside leadership in a group conversation in 2011.

At another level, the survival of BCP ideas and practices can be seen through the establishment of related organizations after 1977. While projects of the Azanian People's Organization (AZAPO, the political organization formed in 1978 to replace the Black People's Convention) lasted only a few years, major projects established by Black Consciousness activists post-1977 still operate today. The nature of these organizations indicates that if the BCP had been allowed to continue, it would have addressed the resource and community ownership questions left unanswered by its early demise. After October 1977, people involved in the BCP and the movement applied Black Consciousness or BCP principles of working *with* people instead of *for* them and addressing root causes of problems in running urban and rural projects with youth, women, and churches. They continued to seek to change the mindset as well as material situation of black people in order to build self-reliance and reach a total liberation. They also shifted their focus according to the needs of the people and the resources available to them and as certain programs became independent. Furthermore, while many former BCP employees started these initiatives, others have moved in to take leadership positions.[8]

In April 1977, the state banished Ramphele to Lenyenye, in the Tzaneen District of the northern Transvaal. Once she recovered from the death of Biko and the difficult birth of their son, Hlumelo, she focused on establishing the Ithuseng Community Health Center. She described the health center as a "scaled-down but much better planned version of Zanempilo."[9] It officially opened in September 1981 to serve surrounding impoverished rural villages and townships. Along with primary health care services, Ithuseng initiated income-generating programs, such as a brick-making cooperative. Vegetable gardens "began to blossom everywhere," and representative village committees established a number of child-care centers based on community participation even after Ramphele left in 1984. Ithuseng also conducted literacy classes and initiated projects to empower women, such as building mud-stoves and cardboard wonder boxes to reduce the need for collecting firewood. It enjoyed support from typical BCP funders such as the Interchurch Organization for Development Co-operation (ICCO) in Holland, the Anglo American Corporation, the International University Exchange Fund, and the South African Council of Churches, as well as the local Catholic church, British Christian Aid, and later Oxfam International.

Thoko and Malusi Mpumlwana established the Zingisa Education Trust in order to salvage the Ginsberg Education Fund initiated by Biko. The latter project had lost funding during the upheaval of the BCP in 1977. To secure financial resources and avoid further state repression, they "needed to make it look like a new project." They thus gave it a new name derived from the Xhosa verb *ukuzingisa*—"to persevere."[10] The project extended beyond Ginsberg to include the entire Eastern Cape. Thoko Mpumlwana created a system to ensure scholarships would be given to both urban and rural areas proportionately. Zingisa tracked the recipients of scholarships and involved them in winter school programs to help tutor younger students. In 1980, it became an affiliate of the Border Council of Churches to facilitate funding.[11] In 1993, Zingisa switched gears to focus more on agricultural programs. It dropped its scholarship component due to problems of scale, resources, and management. Zingisa has since sought to give small-scale farmers a voice by raising awareness about government policies and farmers' rights; facilitating meetings between the government, industries, and farmers; providing technical support; and organizing local discussion groups for women. In August 2007, it helped form Ilizwi Lamafama, a regional farmers' union in the Eastern Cape.

By the mid-1990s, Malusi and Thoko Mpumlwana had left King William's Town and Zingisa, yet had helped secure Zingisa's future by forming an umbrella structure for a number of programs. In the mid-1980s, they created the Trust for Christian Outreach and Education (TCOE) while Malusi trained at the Federal Theological Seminary (then in Pietermaritzburg) as part of the Order of Ethiopia Church.[12] Zingisa, Ithuseng, and Masifundise (an educational project established for students in Langa, Cape Town) were its first three main affiliates. When Malusi Mpumlwana stepped down as TCOE's director in the late 1980s, former Zanempilo nurse Nontobeko Moletsane served as the director. TCOE later evolved into the Trust for Community Outreach and Education and grew to include six regional groupings in the Eastern Cape, Western Cape, and Limpopo provinces. The regional groupings included Khanyisa, an organization established to work with disadvantaged communities surrounding Port Elizabeth, directed by Nohle Mohapi (also its founder) from 1990 to 2003 (when she became a full-time municipal councilor). TCOE affiliates have all adopted a rural focus in recent years, with Masifundise (where Jones serves on the Board of Trustees) working with coastal fishing communities.[13]

Black Consciousness activists in Durban, though not all originally involved in the BCP, were inspired by the organization and initiated programs that drew upon its experience. The Umtapo Center was founded in 1986/87 by members of AZAPO, such as Deena Soliar, who became the full-time director. These activists formed Umtapo for two main reasons. First, it was established to respond to the destructive violence that ravaged KwaZulu-Natal from the mid-1980s to the early 1990s, between Inkatha—a Zulu ethnic nationalist movement—and the United Democratic Front (a movement aligned with the ANC). They thought a community organization could cut across party politics and nurture unity. Second, they believed the Black Consciousness movement of the time did not engage in enough grassroots work (though some had directed development initiatives, such as Pandelani Nefolovhodwe, who ran cooperatives in rural areas). Soliar and others founded a nonprofit organization separate from AZAPO to increase community development efforts and find an easier entrée into communities as an organization that operated independently from a political party.[14]

As they worked on creating the Umtapo Center, Soliar and his colleagues looked to the BCP for an example (even involving Khoapa in the center after his return from the United States in 1990). The way Umtapo continuously evolves to meet perceived needs and cultivate self-reliance suggests that the BCP would have done the same if it had survived. Initially, Umtapo planned to run projects in local communities, establish an information center, and set up an advice office. They used the advice office to ascertain the needs of the surrounding communities as they offered legal assistance. Through this office, Umtapo discovered that illiteracy and the lack of structured youth programs were major problems. Subsequently, Umtapo established a literacy program and youth leadership workshops. In 1992, when it felt the need had passed, Umtapo closed its legal advice office. In its stead, it helped launch the Azanian Workers Union (AZAWO), headed by Patrick Mkhize.[15] The center's local youth workshops evolved into a leadership workshop for young women that expanded to a ten-day course on women and development that was conducted in all of South Africa's nine provinces in 1998 and 1999. Umtapo has also made its programs independent. For example, after joining the African Association for Literacy and Adult Literacy and helping to launch the South African Association for Literacy in 1992, Umtapo relinquished its leadership of the literacy program. It also sponsored an African Peace Education program that spawned Peace Africa Youth Centers and peace clubs around South Africa. The idea for creating a program focused on peace education came from a series of conferences on the family held in Umtapo's resource center in 1993 and 1994. Young participants of the program eager to work in their own communities were then trained in establishing centers for community development and self-help. Like the BCP, Umtapo also publishes a regular newsletter to facilitate cooperation and networking and produces training manuals.

Other Black Consciousness activists found an outlet for their community work at the Wilgespruit Fellowship Center in Johannesburg and have more recently established agricultural programs. Nefolovhodwe and Ishmail Mkhabela both ran training meetings in community organization at Wilgespruit that included economic project planning, discussions on race and class, labor studies, and women. Nefolovhodwe later focused on agricultural projects, working with the People's Agricultural Development organization until he became a member of South Africa's parliament in 2002.[16] At about that same time, he also became the director of the Is'Baya Development Trust, an organization founded by Jones in 2001. Is'Baya focuses on community mobilization and self-reliance in poor rural areas primarily through an Integrated Village Renewal program, which it has implemented in the O. R. Tambo District of the Eastern Cape. Starting at the household level, it first seeks to establish self-sufficient food production, then transition farmers into commercial production of high-value crops (working in partnership with the Agricultural Research Council Institute for Tropical and Subtropical Crops). In September 2013, Is'Baya reported that more than 5,200 households in the Eastern Cape had planted over 110,000 trees through fifty-two villages, including mango, guava, and avocado trees. Over twenty-four trial sites had planted herbs such as lavender, thyme, marjoram, and rosemary. Is'Baya has provided training courses on cooperative management for each village in order to support the formation of local farming cooperative organizations led by local farmers. This is putting the villagers in a position to organize and "represent themselves" in accessing resources and infrastructure. Large-scale commercial farming has not yet developed, but many households have increased their subsistence production and have begun to sell fruit, jams, and juices to their local communities, schools, and guesthouses.[17]

Like the BCP in Zinyoka, Is'Baya also hopes to address a wide range of community issues. The village renewal program includes health management and heritage programs. The organization talks about developing a critical consciousness among villagers and working with people to define themselves and pose solutions so they can take charge of their own development. It also emphasizes drawing upon networks of partners and local resources. Echoing the work of activists in the 1970s, Is'Baya reported in September 2013 that the capacity to organize and manage "their own affairs" has, "as expressed by the village groups, . . . restored their dignity and confidence." Is'Baya stressed the importance of this last result of its programs. As with the BCP, developing individuals by improving their self-perception and capacity for effective collective action was important for the holistic development of the community.[18]

The Steve Biko Foundation is part of the line of organizations that make up the legacy of Black Consciousness community development. It has a different agenda as it also seeks to shape the heritage and legacy of Steve Biko. Still, its emphasis on local development as part of that legacy is evidence of the important place of community development in Biko's life and within the Black Consciousness movement. The foundation's executive office in Johannesburg runs national programs to promote public dialogue. The Steve Biko Center in Ginsberg has focused on community development. It has held an annual sports tournament to promote local sports development and youth leadership conferences. It has worked with a local paprika farming cooperative and supports a theater and arts group, among other programs. The center has expanded the foundation's activities and, similar to the BCP, maintains a museum, library, and archive.

The survival of Black Consciousness community development ideas and practices through organizations like Ithuseng, Umtapo, and Is'Baya is a testament to the effectiveness of those ideas and practices, despite the challenges and contradictions the BCP faced in the 1970s. The significance of the history of the BCP and this aspect of the movement also extends beyond the existence of these organizations. The BCP's history demonstrates the possibilities of black-led, people-centered participatory methods that aim for both a social-psychological liberation and material self-reliance. Even though community health initiatives or black-led cooperatives and publications were not necessarily new in South Africa in the 1970s, Black Consciousness activists built up black people in opposition to apartheid at a time when resistance had generally been quieted. Through its analysis of how activists carried out their projects, this book has revealed the different networks and often messy and paradoxical relationships that advanced the cause of liberation and community development in the country. It highlights the importance of transnational student and church connections of the time, the significant though tacit role of women, the successes and limitations of youth activism, and the cooperation between black people and white people that occurred under a surface of rhetoric that rejected all such associations. The innovation and autonomy activists maintained while still utilizing outside money and multiracial networks shows that the history of twentieth-century development cannot be read simply as the diffusion of ideas and advancements from Europe and North America into Africa, Asia, and Latin America. Furthermore, in contrast to much of the extant history of development in Africa, this history focuses on nongovernmental African-led small-scale development initiatives. In the introduction, I argued that looking at this kind of development history gives us a different perspective on particular aspects of economic and community development. By way of conclusion, I outline some broad issues to which the history of Black Consciousness community development speaks.

First, the history of SASO and BCP community work shows the importance of an overarching ideology that prioritizes what happens to individuals and communities in the process of running a development initiative. This is very similar to Amartya Sen's famous argument that development should be seen "as the process of expanding the real freedoms that people enjoy."[19] But it goes deeper. The Black Consciousness philosophy moved activists to seek to restore human dignity and build black self-reliance by improving skills and abilities to coordinate as well as by conscientizing black people—cultivating in them a critical awareness of their worth and position in society and their potential to change their circumstances. For these activists, self-reliance, political liberation, material security, physical health, and human dignity all had to be addressed simultaneously. This meant that the BCP's fundamental approach to urban and rural areas did not significantly differ and that it worked with village women, although it had not initially set out to. Furthermore, reaching this end result was foremost in the minds of activists rather than the survival of a project for the project's sake. Whether the shoes the Njwaxa factory sold were competitive with PEP stores, whether Zanempilo gave out an increasing number of immunizations, or whether *Black Review* sold more copies than the *Survey* was not the most important priority. The BCP was more concerned with women taking charge of their own health and the nutrition of their children, with black people gaining confidence and discussing how they could address poverty, and with developing entrepreneurial and industrial skills to provide jobs and goods for black communities. Freire's own work was more effective when he emphasized process over results.[20] In Archbishop Njongonkulu Ndungane's words: "We cannot consider development within South Africa, nor upon this continent, without considering what it is to be truly human." As he argued, development efforts that do not seek "the flourishing of the whole human person" will be "too small."[21]

This philosophy shaped Black Consciousness activists' participatory approach to their projects. BCP employees and SASO students were at once both outsiders and insiders in the communities where they worked. They suffered discrimination as black people in South Africa but also at times spoke different languages, came from different socioeconomic classes and geographic communities, and faced different challenges because of their gender or historical origin. Like many development practitioners past and present, activists learned to listen to and work with local communities. This approach did not devalue the leadership and resources the activists provided.

The key was for activists as instigators to ensure the community—with its various actors—took part. Though they may not have adequately recognized it, activists did learn about the reality of "internal differences" that run along the lines of "class, gender, age and geographic location" when putting their ideas into practice.[22] Thus, despite this weakness, Black Consciousness community work is an example of how to practice participatory development at all levels: in the assessment of problems and needs and in devising and carrying out solutions. As Ramphele wrote, this kind of participation that involves people in the whole process not only is more effective but also "brings about growth in the persons involved and their empowerment."[23]

The Black Consciousness liberation philosophy and participatory approach to community programs are both part of one of the most relevant lessons of the history of Black Consciousness development for today: the importance of people-centered leadership. Ramphele has also termed this ethos "person-centered professionalism." For her, this term encapsulates the kind of leadership, dedication, and motivation that is focused on having projects make a deeper and longer-lasting impact on communities and individuals.[24] Ramphele has also argued that South Africa needs to purge the authoritarianism in its social relationships, leadership styles, discussions with those of different viewpoints, and treatment of the most vulnerable. In addition to cultivating "person-centered professionalism" in public services, she has stressed the importance of consultative decision making in government.[25] Echoing similar sentiments, Khoapa compared the BCP's people-centered approach in Njwaxa to current politicians concerned more with obtaining and displaying wealth than the welfare of their people.[26] Mangcu argued that when people ask how South Africa would be different if Biko had survived, they are expressing a social wish for a "return to the kind of leadership that is underpinned by solidarity with the people." He went on to describe the importance of conscientization in the relationship between leadership and its citizenry, writing that people "need to be conscientized to think and act as subjective agents and not objects of other people's sympathy and largesse. And that too requires leadership that speaks and engages with the people—instead of seeing them merely as racial voting cattle."[27]

While a conscientization approach like the one Black Consciousness activists took can be effective, it varies in different contexts and can be problematic.[28] The racial and class dynamics in Brazil and Chile where Freire worked in the 1960s differed from those in South Africa in the 1970s, making the kind of conscientizing projects conducted in each place different. In Brazil, although racial discrimination did exist and had an impact on social, economic, and political development, it was not a pillar of the government as in South Africa. Freire wrote about the need to conscientize workers and peasants about the nature of their socioeconomic oppression before they could critically devise solutions to combat it (and he thought identity politics in the United States were unproductive).[29] Black people in South Africa, on the other hand, already recognized a major source of their oppression: racism. Black Consciousness activists applied Freire's methods more broadly than literacy projects to awaken people to their psychological complicity in their racial oppression and help people then improve their ability to change society.[30] They targeted conscientization through publications and in physical projects based in local communities. The results of their efforts showed that although publications directed at changing a mind-set can effectively bring about conscientization, local projects with a concrete, material impact can have a similar effect—but even deeper, especially for those who cannot read or those who face pressing economic challenges. The BCP's clinic and factory improved villagers' sense of self-worth and sense of agency in a powerful way because it was accompanied by a material change, whereas the *Black Review* was primarily an intellectual project.

In their different contexts, both Freire and Black Consciousness activists learned the importance of having a measure of state support or tolerance. Freire learned how powerful the state could be in his practice even if he did not adequately acknowledge it in his theories. He ran his major literacy campaigns in partnership with governments until politics forced him into exile.[31] The BCP, working in opposition to the government, eventually crumbled under fatal state intervention. The challenges that repressive state action can pose raises the question as to whether conscientization as an approach to development can work when political freedom is severely limited. The history of the Black Consciousness movement indicates that under these circumstances, those working for conscientization would need to mobilize politically to secure the process itself. Yet the danger, and contradiction, in moving in this political direction is that the theory of allowing people to become autonomous critical beings is compromised. Alternatively, a conscientization approach that is less overtly political is more likely to persist under a repressive system, as did the post-1977 Black Consciousness–aligned projects described above. It also may not take hold as activists might hope—in theory, leaders or instigators should relinquish control over the outcome.[32]

Finally, underlying the history of the BCP and Black Consciousness community work is the issue of foreign aid. The role and effectiveness of international aid have come under greater scrutiny.[33] The case of the BCP suggests that outside resources in many projects are necessary for beginning the process of building self-reliance. The BCP could not have accomplished what it did without outside funding. Black Consciousness activists learned through their community work that starting with outside resources was in some ways essential for "people who are struggling with mere survival." Ramphele wrote: "The idea of pulling oneself up by one's own boot-straps presupposes that one has boots to wear in the first instance."[34] The BCP needed money to run its programs and at times accepted it from controversial sources. Yet the deeper concern was maintaining autonomy while still obtaining resources. The BCP was able to retain full control over how it used the money that came into the organization because the ecumenical groups, foreign churches, and Anglo American who made substantial financial contributions respected and supported the BCP's autonomy. When speaking of aid and its merits or demerits, then, the BCP's history reminds us that it is necessary to carefully specify where aid—in all its forms—comes from, where it goes, and who controls it, including churches or religious organizations.

The issue of aid or raising capital (as in the case of the Njwaxa factory) also relates to debates about South African postapartheid economic policies. The ANC has been criticized for stepping back from socialist aims and selling out to global neoliberal agendas.[35] Others have pointed out that the ANC has not been so inconsistent. They have discussed the dilemma the ANC faced in balancing the revival of the South African economy through capitalistic growth strategies with spreading that growth more broadly.[36] Although the BCP ran small-scale initiatives, its experience shows that this dilemma is not new in South African history. But the BCP used entrepreneurial projects to take jobs and skills to people. Thus, the BCP's history also adds weight to arguments that skill development and education are equally or more important to addressing unemployment and economic exclusion than black capital accumulation.

Clearly the end of apartheid did not solve all of the problems and challenges the BCP worked to address. There is still a need for community upliftment—for a psychological awakening, improved self-reliance, and greater cooperation to work toward those end goals. The BCP hoped that its work would inspire broader change, even within the government that opposed its work. A recent program Ramphele and her former Zanempilo colleague Nontobeko Moletsane started is an example of how the ideas and practices employed by the BCP can be applied on a broader scale. Ramphele and Nontobeko Moletsane launched their Letsema Circle initiative in 2010 to improve Eastern Cape health care delivery through a model of government-public consultation. Using a "walking together" method, Letsema's goal is to stimulate members of communities to work together to "find their own solutions towards improving the living conditions within their communities." In 2011, Letsema Circle reported that as a result of its work, nurses in Uitenhage changed their "mind-set," cut waiting times at their clinics, and offered patients a better experience; schools in Cofimvaba saw students increasingly participate in voluntary counseling and testing for HIV/AIDS; and a soup kitchen in Mqanduli (near Mthatha) turned from relying solely on grocery donations to harvesting from the communal gardens.[37] Time will tell how successful Ramphele and Nontobeko Moletsane's efforts will be, yet they show that the history of the BCP can serve as a resource for similar experiments and can further contribute to debates about the theory and practice of development.

Notes

INTRODUCTION

1. Nontozande Nofence James, interview by author and Lindani Ntenteni, June 26, 2008, Njwaxa.
2. M. M. Nakase, B. E. Nakase, and Nokukwaka Cola, interview by author and Lindani Ntenteni, July 3, 2008, Njwaxa.
3. In this case, antipolitical means de-politicizing or discouraging political participation and debate.
4. Some of the influential works within African history on development include the works of Immanuel Wallerstein; Walter Rodney (see *How Europe Underdeveloped Africa* [London: Bogle-L'Ouverture Publications, 1972]); and Allen F. Isaacman, *Cotton Is the Mother of Poverty: Peasants, Work, and Rural Struggle in Colonial Mozambique, 1938–1961* (Portsmouth, N.H.: Heinemann, 1996). See also the works listed in the following note.
5. Frederick Cooper and Randall M. Packard, eds., *International Development and the Social Sciences: Essays on the History and Politics of Knowledge* (Berkeley: University of California Press, 1997), 18. See also Joseph M. Hodge, Gerald Hödl, and Martina Kopf, eds., *Developing Africa: Concepts and Practices in Twentieth-Century Colonialism* (Manchester: Manchester University Press, 2014); Frederick Cooper, *Africa since 1940: The Past of the Present* (Cambridge: Cambridge University Press, 2002); James Ferguson, *The Antipolitics Machine: "Development," Depoliticization, and Bureaucratic Power in Lesotho* (Cambridge: Cambridge University Press, 1990). Histories of health or poverty and hunger have provided insights into the plight of the poor, but the focus has largely been on overarching structures. See John Iliffe, *The African Poor: A History* (Cambridge: Cambridge University Press, 1987); Randall M. Packard, *White Plague, Black Labor: Tuberculosis and the Political Economy of Health and Disease in South Africa* (Berkeley: University of California Press,

1989); Diana Wylie, *Starving on a Full Stomach: Hunger and the Triumph of Cultural Racism in Modern South Africa* (Charlottesville: University Press of Virginia, 2001). The history of development in South Africa has followed a similar pattern, though historians have focused on labor, class, and land dispossession to explain South Africa's economic and sociopolitical history. Scholars have discussed agricultural reorientation programs and the policy of "separate development" as parts of the repressive apartheid regime. For example: Shula Marks and Richard Rathbone, eds., *Industrialization and Social Change in South Africa: African Class Formation, Culture and Consciousness 1870–1930* (New York: Longman, 1982); Charles van Onselen, *Studies in the Social and Economic History of Witwatersrand, 1886–1914* (New York: Longman, 1982); Iris Berger, *Threads of Solidarity: Women in South African Industry, 1900–1980* (Bloomington: Indiana University Press, 1992); Patrick Harries, *Work, Culture, and Identity: Migrant Laborers in Mozambique and South Africa, c. 1860–1910* (Portsmouth, N.H.: Heinemann, 1994); Dunbar Moodie, *Going for Gold: Men, Mines and Migration* (Berkeley: University of California Press, 1994); Jeremy Seekings and Nicoli Nattrass, *Class, Race, and Inequality in South Africa* (New Haven, Conn.: Yale University Press, 2005).

6. Ferguson, *Anti-politics Machine.*

7. Some notable exceptions are Dorothy Louise Hodgson, *Once Intrepid Warriors: Gender, Ethnicity, and the Cultural Politics of Maasai Development* (Bloomington: Indiana University Press, 2001) and Kara Moskowitz, "'Are You Planting Trees or Are You Planting People?' Squatter Resistance and International Development in the Making of a Kenyan Postcolonial Political Order (c. 1963–78)," *Journal of African History* 56, no. 1 (March 2015): 99–118, though they also focus on the role of state interventions. Histories of environmental and health initiatives have certainly demonstrated the importance of local community perspectives and engagement, but are more interested in the interaction between European colonial governments, the environment, and local groups with their differing perspectives on health, conservation, and the environment. For examples of works that relate to environmental initiatives and local communities, see Emmanuel Kwaku Akyeampong, *Between the Sea & the Lagoon: An Eco-social History of the Anlo of Southeastern Ghana, c. 1850 to Recent Times* (Athens: Ohio University Press, 2001); Karen Brown, "'Trees, Forests and Communities': Some Historiographical Approaches to Environmental History on Africa," *Area*, 35, no. 4 (December 2003): 343–56; Jane Carruthers, "Africa: Histories, Ecologies and Societies," *Environment and History* 10, no. 4 (November 2004): 379–406; Jacob Tropp, *Natures of Colonial Change: Environmental Relations in the Making of the Transkei* (Athens: Ohio University Press, 2006). On community health care in South African history,

see Alan Jeeves, "Delivering Primary Health Care in Impoverished Urban and Rural Communities: The Institute of Family and Community Health in the 1940s," in *South Africa's 1940s: Worlds of Possibilities*, ed. Saul Dubow and Alan Jeeves (Cape Town: Double Storey Books, 2005), 87–107; Howard Phillips, "The Grassy Park Health Centre: A Peri-Urban Pholela?," in Dubow and Jeeves, *South Africa's 1940s*, 108–28; Vanessa Noble, "A Medical Education with a Difference: A History of the Training of Black Student Doctors in Social, Preventive and Community-Oriented Primary Health Care at the University of Natal Medical School, 1940s-1960," *South African Historical Journal* 61, no. 3 (September 2009): 550–74.

8. For a synthesis of Africanist thought through these individuals, see Gail M. Gerhart, *Black Power in South Africa: The Evolution of an Ideology* (Berkeley: University of California Press, 1978).

9. Sen argued for a greater recognition of the intertwined relationship between development and freedom. See Amartya Sen, *Development as Freedom* (New York: Alfred A. Knopf, 1999). Yet seeing Black Consciousness as liberation first, with a material or economic aspect, makes it slightly different from a "development as freedom" approach that focuses on development as an outcome instead of holistic liberation as the outcome and development as part of that liberation or a "liberation strategy" as Mamphela Ramphele put it in "Empowerment and Symbols of Hope: Black Consciousness and Community Development," in *Bounds of Possibility: The Legacy of Steve Biko and Black Consciousness*, ed. Barney Pityana et al. (Cape Town: David Philip, 1991), 169.

10. Gerhart, *Black Power in South Africa*; C. R. D. Halisi, *Black Political Thought in the Making of South African Democracy* (Bloomington: Indiana University Press, 1999).

11. Sam Nolutshungu, *Changing South Africa: Political Considerations* (Manchester: Manchester University Press, 1982), 161. See also Raymond Suttner, *The ANC Underground in South Africa, 1950–1976: A Social and Historical Study* (Auckland Park: Jacana Media, 2008), 76–83.

12. Mbulelo V. Mzamane, "The Impact of Black Consciousness on Culture," in Pityana et al., *Bounds of Possibility*, 179–93; Bhekizizwe Peterson, "Culture, Resistance and Representation," in *The Road to Democracy in South Africa*, vol. 2, ed. SADET (Pretoria: Unisa Press, 2006), 161–85; Pumla Gqola, "Black Woman, You Are on Your Own: Images of Black Women in Staffrider Short Stories, 1978–1982" (Master's thesis, University of Cape Town, 1999); Andile Mngxitama, Amanda Alexander, and Nigel Gibson, eds., *Biko Lives!: Contesting the Legacies of Steve Biko* (New York: Palgrave Macmillan, 2008); Matthew P. Keaney, "'I Can Feel My Grin Turn to a Grimace': From the

Sophiatown Shebeens to the Streets of Soweto on the Pages of *Drum, The Classic, New Classic,* and *Staffrider*" (Master's thesis, George Mason University, 2010).

13. Daniel R. Magaziner, *The Law and the Prophets: Black Consciousness in South Africa, 1968–1977* (Athens: Ohio University Press, 2010).

14. Ramphele, "Empowerment and Symbols of Hope." Even while Saleem Badat and Vanessa Noble touched on SASO community work in their studies of SASO and the Natal medical school, both focused on university campuses and not on what happened in and to local communities. See Saleem Badat, *Black Student Politics, Higher Education and Apartheid: From SASO to SANSCO, 1968–1990* (Pretoria: Human Science Research Council, 1999); Vanessa Noble, "Doctors Divided: Gender, Race and Class Anomalies in the Production of Black Medical Doctors in Apartheid South Africa, 1948–1994" (Ph.D. diss., University of Michigan, 2005).

15. Biko was the fourth martyr of the movement, following the deaths of Mthuli ka Shezi (pushed onto a train track in 1972), Tiro (letter-bombed in Botswana in 1974), and Mapetla Mohapi (killed in police detention in 1976).

16. For example, Millard Arnold, *The Testimony of Steve Biko* (London: M. Temple Smith, 1979); Hilda Bernstein, *No. 46—Steve Biko* (London: International Defence and Aid Fund, 1978); Chris van Wyk, ed., *We Write What We Like: Celebrating Steve Biko* (Johannesburg: Wits University Press, 2007); Mngxitama, Alexander, and Gibson, *Biko Lives!*; Andile M-Afrika, *The Eyes That Lit Our Lives: A Tribute to Steve Biko* (King William's Town: Eyeball Publishers, 2010). Biko was one of the first black liberation heroes to be memorialized in post-1994 South Africa. September 12, 1997, marked the twentieth anniversary of his death. In that year, Mandela dedicated the Biko statue in East London, the Biko home, and the Steve Biko Garden of Remembrance as heritage sites. The John Vorster Bridge crossing the Buffalo River on East London's west side was renamed Biko Bridge on the same day. See also Leslie Hadfield, "We Salute a Hero of the Nation: Steve Biko's Place in South Africa's History" (Master's thesis, Ohio University, 2005).

17. As quoted in Aelred Stubbs, C.R., "Martyr of Hope," in Steve Biko, *I Write What I Like* (Randburg: Ravan Press, 1996), 166. See also "Interview with Deborah Matshoba," in Mngxitama, Alexander, and Gibson, *Biko Lives!*, 283.

18. Luyanda ka Msumza, interview by author, December 2, 2008, Mdantsane.

19. On liberation theology in Latin America, see Melissa J. Wilde, *Vatican II: A Sociological Analysis of Religious Change* (Princeton, N.J.: Princeton University Press, 2007); Christian Smith, *The Emergence of Liberation Theology: Radical Religion and Social Movement Theory* (Chicago: University of Chicago Press, 1991); Ondina E. Gonzáles, *Christianity in Latin America: A History*

(Cambridge: Cambridge University Press, 2008); Scott Mainwaring, *The Catholic Church and Politics in Brazil, 1916–1985* (Stanford, Calif.: Stanford University Press, 1986). On community development programs as part of the U.S. civil rights movement, see Peniel E. Joseph, ed., *The Black Power Movement: Rethinking the Civil Rights–Black Power Era* (New York: Routledge, 2006); Peniel E. Joseph, ed., *Neighborhood Rebels: Black Power at the Local Level* (New York: Palgrave Macmillan, 2010); David Hilliard, ed., *The Black Panther Party Service to the People Programs* (Albuquerque: University of New Mexico Press, 2008).

20. See, for example, Andrew Burton and Helene Charton-Bigot, eds., *Generations Past: Youth in East African History* (Athens: Ohio University Press, 2010); Jon Abbink and Ineke van Kessel, eds., *Vanguard or Vandals: Youth, Politics, and Conflict in Africa* (Leiden: Brill, 2005); Alcinda Honwana and Filip De Boeck, eds., *Makers and Breakers: Children and Youth in Postcolonial Africa* (Oxford: James Currey, 2005). Historians of South Africa, particularly after the 1976 student uprisings, examined the role of youth and generational tensions in political events and social change. For example: Badat, *Black Student Politics*; Sifiso Ndlovu, *The Soweto Uprisings: Counter-Memories of June 1976* (Randburg: Ravan Press, 1998); Kumi Naidoo, "The Politics of Youth Resistance in the 1980s: The Dilemmas of a Differentiated Durban," *Journal of Southern African Studies* 18, no. 1 (March 1992): 143–65; Colin Bundy, "Street Sociology and Pavement Politics: Aspects of Youth and Student Resistance in Cape Town, 1985," *Journal of Southern African Studies* 13, no. 3 (April 1987): 303–30; Benedict Carton, *Blood from Your Children: The Colonial Origins of Generational Conflict in South Africa* (Charlottesville: University of Virginia Press, 2000); Clive Glaser, *Bo-Tsotsi: The Youth Gangs of Soweto, 1935–1976* (Portsmouth, N.H.: Heinemann, 2000).

21. Magaziner, *Law and the Prophets*, chap. 2. Magaziner also broadens intellectual history by including Soweto students in his analysis of how ideas of sacrificing for the struggle and finding hope in suffering took hold in the late 1970s. See also Noble, "Doctors Divided," chap. 5.

22. Mamphela Ramphele, "The Dynamics of Gender within Black Consciousness Organisations: A Personal View," in Pityana et al., *Bounds of Possibility*, 214–27; Mamphela Ramphele, *Across Boundaries: The Journey of a South African Woman Leader* (New York: Feminist Press, 1996), 71; Badat, *Black Student Politics*, 112–13, 156–57; Pumla Gqola, "Contradictory Locations: Blackwomen and the Discourse of the Black Consciousness Movement (BCM) in South Africa," *Meridians* 2, no. 1 (2001): 130–52; Magaziner, *Law and the Prophets*, chap. 2. See also Noble's discussion of "Black Masculine Femininities" in "Doctors Divided," chap. 6.

23. Pamela Scully and Denise Walsh, "Altering Politics, Contesting Gender," *Journal of Southern African Studies* 32, no. 1 (2006): 2. See also Cherryl Walker, *Women and Resistance in South Africa* (New York: Monthly Review Press, 1991); Shireen Hassim, *Women's Organizations and Democracy in South Africa: Contesting Authority* (Madison: University of Wisconsin Press, 2006); Cherryl Walker, ed., *Women and Gender in Southern Africa to 1945* (Cape Town: David Philip and James Currey, 1990); Cherryl Walker, "Women and Resistance: In Search of South African Feminism," *Work in Progress*, no. 36 (April 1985): 25–30; Amanda Kemp et al., "The Dawn of a New Day: Redefining South African Feminism," in *The Challenge of Local Feminisms: Women's Movements in Global Perspective*, ed. Amrita Basu (Boulder, Colo.: Westview Press, 1995), 131–62. Meghan Healy adeptly analyzes the historiography on women in politics in the early years of the ANC, providing further insight into the literature, in "Women and the Problem of Family in Early African Nationalist History and Historiography," *South African Historical Journal* 64, no. 3 (September 2012): 450–71.

24. Zine Magubane challenges notions that women who prioritized national liberation necessarily divorced women's issues from national liberation and that those focused on bread-and-butter issues were conservative in her "Attitudes towards Feminism Among Women in the ANC, 1950–1990: A Theoretical Re-interpretation," in *Road to Democracy*, vol. 4, *1980–1990*, ed. SADET (Pretoria: Unisa Press, 2010), 975–1034. Nomboniso Gasa argues for a nonlinear history of women's movements and greater acknowledgment of women's various positions and goals in Nomboniso Gasa, ed., *Women in South African History: Basus'iimbokodo, Bawel'imilambo/They Remove Boulders and Cross Rivers* (Cape Town: Human Science Research Council Press, 2007), xvi–xvii, 214–15, 224–25. See also Raymond Suttner, "Women in the ANC-led Underground" in Gasa, *Women in South African History*, 233–55; Janet Cherry, "'We Were Not Afraid': The Role of Women in the 1980s' Township Uprising in the Eastern Cape," in Gasa, *Women in South African History*, 281–313.

25. Oshadi Mangena, "The Black Consciousness Philosophy and the Women's Question," in Mngxitama et al., *Biko Lives!*, 253–55, 265.

26. Nohle Mohapi, interview by author, October 30, 2008, Port Elizabeth.

27. There is a growing literature on Christian resistance to apartheid. For example, see John de Gruchy and Steve de Gruchy, *The Church Struggle in South Africa* (Minneapolis: Fortress Press, 2005); L. D. Hansen, *The Legacy of Beyers Naudé* (Stellenbosch: SUN Press, 2005); Bob Clarke, *Anglicans Against Apartheid, 1936–1996* (Pietermaritzburg: Cluster Publications, 2008); Peter Walshe, *Prophetic Christianity and the Liberation Movement in South Africa*

(Pietermaritzburg: Cluster Publications, 1995). Other scholars have explored the development of Black Theology in conjunction with Black Consciousness. For example, see contributions to Pityana et al., *Bounds of Possibility*; Martin Prozesky, ed., *Christianity Amidst Apartheid: Selected Perspectives on the Church in South Africa* (New York: St. Martin's Press, 1990); Dwight Hopkins, *Black Theology USA and South Africa: Politics, Culture, and Liberation* (Maryknoll, N.Y.: Orbis Books, 1989); Magaziner, *Law and the Prophets*; Daniel Magaziner, "Christ in Context: Developing a Political Faith in Apartheid South Africa," *Radical History Review*, no. 99 (2007): 80–106.

28. See similar arguments in Steve de Gruchy, Nico Koopman, and Sytse Strijbos, eds., *From Our Side: Emerging Perspectives on Development and Ethics* (Amsterdam: Rozenberg, 2008).

29. Spro-cas director Peter Randall thankfully sent all of his papers to the Wits library. Archived BCP documents are held at the Historical Papers in the William Cullen Library and the African Studies Documentation Centre at the University of South Africa. Other archival and written records include: newspaper articles, especially in East London's *Daily Dispatch*; the Records and Archives services of the Eastern Cape Provincial Department of Sport, Recreation, Arts, and Culture based in King William's Town, with files on Ciskei health care, headmen and chiefs, development, and welfare projects; and government documents from offices in Bhisho, such as the Department of Agriculture and Rural Development Land Use Management. Unfortunately, church records regarding parishes and church buildings connected to the BCP do not exist in archives of the Anglican Church. I was told the records in Alice had been destroyed by fire and that the Anglican Church offices in Zwelitsha did not have what I was looking for. This was after I searched the Church of the Province South Africa (CPSA) collections at both the Historical Papers at the University of the Witwatersrand and Rhodes University. Lovedale Press files from the years it printed BCP materials had also reportedly burned.

30. Particularly pertinent to my project is Cheikh Babou's use of oral sources in writing the history of the Muridiyya as an insider: Cheikh Anta Babou, *Fighting the Greater Jihad: Amadu Bamba and the Founding of the Muridiyya of Senegal, 1853–1913* (Athens: Ohio University Press, 2007), 9–19. See also, for example, Luise White, Stephan F. Miescher, and David William Cohen, eds., *African Words, African Voices: Critical Practices in Oral History* (Bloomington: Indiana University Press, 2001).

31. All interviews were transcribed and translated by myself and native Xhosa speakers: Palesa Mothlabane, Lindani Ntenteni, Nkosinathi Vezi, Buyiswa Mini, Thokozani Langeni, Mzwanele Mduna, Saxola Simakade, and Sonto

Pooe. I deposited copies of the transcripts with the University of Fort Hare and the Steve Biko Foundation.

32. This was in part inspired by Nwando Achebe's introduction to *Farmers, Traders, Warriors, and Kings: Female Power and Authority in Northern Igboland, 1900–1960* (Portsmouth, N.H.: Heinemann, 2005).

33. Sean Field, *Oral History, Community, and Displacement: Imagining Memories in Post-Apartheid South Africa* (New York: Palgrave Macmillan, 2012); Jacob Dlamini, *Native Nostalgia* (Auckland Park: Jacana Media, 2009). See also Joanna Bornat, "Remembering and Reworking Emotions: The Reanalysis of Emotion in an Interview," *Oral History* 38, no. 2 (2010): 43–52; Helena Pohlandt-McCormick, "'I Saw a Nightmare . . .': Violence and the Construction of Memory (Soweto, June 16, 1976)," *History and Theory* 39, no. 4 (2000): 23–44; Anne Kelk Mager, *Gender and the Making of a South African Bantustan: A Social History of the Ciskei, 1945–1959* (Portsmouth, N.H.: Heinemann, 1999), 12.

34. For more on defining communities, see "Class, Community, and Ideology in the Evolution of South African Society," in Belinda Bozzoli, *Class, Community and Conflict: South African Perspectives* (Johannesburg: Ravan Press, 1987), 4–8; Benedict Anderson, *Imagined Communities: Reflections on the Origin and Spread of Nationalism* (New York: Verso, 1991).

CHAPTER 1. LIBERATING CONCEPTS

1. Malusi Mpumlwana, phone interview by author, December 20, 2008. Biko wrote that it was an "absolute duty" for black people to fulfill the economic needs of their people in Steve Biko, *I Write What I Like* (Randburg: Ravan Press, 1996), 97.

2. Ranwedzi Harry Nengwekhulu, "Community Action and Development," 1972, A2176, Historical Papers, Cullen Library, University of the Witwatersrand (hereafter cited as Cullen).

3. "From the President's Desk," [Barney Pityana], *SASO Newsletter* 1, no. 2 (June 1971): 9, Digital Innovation South Africa (DISA). All issues of *SASO Newsletter* were accessed from DISA.

4. For example, see Mamadou Diouf, "Senegalese Development: From Mass Mobilization to Technocratic Elitism," in *International Development and the Social Sciences: Essays on the History and Politics of Knowledge*, ed. Frederick Cooper and Randall M. Packard (Berkeley: University of California Press, 1997), 291–319; John Aerni-Flessner, "'If We Govern Ourselves, Whose Son

Is to Govern Us?': Youth, Independence and the 1960s in Lesotho" (Ph.D. diss., Washington University, 2011); and, for a reevaluation of the history of Ghana's major Akasombo Dam project, Stephan F. Miescher, "Building the City of the Future: Visions and Experiences of Modernity in Ghana's Akasombo Township," *Journal of African History* 53, no. 3 (2012): 367–90.

5. "The Arusha Declaration: Socialism and Self-Reliance," in Julius K. Nyerere, *Freedom and Socialism: A Selection from Writings and Speeches, 1965–1967* (Dar es Salaam: Oxford University Press, 1968), 243.

6. Gilbert Rist, *The History of Development: From Western Origins to Global Faith* (London: Zed Books, 2002), 123.

7. Factors that led to its failure included drought, rising oil prices in the 1970s, and difficulty adapting agricultural techniques. The commercial sector equally failed to grow. Nyerere eventually stepped down, and Tanzania came to rely on international aid more than most other African countries. For classic analyses of *ujamaa*, see Goran Hyden, *Beyond Ujamaa in Tanzania: Underdevelopment and an Uncaptured Peasantry* (London: Heinemann, 1980); James C. Scott, *Seeing Like a State: How Certain Schemes to Improve the Human Condition Have Failed* (New Haven, Conn.: Yale University Press, 1998), chap. 7. See also Rist, *History of Development*, 131–33. For recent reassessments of previous analyses of *ujamaa*, see Priya Lal, "Self-reliance and the State: The Multiple Meanings of Development in Early Post Colonial Tanzania," *Africa: The Journal of the International African Institute* 82, no. 2 (2012): 213–34; and articles by Leander Schneider, including "High on Modernity? Explaining the Failings of Tanzanian Villagisation," *African Studies* 66, no. 1 (2007), 9–38, and "Colonial Legacies and Postcolonial Authoritarianism: Connects and Disconnects," *African Studies Review* 49, no. 1 (2006): 93–118.

8. Mahmood Mamdani, *Citizen and Subject: Contemporary Africa and the Legacy of Late Colonialism* (Princeton, N.J.: Princeton University Press, 1996), 27. Mamdani makes the case for analyzing South Africa in the context of the rest of the continent rather than as a complete exception. Indeed, doing so better situates South Africa into the context of its time and highlights the similarities between South Africa and other African countries. Still, it is also important to recognize the significance of the specific differences. In the case of development in the 1960s and 1970s, the nature of apartheid meant that black South Africans dealt with a very different context.

9. See Philip Bonner, Peter Delius, and Deborah Posel, eds., *Apartheid's Genesis: 1935–1962* (Johannesburg and Braamfontein: Ravan Press and Witwatersrand University Press, 1993); Deborah Posel, *The Making of Apartheid, 1948–1961: Conflict and Compromise* (Oxford: Oxford University Press, 1991); Deborah Posel, "Race as Common Sense: Racial Classification in

Twentieth-Century South Africa," *African Studies Review* 44, no. 2 (2001): 87–113; William Beinart and Saul Dubow, eds., *Segregation and Apartheid in Twentieth-Century South Africa* (New York: Routledge, 1995); Nancy Clark, *Manufacturing Apartheid: State Corporations in South Africa* (New Haven, Conn.: Yale University Press, 1994); Ivan Evans, *Bureaucracy and Race: Native Administration in South Africa* (Berkeley: University of California Press, 1997); Dan O'Meara, *Forty Lost Years: The Apartheid State and the Politics of the National Party, 1948–1994* (Athens: Ohio University Press, 1996); Jeremy Seekings and Nicoli Nattrass, *Class, Race, and Inequality in South Africa* (New Haven, Conn.: Yale University Press, 2005).

10. Jeffrey Butler, Robert I. Rotberg, and John Adams, *The Black Homelands of South Africa: The Political and Economic Development of Bophuthatswana and KwaZulu* (Berkeley: University of California Press, 1977); Fred T. Hendricks, *The Pillars of Apartheid: Land Tenure, Rural Planning and the Chieftaincy* (Uppsala: Academiae Ubsaliensis, 1990); Bernard Magubane et al., "Resistance and Repression in the Bantustans," in *The Road to Democracy*, vol. 2, ed. SADET (Pretoria: University of South Africa, 2006), 749–802.

11. H. F. Verwoerd, *Separate Development: The Positive Side* (Pretoria: Information Service of the Department of Native Affairs, 1958), as quoted in Nancy L. Clark and William H. Worger, *South Africa: The Rise and Fall of Apartheid* (New York: Longman, 2004), 60.

12. House of Assembly Debates, April 10, 1961, as quoted in Magubane et al., "Resistance and Repression in the Bantustans," 750.

13. For more on the history of Bantu Education, see Jonathan Hyslop, *The Classroom Struggle: Policy and Resistance in South Africa, 1940–1990* (Pietermaritzburg: University of Natal Press, 1999). See also Peter Kallaway, ed., *The History of Education Under Apartheid, 1948–1994: The Doors of Learning and Culture Shall Be Opened* (New York: Peter Lang, 2002).

14. Catholic priests also advocated making Christianity relevant to the majority by conducting Mass in vernacular languages. The Vatican II council officially adopted this as part of church policy. For more on Vatican II and its impact, see Melissa J. Wilde, *Vatican II: A Sociological Analysis of Religious Change* (Princeton, N.J.: Princeton University Press, 2007). They also built self-reliant communities (termed "base ecclesial communities," or CEBs) and ran worker programs in both urban and rural regions. See Christian Smith, *The Emergence of Liberation Theology: Radical Religion and Social Movement Theory* (Chicago: University of Chicago Press, 1991); Ondina E. Gonzáles, *Christianity in Latin America: A History* (Cambridge: Cambridge University Press, 2008); Scott Mainwaring, *The Catholic Church and Politics in Brazil, 1916–1985* (Stanford, Calif.: Stanford University Press, 1986).

15. Consequently, a contextual theology school developed in South Africa in the 1980s. See Martin Prozesky, ed., *Christianity Amidst Apartheid: Selected Perspectives on the Church in South Africa* (New York: St. Martin's Press, 1990); Dwight Hopkins, *Black Theology USA and South Africa: Politics, Culture, and Liberation* (Maryknoll, N.Y.: Orbis Books, 1989); Daniel Magaziner, "Christ in Context: Developing a Political Faith in Apartheid South Africa," *Radical History Review*, no. 99 (2007): 80–106; John de Gruchy and Steve de Gruchy, *The Church Struggle in South Africa* (Minneapolis: Fortress Press, 2005); L. D. Hansen, *The Legacy of Beyers Naudé* (Stellenbosch: SUN Press, 2005); Bob Clarke, *Anglicans Against Apartheid, 1936–1996* (Pietermaritzburg: Cluster, 2008).

16. South African Council of Churches, "A Message to the People of South Africa," June 1968, South African Council of Churches. It affirmed that the message of Christianity was that God is love and that as Christ had liberated men from sin and "broken down the walls of division between God and man," he had also overcome the division between man and man. Yet South African society had replaced faith in Christ with faith in racial identity and racial separation, "[amounting] to a denial of the central statements of the Gospel" and limiting the "ability of a person to obey the Gospel's command to love his neighbor as himself."

17. See back cover of South African Institute of Race Relations, *Survey* (Johannesburg: South African Institute of Race Relations, n.d.), all editions.

18. For a discussion on the context of the founding of the SAIRR and the *Survey*, see Paul Rich, *White Power and the Liberal Conscience: Racial Segregation and South African Liberalism, 1921–60* (Manchester: Manchester University Press, 1984), 27–30.

19. See back cover of SAIRR, *Survey*, all editions.

20. Archbishop Denis Hurley to Peter Randall, November 4, 1970, A835, Da 1, Cullen; see also Colin Gardner to Peter Randall, December 22, 1970 and Peter Randall to Rev. Theo Kotze, June 1, 1971, both in A835, Da 1, Cullen.

21. Saleem Badat, *Black Student Politics, Higher Education and Apartheid: From SASO to SANSCO, 1968–1990* (Pretoria: Human Science Research Council, 1999); Thomas Karis and Gail M. Gerhart, *From Protest to Challenge: A Documentary History of African Politics in South Africa, 1882–1990*, vol. 5, *Nadir and Resurgence, 1964–1979* (Bloomington: Indiana University Press, 1997), 62–75. On the unintended consequences of NUSAS's gathering of statistics on worker wages, see Grace Davies, "Strength in Numbers: The Durban Student Wages Commission, Dockworkers and the Poverty Datum Line, 1971–1973," *Journal of Southern African Studies* 33, no. 2 (2007): 401–20. See also Ian Macqueen, "Re-imagining South Africa: Black Consciousness,

Radical Christianity and the New Left, 1967–1977" (Ph.D. diss., University of Sussex, 2011).

22. See Peter Limb, *The ANC's Early Years: Nation, Class and Place in South Africa before 1940* (Pretoria: UNISA University Press, 2010); Govan Mbeki, *Let's Do It Together: What Cooperative Societies Are and Do* (Cape Town: African Bookman, 1944); Norman Etherington, "African Economic Experiments in Colonial Natal 1845–1880," *African Economic History* 5 (Spring 1978): 1–14; Xolela Mangcu, *Biko: A Biography* (Cape Town: Tafelburg, 2012), 234–35. See also the discussion of Ethiopian movements below.

23. See Alan Gregor Cobley, *The Rules of the Game: Struggles in Black Recreation and Social Welfare Policy in South Africa* (London: Greenwood Press, 1997). For records on the small trading and farming cooperatives, see folders on Cooperative Movements C.1.2.9, and Correspondence with Cooperatives C2.3.1, in Ballinger Papers, Cullen, and various editions of the South African Institute of Race Relations *Survey*.

24. See Cobley, *Rules of the Game*, chap. 3, on social welfare groups for women up to the 1960s.

25. Catherine Higgs, "Zenzele: African Women's Self-Help Organizations in South Africa 1927–98," *African Studies Review* 47, no. 3 (December 2004): 119–41.

26. The Jan Hofmeyer School of Social Work was founded in 1941 by white men associated with the YMCA and was funded by white philanthropists and the government. Students were trained in conducting sociological research, organizational/operational skills, community relations, community health, and recreation. Cobley wrote, "Notably absent from the curriculum was any in-depth discussion of the socioeconomic and political context in which the trainees would have to practice their profession." Cobley, *Rules of the Game*, 147. The school was closed in the late 1950s as the government took over higher education and shut down more liberal education.

27. For example, O. F. Raum, "Self-Help Associations," *African Studies Review* 28, no. 2 (1969): 119–41. Other information in this section comes from all issues of *Black Review* and SAIRR *Survey*, years 1965–75.

28. Badat, *Black Student Politics*, 62. See also Daniel R. Magaziner, *The Law and the Prophets: Black Consciousness in South Africa, 1968–1977* (Athens: Ohio University Press, 2010), 21–24; Hyslop, *Classroom Struggle*.

29. SASO, "Report on the 1st National Formation School, held at the University of Natal Black Section, 1–4 Dec, 1969," DISA. Note the use of the term "non-white" at this point. SASO members would later embrace the term "black" as a more positive way of identifying themselves.

30. See, for example, Steve Biko, SASO President, to Justice Moloto, President of University Christian Movement, April 2, 1970, DISA. SASO took over the UCM's literacy project when the UCM disbanded in 1973. See SASO, "Minutes of the Proceedings of the 3rd General Student's Council," held at St. Peter's Seminary, Hammanskraal, July 2–9, 1972, 23, The Black Consciousness movement of South Africa—Material from the collection of Gail Gerhart (hereafter cited as GG), Reel 2.

31. Dr. Siyolo Solombela, interview by author, May 25, 2008, Bonnie Doon, East London; Dr. Mncedisi W. Jekwa, interview by author, May 11, 2008, Beacon Bay, East London. See also Vanessa Noble, "Doctors Divided: Gender, Race and Class Anomalies in the Production of Black Medical Doctors in Apartheid South Africa, 1948–1994" (Ph.D. diss., University of Michigan, 2005), 72.

32. Noble, "Doctors Divided," 72–73; Magaziner, *Law and the Prophets*, 21–25. See also Xolela Mangcu's discussion of these aspects in Mangcu, *Biko*, chap. 3.

33. Mamphela Ramphele, *Across Boundaries: The Journey of a South African Woman Leader* (New York: Feminist Press, 1996), 47. See also Mamphela Ramphele, interview with Mary Marshall Clark, August 2, 1999, Cape Town, Carnegie Corporation Oral History Project.

34. Mangcu, *Biko*, 233.

35. Peter Jones, interview by author, April 22, 2006, Athens, Ohio.

36. Barney Pityana, interview by author, March 20, 2008, East London.

37. "Campus News," *SASO Newsletter* 1, no. 1 (May 1971).

38. Peter Jones, interview by author, September 4, 2004, Somerset West.

39. Nobandile Biko, interview by author, September 9, 2008, Cape Town. Biko's older sister Bukelwa was a nurse, and Nobandile Biko was involved in running and setting up child-care programs, working for organizations such as the Border Council of Churches, Institute of Race Relations, and numerous NGOs. She worked alongside her brother when he ran BCP programs in the Eastern Cape.

40. Malusi Mpumlwana, interview by author, April 16, 2008, Johannesburg. African American churches also played an important role in the spread of Ethiopian and African independent churches and inspired hope of African independence. See J. Mutero Chirenje, *Ethiopianism and Afro-Americans in Southern Africa, 1883–1916* (Baton Rouge: Louisiana State University Press, 1987); James T. Campbell, *Songs of Zion: The African Methodist Episcopal Church in the United States and South Africa* (New York: Oxford University Press, 1995); Robert Trent Vinson, *The Americans Are Coming!: Dreams of African American Liberation in Segregationist South Africa* (Athens: Ohio University Press, 2012).

41. Dr. Vuyo Mpumlwana, interview by author, October 3, 2008, Mthatha.
42. Biko, *I Write*, 89.
43. Steve Biko, interview by Gail M. Gerhart, October 24, 1972, in Andile Mngxitama, Amanda Alexander, and Nigel Gibson, eds., *Biko Lives!: Contesting the Legacies of Steve Biko* (New York: Palgrave Macmillan, 2008), 34.
44. Magaziner, *Law and the Prophets*, 44–45.
45. See, for example, Nyerere's 1962 speech, "*Ujamaa*—the Basis of African Socialism," in Julius Nyerere, *Freedom and Unity: A Selection from Writings and Speeches* (London: Oxford University Press, 1967), 162; Nengwekhulu, "Community Action and Development"; Barney Pityana, "Priorities in Community Development—An Appeal to the Blackman's Compassion," *SASO Newsletter* 1, no. 4 (September 1971).
46. Magaziner, *Law and the Prophets*, 41. For more on SASO's reading materials, see Magaziner, *Law and the Prophets*, chap. 3; Pityana et al., *Bounds of Possibility*, 28–30, 146, 155, 218.
47. Biko, *I Write*, 49. See also Harry Nengwekhulu, interview by Gail Gerhart, October 17, 1972, Johannesburg, Karis-Gerhart Collection: From Protest to Challenge, 1964–1990, Reel 2, folder 28.
48. Biko, *I Write*, 68.
49. Steve Biko, "I Write What I Like: We Blacks," *SASO Newsletter* 1, no. 2 (September 1970): 16. See also "SASO Student Manifesto," point b.ii, *SASO Newsletter* 1, no. 3 (August 1971). For a discussion on the gendered language of SASO, see Magaziner, *Law and the Prophets*, chap. 2.
50. The turn to a Marxist analysis after 1977 should not then be completely surprising, though other factors played into this shift as well. See Badat's discussion of this in *Black Student Politics*, 99–103. For more on the shift after 1977, see the essays by Nurina Ally and Shireen Ally and Nigel Gibson in Mngxitama, Alexander, and Gibson, *Biko Lives!*; Sam Nolutshungu, *Changing South Africa: Political Considerations* (Manchester: Manchester University Press, 1982); and Robert Fatton Jr., *Black Consciousness in South Africa: The Dialectics of Ideological Resistance to White Supremacy* (Albany: State University of New York Press, 1986).
51. Pityana highlighted how ill-health caused by malnutrition stifled black development in Pityana, "Priorities in Community Development," 14.
52. Biko, *I Write*, 28.
53. SASO, "Minutes of the Proceedings of the 3rd General Student's Council," Resolution 41, 29.
54. Pandelani Nefolovhodwe, interview by author, November 5, 2008, Midrand.
55. SASO, "Report of Leadership Training Seminar at Edendale Lay Ecumenical Center, Pietermaritzburg, 5–8 Dec, 1971," GG, Reel 1.

56. "From the President's Desk," 9.

57. Pityana, "Priorities in Community Development," 13.

58. Ramphele interview.

59. Bennie Khoapa, "Spro-Cas 2: Black Community Programmes: Tentative Suggestions for Action," 2, GG, Reel 3. See also page 3.

60. Spro-Cas Black Community Programmes, "Proposal to the Ford Foundation," n.d., 2, A835, C9, Cullen.

61. This part of the report does not have a clear author, though it could be V. Mafungo.

62. See "Liberals, Radicals and the Politics of Black Consciousness," in Paul Rich, *Hope and Despair: English-Speaking Intellectuals and South African Politics, 1896–1976* (London: British Academic Press, 1993), 90–118; Rich, *White Power and the Liberal Conscience*.

63. See Nurina Ally and Shireen Ally, "Critical Intellectualism," in Mngxitama, Alexander, and Gibson, *Biko Lives!*, 173, 171–89.

64. "Spro-Cas Black Community Programmes Budget Proposals–1973," A835, C1, Cullen.

65. Barney Pityana, "Power and Social Change," in *Student Perspectives on South Africa*, ed. David Welsh and Hendrik W. van der Merwe (Cape Town: David Philip, 1972), 181; Donald Woods, *Biko*, 3rd ed. (New York: Henry Holt, 1991), 39.

66. Spro-Cas Black Community Programmes, "Proposal to the Ford Foundation," 1.

67. SASO, "Minutes of the Proceedings of the 3rd General Student's Council," 20–22; Interview with SASO leaders by Gail Gerhart, October 23, 1972, Durban, from Gerhart Interviews, in Aluka digital library, Struggles for Freedom in Southern Africa Collection.

68. SASO, "Report of Leadership Training Seminar Edendale at Lay Ecumenical Center." Students were also taught in a leadership training program that an "aura of dependency kills the initiative, originality and the will to be of a people." See SASO, "Leadership Training Program," December 1971, 1, from Karis-Gerhart Collection in Struggles for Freedom in Southern Africa, Aluka digital library.

69. Khoapa, "Spro-Cas 2: Black Community Programmes," 2–3, GG, Reel 3.

70. Nengwekhulu, "Community Action and Development."

71. Khoapa, "Spro-Cas 2: Black Community Programmes"; Nengwekhulu, "Community Action and Development."

72. See Magaziner, *Law and the Prophets*, 51–52.

73. Malusi Mpumlwana interview, December 20, 2008; Mamphela Ramphele, "Empowerment and Symbols of Hope: Black Consciousness and Community

Development," in *Bounds of Possibility: The Legacy of Steve Biko and Black Consciousness*, ed. Barney Pityana et al. (Cape Town: David Philip, 1991), 158.

74. See Noble, "Doctors Divided," 135–42.

75. "From the President's Desk," 9.

76. Just as Pan-Africanists across the continent preached. See Nkrumah's oft-quoted *I Speak of Freedom: A Statement of African Ideology* (London: William Heinemann, 1961). Nkrumah wrote: "Divided we are weak; united, Africa could become one of the greatest forces for good in the world" (xi–xiv).

77. Pityana interview. See also SASO, "Report on the 1st National Formation School."

78. Malusi Mpumlwana interview, December 20, 2008. As discussed below, it made sense to include Ramphele in drawing up the plans for the clinic and to head the clinic because of her expertise, but recruiting her also allowed her to be closer to Biko. Biko's wife, Nontsikelelo Mashalaba, was a nurse. After he was banned to the King William's Town District, she worked at the rural St. Matthews Mission hospital in Keiskammahoek, about 22 miles (35 km) from King William's Town.

79. Barney Pityana, "The 2nd General Students Council: An Assessment," *SASO Newsletter* 1, no. 3 (August 1971): 3.

80. Khoapa, "Spro-Cas 2: Black Community Programmes," 5–6.

81. Jones interview, April 22, 2006.

CHAPTER 2. CREATIVE INTERACTIONS

1. Mosibudi Mangena, *On Your Own: Evolution of Black Consciousness in South Africa/Azania* (Braamfontein: Skotaville, 1989), 27. Freire would have been pleased to know that practitioners of his methods received an informal education since he stressed the importance of constantly modifying one's praxis and ideology while putting ideas into practice.

2. Saleem Badat, *Black Student Politics, Higher Education and Apartheid: From SASO to SANSCO, 1968–1990* (Pretoria: Human Science Research Council, 1999), 150. Ramphele remembered that the older Bennie Khoapa, director of the BCP who began to share office space with SASO at Beatrice Street in Durban in 1972, "remained a restraining yet supportive influence on youthful over-enthusiasm." Mamphela Ramphele, *Across Boundaries: The Journey of a South African Woman Leader* (New York: Feminist Press, 1996), 68.

3. SASO, "Report of Leadership Training Seminar at Edendale Lay Ecumenical Center, Pietermaritzburg, 5–8 Dec, 1971," The Black Consciousness movement of South Africa—Material from the collection of Gail Gerhart (hereafter cited as GG), Reel 1. The students also counted it a success that they "thwarted" the "freehand of the liberals" in New Farm.

4. Mamphela Ramphele, "Empowerment and Symbols of Hope: Black Consciousness and Community Development," in *Bounds of Possibility: The Legacy of Steve Biko and Black Consciousness*, ed. Barney Pityana et al. (Cape Town: David Philip, 1991), 157–58. See also Report Back Session of SASO, "Report of Leadership Training Seminar Edendale Lay Ecumenical Center," 6–7.

5. SASO, "Report of Leadership Training Seminar at Edendale Lay Ecumenical Center," 9.

6. Steve Biko, "I Write What I Like: We Blacks," *SASO Newsletter* 1, no. 2 (September 1970): 17.

7. On the history of Ginsberg, see Luyanda ka Msumza, "From Half-way Station to Permanent Settlement: A Study in the Evolution of Ginsberg Township, 1939 to 1964" (Honors thesis, University of Cape Town, 1993); Stephanie Victor, "Segregated Housing and Contested Identities: The Case of the King William's Town Coloured Community, 1895–1946" (M.Sc. Thesis, Rhodes University, 2007); Xolela Mangcu, *Biko: A Biography* (Cape Town: Tafelburg, 2012), chap. 3; and interviews conducted by the Ginsberg Youth Council, held at the Steve Biko Foundation.

8. SASO, "Report of Leadership Training Seminar at Edendale Lay Ecumenical Center," 4, 7.

9. Ibid.

10. Ramphele, *Across Boundaries*, 63–64.

11. Ramphele, "Empowerment and Symbols of Hope," 178.

12. Reports presented at 3rd General Students Council, 1972, UNB Report, 2.

13. "Commissions presented at 4th General Students Council of the South African Students Organ, St. Peter's Seminary, Hammanskraal, July 14–22, 1973," Community Development report, 4, GG, Reel 2.

14. For a brief narration of this, see Thomas Karis and Gail M. Gerhart, *From Protest to Challenge: A Documentary History of African Politics in South Africa, 1882–1990*, vol. 5, *Nadir and Resurgence, 1964–1979* (Bloomington: Indiana University Press, 1997), 121–22.

15. See SASO, "Report of Leadership Training Seminar at Edendale Lay Ecumenical Center." The Turfloop students reported that their project at the local clinic did not initially succeed because they met with suspicion from the clinic staff and it was seen as a "paternalistic handout."

16. Peter Jones, interview by author, April 22, 2006, Athens, Ohio. Njabulo S. Ndebele, university student in Lesotho at the time and later vice chancellor of the University of Cape Town, said, "The Freirian perspective had an even greater resonance because of the affinity between that perspective and the Black Consciousness Movement in respect of their common recognition for the role of awareness, consciousness, pride in oneself, self esteem, definition of self within community in the quest for freedom." Barbara Nussbaum, "An Exemplar of Conscious Leadership," Leadership website article, Centre for Conscious Leadership.

17. Scott Mainwaring, *The Catholic Church and Politics in Brazil, 1916–1985* (Stanford, Calif.: Stanford University Press, 1986).

18. See Andrew Kirkendall, "Reentering History: Paulo Freire and the Politics of the Brazilian Northeast, 1958–1964," *Luso-Brazilian Review* 41, no. 1 (2004): 169–71. Kirkendall wrote that Freire's ideas were "heavily influenced by developmental nationalism" along with his "own deeply held religious convictions" as a Catholic (72).

19. Paulo Freire, *Pedagogy of the Oppressed*, trans. Myra Bergman Ramos (New York: Herder and Herder, 1971); Paulo Freire, *Education for Critical Consciousness* (New York: Continuum, 1973). Black Consciousness activists also drew upon Freire's *Cultural Action for Freedom* (Harmondsworth: Penguin, 1970). For a brief assessment of Freire's broader impact on South Africa, see Fhulu Nekhwevha, "The Influence of Paulo Freire's 'Pedagogy of Knowing' in South African Education Struggle in the 1970s and 1980s," in *The History of Education Under Apartheid, 1948–1994: The Doors of Learning and Culture Shall Be Opened*, ed. Peter Kallaway (New York: Peter Lang, 2002), 134–44. Many of Freire's works were banned by the South African government in 1974, under the Publication Act No. 42 of 1974. Jacobsen's Index of Objectionable Literature, South Africa, Beacon for Freedom of Expression website.

20. Richard Shaull, foreword to Freire, *Pedagogy of the Oppressed*, 12.

21. Freire, *Pedagogy of the Oppressed*, 159, 41.

22. The goal of the MCP was to create a service agency that would empower people and affect a "political, social, economic transformation of society." Freire, *Cultural Action for Freedom*, 111–15. Freire specifically worked as the coordinator of the MCP's Adult Education Project. The MCP began working jointly with the SEC in 1962 on expanding cultural circles into Popular Institutes of Brazilian Studies (ISEB), autonomous groups run by local people.

23. Freire, *Pedagogy of the Oppressed*, 103–4.

24. Freire, *Education for Critical Consciousness*, 49.

25. Ibid., 176; Paulo Freire, *Letters to Cristina: Reflections on My Life and Work*, trans. Donaldo Macedo et al. (New York: Routledge, 1996), 141.

26. Daniel R. Magaziner, *The Law and the Prophets: Black Consciousness in South Africa, 1968–1977* (Athens: Ohio University Press, 2010), chaps. 3 and 7 (especially p. 251). As Magaziner argues, activists in South Africa used the term "to conscientize" in two ways: to describe a personal, psychological awakening to a critical consciousness and to refer to the process of being politicized to the beliefs of Black Consciousness.

27. Patricia Romero, *Profiles in Diversity: Women in the New South Africa* (East Lansing: Michigan State University Press, 1998), 173. The above biographical information comes from this book as well as Anne Hope, interview by author, May 16, 2008, Lakeside.

28. Mangena, *On Your Own*, 25.

29. Romero, *Profiles in Diversity*, 173. See also Hope interview.

30. Ramphele, "Empowerment and Symbols of Hope," 159–60.

31. "Winterveld Community Project: A Progress Report," n.d. [1972?], 9–10, GG, Reel 1.

32. Mbulelo V. Mzamane, Bavusile Maaba, and Nkosinathi Biko, "The Black Consciousness Movement," in *The Road to Democracy in South Africa*, vol. 2, ed. SADET (Pretoria: University of South Africa, 2006), 130.

33. Asha Rambally Moodley, telephone interview by author, August 3, 2011. She also applied this approach to teaching, stating: "Those ideas were part of our literacy programs, and I also thought they played a hell of an important role in my own personal teaching because you also saw your students as coming from particular communities and as younger people, little people, who had ideas of their own and also thought about the world in a particular way so that you had to construct a kind of pedagogy . . . which enabled you to dialogue with them instead of going to them with a top-down approach."

34. Malusi Mpumlwana, telephone interview by author, December 20, 2008. Ramphele cited the careful work of Malusi Mpumlwana in nurturing a working relationship between the students and residents in "Empowerment and Symbols of Hope," 158. Further attempts were made to continue the New Farm project beyond the clinic, but SASO suspended it in 1973. Mpumlwana and Solombela left the project in 1973, tensions between landlords stalled the project, and the relationship between community leaders and SASO deteriorated. SASO students decided to concentrate their efforts on a more successful project in Dududu, a village on the South Coast of Natal.

35. "Maitshe Nchaupe Aubrey Mokoape Testimony," *State v. Cooper et al.*, reel 5, 4943, AD1719, Historical Papers, Cullen Library, University of the Witwatersrand (hereafter cited as Cullen).

36. Steve Biko, *I Write What I Like* (Randburg: Ravan Press, 1996), 114.

37. Badat, *Black Student Politics*, 149–56; Ramphele, "Empowerment and Symbols of Hope," 172, 174–75. Badat also pointed out that other students looking for more militant political action did not see the importance of community work.

38. For example, see "Report on the Proceedings at the National Formation School held at the Fedsem (Federal Theological Seminary) May 11–13, 1973," 5, GG, Reel 2; "Composite Executive Report to the 6th G.S.C., at the Wilgespruit Conference Center, Roodepoort, Transvaal, June 30–July 7, 1974," GG, Reel 2.

39. SASO, "Estimated Expenditure 1970–1971," Digital Innovation South Africa (DISA); Harry Nengwekhulu, interview by Gail Gerhart, October 17, 1972.

40. "The 'New Farm' Project on Preventive Medicine," n.d. [1972?], GG, Reel 1.

41. For more on funding, see Tor Sellström, "Sweden and the Nordic Countries: Official Solidarity and Assistance from the West," in *The Road to Democracy in South Africa*, vol. 3, *International Solidarity*, ed. SADET (Pretoria: University of South Africa, 2008), 471–76.

42. Peter Jones, interview by author, May 14, 2008, Somerset West. Records indicate that Father Aelred Stubbs initiated this relationship. See page 15 of document designated as "Appeal Case to Chairman's Fund" [n.d.] in Anglo American Chairman's Fund records provided to me in March 2010 by Tshikululu Social Investments, the agency into which the Chairman's Fund evolved.

43. Barney Pityana, "Priorities in Community Development—An Appeal to the Blackman's Compassion," *SASO Newsletter* 1, no. 4 (September 1971): 14–15.

44. Nengwekhulu interview; Karis and Gerhart, *From Protest to Challenge*, 122.

45. See "Sathasivan Cooper Testimony," *State v. Cooper et al.*, reel 4, 3632–3634, AD1719, Cullen. See also "Strinivasa Rajoo Moodley Testimony," reel 7, 7278, AD1719, Cullen, where Moodley says they had relationships with companies to get subsidies but that he does not believe they had detailed conversations about the issue of foreign investment.

46. Ramphele, *Across Boundaries*, 65.

47. Ramphele, "Empowerment and Symbols of Hope," 170.

48. For those wanting to place this on the multiracial versus nonracial spectrum of liberation movement ideology, they can think of it as nonracial. Black Consciousness activists welcomed white involvement as long as they were involved on the terms of the black majority.

49. While a student at the Natal Teachers' Training College from 1954 to 1956, he became interested in politics and spent time with lecturer Peter

Hunter in Sobantu Village in Pietermaritzburg learning Zulu and helping to teach Afrikaans to teachers required under the new Bantu Education Acts to use Afrikaans as a medium of instruction. Randall studied through the University of South Africa and the University of the Witwatersrand to earn his B.A., M.Ed., and Ph.D.

50. Peter Randall, *Taste of Power* (Johannesburg: Spro-cas, 1973), 6.

51. "Minutes of Spro-cas 2 Planning Meeting: 15–16 October 1971," n.d., A835, C1, Cullen; Spro-cas, "Black Community Programmes," n.d., GG, Reel 3.

52. In 1960, having finished his training, he took a job as a personnel manager with the South African Rubber Manufacturing Company, based in Howick, Natal, before working for the YMCA. This biographical information is drawn from three different interviews with Khoapa: by Gail Gerhart and Thomas Karis, June 16, 1989, New York; by David Wiley, May 7, 2006, Durban, *South Africa: Overcoming Apartheid, Building Democracy* website; and by author, June 4, 2008, Durban.

53. Khoapa interview, May 7, 2006; Bennie Khoapa, telephone interview by author, October 8, 2009. See also Magaziner's discussion of Khoapa's use of Bennett in *Law and the Prophets*, chap. 3.

54. Khoapa interview, June 4, 2008; Khoapa interview, May 7, 2006. Khoapa claimed in the May 7, 2006, interview that Vuyo Mashalaba told Biko that Khoapa had said some controversial things regarding gender roles, and they set up the debate to challenge him more. In his view, the students did not have a sophisticated understanding of blackness at that time. Khoapa called himself, along with Lewis Skweyiya and a Professor Sibisi at the University of Zululand, adult advisers to SASO. Khoapa interview, June 16, 1989.

55. Khoapa interview, June 4, 2008. Also Khoapa interview, May 7, 2006.

56. See Minutes of Spro-cas staff meeting, July 28, 1972, A835, B10.ii, Cullen. A police memo argued this was the intention of Spro-cas and the Christian Institute—to bring the two radical strands working for change in South Africa together. See Security Police, "Memorandum: Black Community Programmes," sec. 22, provided to me by the South African National Intelligence Agency.

57. "Spro-Cas Black Community Programmes Budget Proposals—1973," A835, C1, Cullen; Khoapa interview, June 4, 2008. See also Peter Randall, telephone interview by author, May 13, 2009.

58. Randall interview. The Christian Institute was also significantly influenced by Black Consciousness activists and became a more radical organization because of its association with these activists in the early 1970s.

59. See "Spro-cas 2: Budget for 1972–1973," Spro-cas 2 booklet, 6, A835, C1, Cullen.

60. Bennie Khoapa to Peter Randall, December 3, 1973, A835, C9, Cullen. Randall received "a ban" along with most of the leadership of the Christian Institute in October 1977. See also Randall interview; Khoapa interview, June 4, 2008. See also Brian Brown to Bennie Khoapa, September 5, 1972, A835, B9.ii, Cullen.

61. Peter Randall, "SPRO-CAS: Motivations and Assumptions," reprinted from *Reality*, March 1973, A835, C1, Cullen; Minutes of Spro-Cas 2 Planning Meeting October 1971. In the October 1971 meeting, it was stated that black programs "may call on white experts who can contribute insights etc.," perhaps reflecting an initial hesitation or uneasiness about the BCP acting independently.

62. When the BCP office opened in Durban in 1972, Khoapa and Hester (née Fortune) Joseph, the office administrator, were the only employees, but the Spro-cas 2 budget had provisions for the hiring of two field workers if needed. See Bennie Khoapa to Steve Biko, January 11, 1972; Peter Randall to Beyers Naudé and John Rees, July 31, 1972, both in A835, C9, Cullen. In the interview on May 7, 2006, Khoapa said that Biko's mother called him to ask him to give Biko a job.

63. John Rees to Peter Randall, August 2, 1972, A835, C9, Cullen. He was "very interested" that Biko should take up the post, but "a little worried as to his relationship as it were to the Church [as in the Body of Christ]." Rees saw Spro-cas as a church action program, but Biko was "very heavily identified with an organization which is not overtly Christian."

64. Randall stated, "I also personally came in for some criticism because I wasn't particularly religious or theological. I was probably agnostic." Randall interview. See also email correspondence with the author, October 17, 2009.

65. Diana Wylie, *Art + Revolution: The Life and Death of Thami Mnyele, South African Artist* (Charlottesville: University of Virginia Press, 2008), 53–55, 86–90.

66. Oshadi Mangena, interview by author, May 26, 2011, Johannesburg.

67. Khoapa interview, October 8, 2009.

68. Aside from the BCP, Khoapa pointed out that the majority of the Spro-cas leadership was white. "Report of the Spro-Cas Staff Seminar Held from May 26–27," n.d. (content suggests 1972), A835, C1, Cullen.

69. "Memorandum from Mr. Khoapa on Sponsorship of Spro-cas," A835, C1, Cullen.

70. "Black Community Programmes: Spro-cas 2" pamphlet.

71. Khoapa interview, October 8, 2009.

72. The early Cape Town panel included Coloured community leaders, evidence of the strong presence of Black Consciousness in the Western Cape that

helped legitimize the movement's definition of "black." Yet the BCP ended up not establishing an office in Cape Town. Bans on employees took the BCP elsewhere, and its Cape Town advisory panel contact lost interest. Bennie Khoapa, telephone interview by author, May 3, 2010. Khoapa suspected that while some advisory panel members spoke the language of Black Consciousness, they were more interested in obtaining resources.

73. A concern that this clarification was needed in the black community may have been sparked by Reverend Clive McBride from Cape Town, who complained that "liberal organizations like CI [Christian Institute] and SAIRR etc. get money on our ticket (blacks) and very little of the money really filters through to the grass roots." As quoted in Security Police, "Memorandum: Black Community Programmes," sec. 34. The police report also mentions criticism from the Cape Panel of the way the BCP operated. The panels wanted to conduct more programs themselves. Khoapa speculated in a telephone interview on May 3, 2010, that McBride was more concerned about obtaining resources rather than the Black Consciousness principles he expressed at this meeting.

74. Randall, "SPRO-CAS: Motivations and Assumptions," 1, 6; Randall interview.

75. "Memorandum to South African Council of Churches and Christian Institute of S.A. from Bennie Khoapa regarding Meeting of the Black Panel of the B.C.P.," December 4, 1972, A835, B10.ii, Cullen; Peter Randall to Beyers Naudé, December 18, 1972, A835, B6, Cullen.

76. "Spro-Cas Black Community Programmes Budget Proposals—1973," 9–11. See also Peter Randall to Beyers Naudé, June 29, 1972, A835, B9.ii, Cullen; "Memo to all Spro-cas staff" from Bennie Khoapa, October 17, 1972, A835, B4, Cullen; Beyers Naudé to Peter Randall and Bennie Khoapa, December 21, 1972, A835, B9, Cullen.

77. In other words, at this point, the BCP was a private company but did not have capital shares. Instead, members acted as guarantors. Randall told Naudé in May 1973 that he thought Spro-cas should be disbanded at the end of July, leaving the BCP to operate on its own and Ravan Press to take over Spro-cas publishing. Peter Randall to Beyers Naudé, May 29, 1973, A835, B5, Cullen. Naudé wrote to Khoapa in March that the Christian Institute fully supported the BCP's move toward autonomy. Beyers Naudé to Bennie Khoapa, March 8, 1973, A835, C9, Cullen. The Christian Institute proved this commitment with continued financial support of the BCP until both organizations were banned in 1977.

78. "R300 000 BCP Assets Seized," *Daily Dispatch*, October 21, 1977. Khoapa told Sam Nolutshungu that when the government shut down the BCP, it had a payroll of R66,000 for fifty permanent staff, a total operating budget of

over R0.5 million with assets of over R1 million. With the home-industries and the garment factory in Cape Town, he estimated the BCP had 400 more employees. See Nolutshungu, *Changing South Africa*, 203.

79. These numbers are based on inflation rates reported on Statistics South Africa "CPI History 1960 Onwards," www. statssa.gov.za and an average exchange rate in 2014 of R10.8 to the U.S. dollar.

80. "Memo to Spro-cas—from C.I. [Brian Brown]," May 16, 1973; Bennie Khoapa to Peter Randall, August 1, 1973, both in A835, B9.i, Cullen; ? to Bennie Khoapa (regarding Spro-cas finances) June 18, 1973, A835, B9.ii, Cullen; Brian Brown to Bennie Khoapa (regarding vehicle registration/ licensing), April 10, 1973; Brian Brown to Peter Randall (regarding use of office after end of Spro-cas), May 25, 1973; Bennie Khoapa to Peter Randall, July 13, 1973 (acknowledging the receipt of financial statements from Spro-cas but wanting to meet with BCP panel to discuss them), all in A835, C9, Cullen. Indeed, Tor Sellström indicated that donations to Black Consciousness organizations by the Nordic countries through church and NGOs almost doubled over time, while the ANC's aid remained relatively the same. See Sellström, "Sweden and the Nordic Countries," 471–76.

81. Security Police, "Memorandum: Black Community Programmes," secs. 65–66, 70.

82. As discussed further in chapter 5, the BCP made plans to generate income on its own in part by investing in a Cape Town clothing factory in 1976 and 1977, but was shut down before this initiative really got off the ground.

83. This conference involved black leaders from different denominations of "so-called Multi-racial churches in South Africa, with the view to examining their role within these churches and ways and means of increasing the effectiveness of their leadership." As a result, ministers planned to form regional caucuses to work on literacy and social services projects. The BCP held a follow-up meeting in August and organized a conference on Black Theology in 1973. "Report of Conference for Black Church Leaders at Edendale Lay Ecumenical Centre in Pietermaritzburg, May 15–18, 1972," A835, C1, Cullen. See also BCP, "Year Report 1972," n.d., Karis-Gerhart Collection in Struggles for Freedom in Southern Africa, Aluka digital library (hereafter cited as KG-Aluka); BCP, "1973 Report," n.d., KG-Aluka.

84. "Spro-cas 2," 5, GG, Reel 3. Training for organizations could follow if necessary. "Spro-Cas Black Community Programmes Budget Proposals—1973"; Proposal to the Ford Foundation; and Peter Randall to Beyers Naudé, June 29, 1972, all in A835, B9.ii, Cullen.

85. After giving up on becoming a Catholic priest because of racial discrimination in the church, and an attempt to work with the trade union movement,

he became a journalist for the *Rand Daily Mail*. He and other like-minded people in the area (including the poet and writer Wally Serote) often met to share their political views and hold discussions. The only woman among them, Cindy Ramarumo, met Biko during a visit to Ramphele at UNB. Ramarumo took the news of a newly organized student group back to her friends in Alexandra. Mafuna soon after developed a close friendship with SASO leaders such as Biko, Pityana, and Nengwekhulu, and enrolled as a student in UNISA so he could join SASO's Reef branch. Bokwe Mafuna, "The Impact of Steve Biko on My Life," in *We Write What We Like: Celebrating Steve Biko*, ed. Chris van Wyk (Johannesburg: Wits University Press, 2007), 77–89; Bokwe Mafuna, interview by Gail Gerhart, June 21, 1990, Harare, Zimbabwe, Karis-Gerhart Collection: From Protest to Challenge, 1964–1990, Reel 2; Bokwe Mafuna, interview by author, November 6, 2008, Roodepoort.

86. Khoapa interview, June 4, 2008. See also letter confirming Biko's and Mafuna's continued employment, Beyers Naudé to Bennie Khoapa, March 8, 1973, A835, C9, Cullen.

87. Bennie Khoapa, interview by author, November 3, 2008, Durban.

88. Thus, with the bannings, "the months and years ahead" would see "a more deliberate application of our total organizational resources in these directions." See BCP, "1973 Report." 11. The BCP may have also felt some pressure from donors to spend money "in the direction of alleviation of human needs in terms of their immediate conditions and social situation," as stated by Randall regarding a Church of Norway grant in Peter Randall to Beyers Naudé, June 29, 1972, A835, B9, Cullen.

89. Khoapa interview, June 4, 2008.

90. Aelred Stubbs, "Martyr of Hope," in Biko, *I Write*, 166.

91. Malusi Mpumlwana interview.

92. Khoapa interview, October 8, 2009.

93. Jones interview, April 22, 2006 (partly unrecorded). See also Malusi Mpumlwana interview.

94. They left with the initial goal of becoming part of the armed struggle. They found difficulty maneuvering in exile politics, and Mafuna was banished from Botswana in 1978. See Mafuna, "Impact of Steve Biko on My Life," 85–86.

95. In 1976, Ramokgopa held a position with IBM as a systems engineer. He had taught mathematics in Swaziland and returned to South Africa to do an advanced degree in physics. When his supervisor left for a sabbatical in Canada, the Council for Scientific and Industrial Research that provided his scholarship cut off his funding. Ramsey Ramokgopa, interview by author, November 10, 2008, Johannesburg.

96. BCP, "1975 Report," n.d., AAS20 Black Community Programmes, Documentation Centre for African Studies, UNISA Archives; BCP Limited, "1976 Report," n.d., KG-Aluka. This number does not include the employees of the Njwaxa factory.

97. Malusi Mpumlwana interview. The security police also frequented the Leopold Street office, even disguising at least one nighttime visit as criminal vandalism. For more on the break-in of the offices in 1976 when Donald Card, a former security police officer, offered his opinion that General Hattingh was capable of such an act, see Cornelius Thomas, *Tangling the Lion's Tale: Donald Card, from Apartheid Era Cop to Crusader for Justice* (East London: Donald Card, 2007), 193–96; Donald Card, interview by author, October 15, 2008, Gonubie, East London.

98. Pumla Gqola, "Contradictory Locations: Blackwomen and the Discourse of the Black Consciousness Movement (BCM) in South Africa," *Meridians* 2, no. 1 (2001): 130–52; Magaziner, *Law and the Prophets*.

99. Ramphele, *Across Boundaries*, 71.

100. Mamphela Ramphele, "The Dynamics of Gender within Black Consciousness Organisations: A Personal View," in Pityana et al., *Bounds of Possibility*, 214–27; Badat, *Black Student Politics*, 112–13, 156–57. See also "Interview with Deborah Matshoba," in *Biko Lives!: Contesting the Legacies of Steve Biko*, ed. Andile Mngxitama, Amanda Alexander, and Nigel Gibson (New York: Palgrave Macmillan, 2008), 280.

101. Ramphele, "Dynamics of Gender," 220.

102. Matshoba remembered how Biko discouraged her and others from forming a women's group so as to maintain unity as black people. "Interview with Deborah Matshoba," 279.

103. Khoapa interview, June 4, 2008; Malusi Mpumlwana interview, December 20, 2008; Thoko Mpumlwana, interview by the author, July 24, 2008, Pretoria; Luyanda ka Msumza, interview, December 2, 2008; Khoapa interview, November 3, 2008; Mangena interview; Moodley interview.

104. "Spro-Cas 2 Planning Meeting: 15–16 October 1971."

105. It did not create the leadership training center it had planned, and Peter Jones said that he and Biko viewed the project in Mthatha as mediocre. Jones interview, May 14, 2008. Ndamse was the wife/widow of a homeland politician who supported the BCP. Ramphele wrote about how she disagreed with Ndamse over the politics of homeland independence in Ramphele, *Across Boundaries*, 103. Khoapa and Reverend Mcebisi Xundu, who worked for the BCP in the Transkei, explained that some tensions arose within the movement over working with the Ndamses, but that this was seen as an effort to gain a foothold in the Transkei, and Xundu was supposed to keep a check on

Ndamse. Khoapa interview, November 3, 2008; Reverend Mcebisi Xundu, interview by author, October 30, 2008, Port Elizabeth. For more on Ndamse, Xundu, the BCP, and Transkei politics, see Timothy Gibbs, *Mandela's Kinsmen: Nationalist Elites and Apartheid's First Bantustan* (Johannesburg: James Currey, 2014), chap. 4.

106. Charles Nqakula, "1(b): 15 Leopold Street," in *Umhlaba Wethu: A Historical Indictment*, ed. Mothobi Mutloatse (Johannesburg: Skotaville, 1987), 21–24.

CHAPTER 3. *BLACK REVIEW*

1. "Spro-Cas Black Community Programmes Budget Proposals—1973," n.d., 8, A835 Spro-cas 1969–1973, Historical Papers, Cullen Library, University of the Witwatersrand (hereafter cited as Cullen).
2. Thoko Mbanjwa, *Black Review 1974/75* (Durban: Black Community Programmes, 1975), v.
3. With this definition, I adhere to the view of Dick Cloete, "Alternative Publishing in South Africa in the 1970s and 1980s," in *The Politics of Publishing in South Africa*, ed. Nicholas Evans and Monica Seeber (London and Scottsville: Holger Ehling Publishing and University of Natal Press, 2000), 43. Since it is less concerned with market considerations, the alternative press is more likely to challenge the status quo. Les Switzer breaks the history of the alternative press into four periods: Mission Press (1830s–1880s); Independent Protest Press (1880s–1930s); Early Resistance Press (1930s–1960); and Later Resistance (1970s–1990s), in Les Switzer ed., *South Africa's Alternative Press: Voices of Protest and Resistance, 1880s–1960s* (Cambridge: Cambridge University Press, 1997), 1–5.
4. Besides his work with Tswana-English newspapers, Plaatje's notable literary works include his novel *Mhudi: An Epic of South African Native Life a Hundred Years Ago* (1930) and *Native Life in South Africa* (1916), a response to the Native Lands Act of 1913.
5. Switzer, *South Africa's Alternative Press*; Les Switzer and Mohamed Adhikari, eds., *South Africa's Resistance Press: Alternative Voices in the Last Generation Under Apartheid* (Athens: Ohio University Center for International Studies, 2000); Karin Barber, ed., *Africa's Hidden Histories: Everyday Literacy and Making the Self* (Bloomington: Indiana University Press, 2006); David Attwell, *Rewriting Modernity: Studies in Black South African Literary History* (Athens: Ohio University Press, 2005). Matthew Keaney has also shown that Soweto literary magazines reflected various approaches to building communities and

cultures, along with debates among writers about the role of literature in doing so. See Matthew Keaney, "'I Can Feel My Grin Turn to a Grimace': From the Sophiatown Shebeens to the Streets of Soweto on the Pages of *Drum, The Classic, New Classic,* and *Staffrider*" (Master's thesis, George Mason University, 2010). For East African perspectives, see Derek R. Peterson, *Creative Writing: Translation, Bookkeeping, and the Work of Imagination in Colonial Kenya* (Portsmouth, N.H.: Heinemann, 2004); Corrie Decker, "Reading, Writing, and Respectability: How Schoolgirls Developed Modern Literacies in Colonial Zanzibar," *International Journal of African Historical Studies* 43, no. 1 (2010): 89–114.

6. See David Atwell's discussion of alternative modernities and transculturation as better ways of understanding South African literature than postcolonial or postmodern theories in *Rewriting Modernity*.

7. Alan Gregor Cobley, *The Rules of the Game: Struggles in Black Recreation and Social Welfare Policy in South Africa* (London: Greenwood Press, 1997), chap. 2; Tim Couzens, *The New African: A Study of the Life and Work of H. I. E. Dhlomo* (Johannesburg: Ravan Press, 1985); Bhekizizwe Peterson, "The *Bantu World* and the World of the Book: Reading, Writing, and 'Enlightenment,'" in Barber, *Africa's Hidden Histories*, 236–57. For more comments on how reading is necessary for social and economic development, see also Evans and Seeber, *Politics of Publishing in South Africa*, 3, 44.

8. Benedict Anderson, *Imagined Communities: Reflections on the Origin and Spread of Nationalism* (New York: Verso, 1991), 24–36.

9. Barber, *Africa's Hidden Histories*, 15–16.

10. Peter Limb, *The People's Paper: A Centenary History and Anthology of Abantu-Batho* (Johannesburg: Wits University Press, 2012).

11. Switzer, *South Africa's Alternative Press*, 2.

12. Benedict Anderson, Hannah Barker, and Simon Burrows, "Introduction," in *Press, Politics, and the Public Sphere in Europe and North America, 1760–1820,* ed. Hannah Barker and Simon Burrows (Cambridge: Cambridge University Press, 2002), 17. See also Switzer, *South Africa's Alternative Press*, 2.

13. Richard Turner, *The Eye of the Needle: An Essay on Participatory Democracy* (Johannesburg: Spro-cas, 1972).

14. Many published from abroad. See Frederick Johnstone, *Class Race and Gold: A Study of Class Relations and Racial Discrimination in South Africa* (Boston: Routledge and K. Paul, 1976); William Beinart and Saul Dubow, eds., *Segregation and Apartheid in Twentieth-Century South Africa* (New York: Routledge, 1995); Christopher Saunders, *The Making of the South African Past* (Cape Town: David Philip, 1988), chaps. 16–17.

15. Daniel R. Magaziner, *The Law and the Prophets: Black Consciousness in South Africa, 1968–1977* (Athens: Ohio University Press, 2010), 127.

16. Community newspapers and serials like *Grassroots* worked to conscientize, but the BCP focused less on political mobilization. See Switzer and Adhikari, *South Africa's Resistance Press*; Evans and Seeber, *Politics of Publishing in South Africa*; Ineke van Kessel, *"Beyond Our Wildest Dreams": The United Democratic Front and the Transformation of South Africa* (Charlottesville: University Press of Virginia, 2000).

17. BCP, "Black Review 1972 Press Release," n.d., A835, Cullen.

18. Steve Biko, *Black Viewpoint* (Durban: Spro-cas/BCP, 1972), introduction.

19. Mamphela Ramphele, "Empowerment and Symbols of Hope: Black Consciousness and Community Development," in *Bounds of Possibility: The Legacy of Steve Biko and Black Consciousness*, ed. Barney Pityana et al. (Cape Town: David Philip, 1991), 161.

20. Peter Jones, interview by author, April 22, 2006, Athens, Ohio.

21. Switzer, *South Africa's Alternative Press*, 45; Les Switzer, "Politics and Communication in the Ciskei: An African Homeland in South Africa," Occasional Papers, Rhodes University. Institute of Social and Economic Research, 23 (Grahamstown: Institute for Social and Economic Research, Rhodes University, 1979), 9; Magaziner, *Law and the Prophets*, 128.

22. B. A. Khoapa, ed., *Black Review 1972* (Durban: Black Community Programmes, 1973), 44.

23. For more, see Bokwe Mafuna, "The Impact of Steve Biko on My Life," in Chris van Wyk, *We Write What We Like: Celebrating Steve Biko* (Johannesburg: Wits University Press, 2007), 77–89; Switzer, *South Africa's Alternative Press*, 2; Keyan Tomaselli and P. Eric Louw, eds., *The Alternative Press in South Africa* (Bellville: Anthropos and James Currey, 1991), 93–130.

24. Khoapa, *Black Review 1972*, 44. Mafuna contributed to *Black Review 1972*, but the names of the authors of individual sections do not appear in print.

25. Steve Biko, *I Write What I Like* (Randburg: Ravan Press, 1996), 52. Activists grouped Bantu Education with biased reporting and white production of knowledge; however, they did not succeed in creating a new educational curriculum as they had hoped (they at one time proposed to establish a "Black University"). For the most part, while SASO critiqued Bantu Education, it ran programs to increase access to education to build black self-reliance. SASO students ran literacy campaigns, and activists helped black students prepare for their matric exams. Badat describes the evolution of SASO's views on education and contrasts this with the South African National Students' Congress focus on education as a site of struggle in Saleem Badat, *Black Student Politics, Higher Education and Apartheid:*

From SASO to SANSCO, 1968–1990 (Pretoria: Human Science Research Council, 1999), 95–99, 162. Daniel Massey details the friction with the educational system at Fort Hare and the eventual expulsion and withdrawals of many SASO students in Daniel Massey, *Under Protest: The Rise of Student Resistance at the University of Fort Hare*, Hidden Histories (Pretoria: Unisa Press, 2010), chap. 5. Later, BCP resource centers made informational, cultural, and literary materials by and about black people available to provide a black-centered education.

26. See Mbulelo V. Mzamane and David Howarth, "Representing Blackness: Steve Biko and the Black Consciousness Movement," in Switzer, *South Africa's Alternative Press*, 176–211; Magaziner, *Law and the Prophets*, chap. 7.

27. For Lembede's writings on this point, see Robert Edgar and Luyanda ka Msumza, eds., *Freedom in Our Lifetime: The Collected Writings of Anton Muziwakhe Lembede* (Athens: Ohio University Press, 1996), 24, 85–86; Gail M. Gerhart, *Black Power in South Africa: The Evolution of an Ideology* (Berkeley: University of California Press, 1978), 58–60.

28. Biko, *I Write*, 52. Biko also wrote, "A people without a positive history is like a vehicle without an engine," (29).

29. Khoapa, ed., *Black Review 1972*, 1. Biko was the editor until the government banned him and prohibited any of his words from being published. Khoapa assumed the editorship of *Black Review* to allow the review to be published. Thus, it is possible that these were Biko's words with Khoapa's name on them.

30. "Proposal to the Ford Foundation," 7; BCP, "Year Report 1972," n.d., 4, A2675, Johannesburg, Karis-Gerhart Collection: From Protest to Challenge, 1964–1990 (hereafter cited as KG), folder 270, Reel 27.

31. BCP, "Black Review 1972 Press Release."

32. BCP Limited, "BCP 1976 Report,"; H. H. Dlamlenze to P. P. Nketi, March 24, 1977, regarding "Black Viewpoint 6: The Country Wide Disturbances," both in KG, folder 271, Reel 27. The published issues thus included: B. S. Biko, ed., *Black Viewpoint*, with contributions by Njabulo Ndebele, C. M. C. Ndamse, M. G. Buthelezi, and Bennie Khoapa (Durban: Spro-cas/BCP, 1972); Thoko Mbanjwa, ed., *Black Viewpoint Number 2: Détente*, with essays by A. J. Thembela, Stan Mogoba, S. Sokupa, R. E. van der Ross, and T. T. S. Farisani (1975); Thoko Mbanjwa, ed., *Black Viewpoint Number 3: Apartheid: Hope or Despair for Blacks?* (1976); and *Black Viewpoint Number 4: Transkei Independence*, with essays by Mlahleni Njisane, Hector Ncokazi, M. G. Buthelezi, Justice Mabandla, and Hlaku Kenneth Richidi (1976), in KG, folder 270–71, Reel 27.

33. Asha Rambally, ed., *Black Review 1975–1976* (Durban: Black Community Programmes, 1977), 130.

34. Bennie Khoapa, email correspondence with author, July 18, 2011. The BCP managed to hold a conference on education before October 1977, but never published an issue based on the conference. See also "Black Community Programmes: Spro-cas 2" pamphlet, 3, The Black Consciousness movement of South Africa—Material from the collection of Gail Gerhart, Reel 3; "Report on the First Meeting of the Joint Liaison Committee of Spro-Cas Sponsors," March 13, 1972, A835, C1, Cullen; "Spro-Cas Black Community Programmes Budget Proposals—1973," Proposal to the Ford Foundation, and Peter Randall to Beyers Naudé, June 29, 1972, all in A835, B9.ii, Cullen; BCP Limited, "Projects and People," 1977, AAS20, UNISA Archives; and all BCP Yearly Reports.

35. *Handbook of Black Organizations* (Durban: Black Community Programmes, 1973), 1. See the discussion of *The African Yearly Register: Being an Illustrated National Biographical Dictionary (Who's Who) of Black Folks in Africa*, compiled by Skota, ANC General Secretary at the time, in Couzens, *New African*, chap. 1.

36. "Spro-Cas Black Community Programmes Budget Proposals—1973," n.d., A835, Cullen; *Handbook of Black Organizations*, 1.

37. Bennie Khoapa, interview by author, June 4, 2008, Durban.

38. Ibid.

39. "Black Review 1972 Press Release."

40. Khoapa, *Black Review 1972*; Mbanjwa, *Black Review 1974/75*; Rambally, *Black Review 1975–1976*.

41. Malusi Mpumlwana, telephone interview by author, May 5, 2010.

42. Khoapa, *Black Review 1972*, 44; see also 26.

43. Mafika Pascal Gwala, ed., *Black Review 1973* (Durban: Black Community Programmes, 1974), 101–2.

44. Malusi Mpumlwana explained that the BCP particularly focused on Namibia also to inform Namibian students studying at South African universities. Malusi Mpumlwana interview. South Africa finally began to pull out of Namibia in 1989.

45. See Rambally, *Black Review 1975–1976*.

46. South African Institute of Race Relations, *Survey, 1971* (Johannesburg: South African Institute of Race Relations), 38–46.

47. Ibid., 245.

48. Peter Jones, interview by author, May 14, 2008, Somerset West.

49. Peter Randall, telephone interview by author, May 13, 2009.

50. Keaney provides further insight into the difficulties of finding funding for publications that did not want to pander to commercial demands in his discussion about funding sources for *The Classic* and *New Classic* in "'I Can Feel My Grin Turn to a Grimace.'"

51. Khoapa interview, June 4, 2008.
52. Bokwe Mafuna, interview by author, November 6, 2008 (first quotation unrecorded), Roodepoort.
53. Ibid.
54. Khoapa interview, June 4, 2008. Ramphele also wrote of the long nights and weekend work at the Beatrice Street office that went into the first edition. See Ramphele, "Empowerment and Symbols of Hope," 162.
55. Bennie Khoapa, telephone interview by author, October 8, 2009.
56. Jones interview, April 22, 2006.
57. Thoko Mpumlwana, interview by author, July 24, 2008, Pretoria.
58. Mbanjwa, *Black Review 1974/75*, v.
59. Thoko Mpumlwana interview.
60. Keaney, "'I Can Feel My Grin Turn to a Grimace.'" See also Andries Walter Opliphant and Ivan Vladislavic, eds., *Ten Years of Staffrider, 1978–1988* (Johannesburg: Ravan Press, 1988); Bhekizizwe Peterson, "Culture, Resistance and Representation," in *The Road to Democracy in South Africa*, vol. 2, ed. SADET (Pretoria: University of South Africa, 2006); Mbulelo V. Mzamane, "The Impact of Black Consciousness on Culture," in *Bounds of Possibility: The Legacy of Steve Biko and Black Consciousness*, ed. Barney Pityana et al. (Cape Town: David Philip, 1991), 179–93; Mphutlane wa Bofelo, "The Influences and Representations of Biko and Black Consciousness in Poetry in Apartheid and Postapartheid South Africa/Azania," in *Biko Lives!: Contesting the Legacies of Steve Biko*, ed. Andile Mngxitama, Amanda Alexander, and Nigel C. Gibson (New York: Palgrave Macmillan, 2008), 191–212; Pumla Gqola, "Black Woman, You Are on Your Own: Images of Black Women in Staffrider Short Stories, 1978–1982" (Master's thesis, University of Cape Town, 1999); Atwell, *Rewriting Modernity*, chap. 5.
61. Mafuna interview.
62. Mzamane and Howarth, "Representing Blackness," 187; Evans and Seeber, *Politics of Publishing in South Africa*, 75, 81; Magaziner, *Law and the Prophets*, 148. Influencing Donald Woods to promote Black Consciousness and hire Thenjiwe Mtintso as a reporter was another way activists had an impact on journalism.
63. Cloete, "Alternative Publishing in South Africa," 43, 46–51; Mzamane and Howarth, "Representing Blackness"; Mzamane, "Impact of Black Consciousness on Culture"; Peterson, "Culture, Resistance and Representation."
64. Frustrated black writers broke away from the Johannesburg branch of PEN, a multiracial international writers association, to form the African Writers Association. Differences in political viewpoints contributed to the rise in tension between black and white Ravan press employees. Skotaville focused

on educational and children's books as well as black theological texts. It was supported by international churches and some local corporate organizations. See Phaswane Mpe and Monica Seeber, "The Politics of Book Publishing in South Africa: A Critical Overview," in Evans and Seeber, *Politics of Publishing in South Africa*, 27; Cloete, "Alternative Publishing in South Africa," 48–51.

65. Khoapa interview, June 4, 2008.
66. Thoko Mpumlwana interview. Mangcu also argues that Biko was an example of enabling leadership in Xolela Mangcu, *Biko: A Biography* (Cape Town: Tafelburg, 2012), 300–303.
67. Thoko Mpumlwana interview.
68. Thoko Mpumlwana, email correspondence with author, September 14, 2009.
69. Khoapa interview, October 8, 2009.
70. Asha Rambally Moodley, telephone interview by author, August 3, 2011. See also Magaziner, *Law and the Prophets*, 134–36; Mzamane, "Impact of Black Consciousness on Culture," 186–88; Peterson, "Culture, Resistance and Representation."
71. Moodley interview. In between the time she helped the BCP in Durban and moved to King William's Town, Moodley stayed in Pretoria, where she "[took] care of the guys" in the SASO and Black People's Convention trial, providing meals, hosting visitors, and helping with paperwork.
72. Ibid.
73. Ibid. Incidentally, Moodley acted as the editor of a feminist journal, *Agenda*, published in the 1990s. See her various articles in the journal as well as Debby Bonnin et al., "Editorial: Celebrating 10 Years," *Agenda*, no. 34 (1997): 2–3.
74. Thoko Mpumlwana interview. Moodley said, "Maybe I was too busy working." Moodley interview.
75. Peterson, "Culture, Resistance and Representation," 182–85.
76. Mpe and Seeber, "Politics of Book Publishing," 27.
77. According to Khoapa, the BCP continued to rely on Randall's advice even after Ravan stopped printing for the BCP. Khoapa interview, October 8, 2009. For more on Ravan Press, see G. E. de Villiers, ed., *Ravan—Twenty Five Years (1972–1997): A Commemorative Volume of New Writing* (Randburg: Ravan Press, 1997). The press had many black employees throughout the 1970s and was even unintentionally important to promoting black ownership in publishing when differences over the choice of texts and publication standards led black employees to leave and help found Skotaville Press.
78. Jeff Peires, "The Lovedale Press: Literature for the Bantu Revisited," *History in Africa* 6 (1979): 155–75.
79. Jones interview, May 14, 2008.
80. Khoapa interview, June 4, 2008.

81. Randall interview.
82. Switzer, *South Africa's Alternative Press*, 45.
83. South African Institute of Race Relations, *Survey 1973*, 202–5.
84. See Khoapa interview, June 4, 2008.
85. Les Switzer, *Media and Dependency in South Africa*, Africa Series 47 (Athens: Ohio University Monographs in International Studies, 1985), 28; Switzer, "Politics and Communication in the Ciskei," 9.
86. Khoapa interview, June 4, 2008. See also editions that list the price for previous editions.
87. Jones interview, May 14, 2008.
88. Thoko Mpumlwana interview.
89. Jones interview, May 14, 2008.
90. After the end of apartheid, Ravan Press found it difficult to operate successfully in a more open commercial environment. See de Villiers, *Ravan—Twenty Five Years*, 19–23. By the late 1990s, the press was subsumed by Pan Macmillan, South Africa. Pan Macmillan employees were unable to locate the records of *Black Review* or Ravan Press in their archives in 2011. This is not surprising since Glenn Moss, Ravan's third head editor, said the press was "not . . . particularly good at record keeping." When he took over in 1988, he attempted to put together a set of "retrospective title files" and does not remember *Black Review* in that collection. He speculated that *Black Review* records got lost when Ravan transitioned from being a printing house to a publishing company and Zenith printers emerged. Glenn Moss, email correspondence with author, April 19, 2011. I was told in a phone conversation with Lovedale Press in March 2010 that the press's records from the 1970s were burned in 1985.
91. Luyanda ka Msumza, interview by author and Lindani Ntenteni, December 2, 2008, Mdantsane. Switzer argued that *Daily Dispatch* readership among Ciskei residents increased during 1976 to 1979, in large part because of a greater interest in the news of state action against Black Consciousness activists and organizations, reported frequently in the newspaper. Switzer, *Media and Dependency in South Africa*, 43.
92. Bennie Khoapa, telephone interview by author, May 3, 2010; Peter Randall, email correspondence with author, May 4, 2010.
93. Khoapa interview, May 3, 2010.
94. Malusi Mpumlwana remembered that they ordered 1,000 copies at a time for each edition, and that they had ordered more for some of the editions (he did not remember which ones in particular). Malusi Mpumwlana interview.
95. Khoapa interview, May 3, 2010.
96. Gwala, *Black Review 1973*, front matter.

97. Mbanjwa, *Black Review 1974/1975*, v.
98. Jones interview, April 22, 2006.
99. See Spro-cas Black Community Programmes, "Proposal to The Ford Foundation," n.d., 12, A835, C9, Cullen; BCP, "Year Report 1972," n.d., 6, Karis-Gerhart Collection in Struggles for Freedom in Southern Africa, Aluka digital library (hereafter cited as KG-Aluka); "Spro-Cas Black Community Programmes Budget Proposals—1973," n.d., A835, Cullen.
100. "Spro-Cas Black Community Programmes Budget Proposals—1973," n.d., A835, Cullen
101. Spro-cas Black Community Programmes, "Proposal to the Ford Foundation," n.d., 13, A835, C9, UNISA Archives.
102. BCP, "Year Report 1972," n.d., 6, A2675, KG, folder 270, Reel 27.
103. BCP, "1974 Report", n.d., 10, KG-Aluka.
104. Khoapa interview, June 4, 2008.
105. BCP Limited, "BCP 1976 Report." The idea of a resource center was not unique to the BCP. For example, the Christian Institute had a resource center in Cape Town. The Wilgespruit Center and the Edendale Lay Ecumenical Centre had similar functions.
106. Barber, *Africa's Hidden Histories*, 2–3, 13.
107. Switzer, *Media and Dependency in South Africa*, 53–55.
108. Nohle Mohapi, interview by author, October 30, 2008, Port Elizabeth.
109. See Msumza interview. Msumza went into exile in 1977, joined the PAC and stayed in Lesotho and Tanzania, then lived and worked in the United States before returning to South Africa after 1994.

CHAPTER 4. THE ZANEMPILO COMMUNITY HEALTH CENTER

1. Mzwandile Manyela, interview by author and Lindani Ntenteni, August 20, 2008, Zinyoka. Manyela had done some carpentry work for this man.
2. Nosingile Sijama, interview by author and Lindani Ntenteni, September 17, 2008, Zinyoka.
3. Zanempilo was officially named a "Community Health Center," representing its broader aims. I use the more widely used colloquial word and current name—clinic, or *ikliniki*—for convenience.
4. Dina Mjondo and Nomnyaka Miti, interview by author and Lindani Ntenteni, August 27, 2008, Zinyoka.
5. The "more human face" phrase comes from the oft-quoted conclusion to Biko's essay, "Black Consciousness and the Quest for a True Humanity,"

found in any version of Biko, *I Write I Write What I Like*: "We have set out on a quest for true humanity, and somewhere on the distant horizon we can see the glittering prize. Let us march forth with courage and determination, drawing strength from our common plight and our brotherhood. In time we shall be in a position to bestow upon South Africa the greatest gift possible—a more human face."

6. As Noble wrote, "medicine was one of the most prestigious and highest paying professions" for black South Africans and promised to elevate one's social status. Vanessa Noble, "Doctors Divided: Gender, Race and Class Anomalies in the Production of Black Medical Doctors in Apartheid South Africa, 1948–1994" (Ph.D. diss., University of Michigan, 2005), 76–77. This idea was also expressed by Vuyo Mpumlwana, interview by author, October 3, 2008, Mthatha; and by Dr. Sydney Moletsane, interview by author, November 4, 2008, Port Shepstone. Ramphele wrote that she decided to become a doctor because she enjoyed science, and it offered her "the greatest professional freedom and satisfaction." Mamphela Ramphele, *Across Boundaries: The Journey of a South African Woman Leader* (New York: Feminist Press, 1996), 44–45.

7. Malusi Mpumlwana, telephone interview by author, December 20, 2008. As discussed below, it made sense to include Ramphele in drawing up the plans for the clinic and to head the clinic because of her expertise, but recruiting her also allowed her to be closer to Biko. Biko's wife, Nontsikelelo Mashalaba, was a nurse. After he was banned to the King William's Town District, she worked at the rural St. Matthews Mission hospital in Keiskammahoek, about 26 miles (42 km) from King William's Town.

8. Simonne Horwitz reminds us that although apartheid was oppressive, people still retained some agency to act independently or in opposition to the state. She demonstrated that apartheid negatively affected the type of health care available to black South Africans, but that at the same time, Baragwanath did have success and positive growth in the apartheid years. Simonne Horwitz, *Baragwanath Hospital, Soweto: A History of Medical Care 1941–1990* (Johannesburg: Wits University Press, 2013).

9. Groote Schuur saw this contradiction of medical care manifested even within the hospital. See Anne Digby and Howard Phillips, *At the Heart of Healing: Groote Schuur Hospital 1938–2008* (Auckland Park: Jacana Media, 2008). See Randall M. Packard, *White Plague, Black Labor: Tuberculosis and the Political Economy of Health and Disease in South Africa* (Berkeley: University of California Press, 1989), and Diana Wylie, *Starving on a Full Stomach: Hunger and the Triumph of Cultural Racism in Modern South Africa* (Charlottesville: University Press of Virginia, 2001), for more on how cultural and political racism

influenced how poverty and hunger developed among black South Africans. Paul Farmer also addresses these issues in *Pathologies of Power: Health, Human Rights, and the New War on the Poor* (Berkeley: University of California Press, 2003). Alan Jeeves has pointed to a deficiency in what he calls "liberal and radical accounts of the political economy of health," as the literature tends to focus mostly on "European medicine as applied to the subordinate groups, who are merely acted upon." See Alan Jeeves, "Health, Surveillance and Community: South Africa's Experiment with Medical Reform in the 1940s and 1950s," *South African Historical Journal* 43, no. 1 (November 2000): 263.

10. See South African Institute of Race Relations, *Survey*, 1960–78 (Johannesburg: South African Institute of Race Relations).

11. Jeffrey Butler, Robert I. Rotberg, and John Adams, *The Black Homelands of South Africa: The Political and Economic Development of Bophuthatswana and KwaZulu* (Berkeley: University of California Press, 1977), 132; South African Institute of Race Relations, *Survey*, 241; Saldru Community Health Project, *Health and Health Services in the Ciskei*, Saldru Working Papers No. 54 (Cape Town: Saldru, 1983), 35; Les Switzer, *Power and Resistance in an African Society: The Ciskei Xhosa and the Making of South Africa* (Madison: University of Wisconsin Press, 1993), 340.

12. *Health Implications of Apartheid in South Africa* (United Nations, Dept. of Political and Security Council Affairs, 1975), 5. The second statistic comes from Anne Digby, "Early Black Doctors in South Africa," *Journal of African History* 46, no. 3 (November 2005): 445.

13. Malusi Mpumlwana interview, December 20, 2008.

14. Mafika Pascal Gwala, ed., *Black Review 1973* (Durban: Black Community Programmes, 1974), 14; South African Institute of Race Relations, *Survey*.

15. Gwala, *Black Review 1973*, 13–14. *Black Review* also pointed out that there were "no black dentists" (though some were in training) and only ten African pharmacists.

16. In the homelands in 1972, African nurses and midwives numbered 10,725, while only fifty-four doctors (including nine Africans) worked in the homelands. See South African Institute of Race Relations, *Survey, 1973*. For more on black nurses, see Shula Marks, *Divided Sisterhood: Race, Class, and Gender in the South African Nursing Profession* (New York: St. Martin's Press, 1994); Grace Mashaba, *Rising to the Challenge of Change: A History of Black Nursing in South Africa* (Kenwyn: Juta Press, 1995); Horwitz, *Baragwanath Hospital*, chap. 5.

17. After studying the incidence and recovery rate of kwashiorkor in the early 1970s, Dr. Trudi Thomas, a medical officer at the Ciskei's St. Matthews mission hospital in Keiskammahoek, vehemently argued that migrant labor caused rural poverty and social disruption. This particularly affected the

health of children without supporting fathers. In a study she conducted in rural Ciskei, she found that 60 percent of malnourished children had not been born within marriage; 80 percent had been deserted by their fathers, most of whom were working in the cities; 80 percent of well-nourished children had been born to married parents and were supported by fathers; 50 percent of well-nourished children born to married parents were supported by fathers. Trudi Thomas, *The Children of Apartheid: A Study of the Effects of Migratory Labour on Family Life in the Ciskei* (London: Africa Publications Trust, 1974), 17–18.

18. The hallmarks of this movement were the 1942–44 Gluckman Commission and the community health center experiments that recognized the impact of social and economic conditions on health and sought to establish integrative curative, preventive, and promotive (education) health care services. See Shula Marks, "South Africa's Early Experiment in Social Medicine: Its Pioneers and Politics," *American Journal of Public Health* 87, no. 3 (March 1997): 452–59; Jeeves, "Health, Surveillance and Community"; Alan Jeeves, "Delivering Primary Health Care in Impoverished Urban and Rural Communities: The Institute of Family and Community Health in the 1940s," in *South Africa's 1940s: Worlds of Possibilities*, ed. Saul Dubow and Alan Jeeves (Cape Town: Double Storey Books, 2005), 87–107; Howard Phillips, "The Grassy Park Health Centre: A Peri-Urban Pholela?," in Dubow and Jeeves, *South Africa's 1940s*, 108–28; Steve Tollman and Derek Yach, "Public Health Initiatives in South Africa in the 1940s and 1950s: Lessons for a Post-Apartheid Era," *American Journal of Public Health* 83, no. 7 (July 1993): 1043–50; Neil Andersson and Shula Marks, "Industrialization, Rural Health, and the 1944 National Health Services Commission in South Africa," in *The Social Basis of Health and Healing in Africa*, ed. Steven Feierman and John M. Janzen (Berkeley: University of California Press, 1992), 131–61.

19. Digby and Phillips, *At the Heart of Healing*, 44–47; Horwitz, *Baragwanath Hospital*. Much of the public health care was still uncoordinated and under the control of provincial governments at the time; private practices and specialists thrived as competition.

20. The above statistics come from the South African Institute of Race Relations, *Survey, 1965*, 284, and *Survey, 1973*, 352. See also *Survey 1972*, 409, which gives these figures: 1:95 whites; 1:184 blacks. In 1980, the Baragwanath hospital in Soweto was short 2,300 beds of the estimated 5,000 needed. Cedric de Beer, *The South African Disease: Apartheid Health and Health Services* (Trenton, N.J.: Africa World Press, 1986), 36.

21. South African Institute of Race Relations, *Survey, 1965*, 284; South African Institute of Race Relations, *Survey, 1973*, 351. Mission hospitals, as with

education, provided this social service in the rural areas where the government or private practice did not go. When the national government began to take over provincial hospitals and consolidate homeland governments, it took over the mission hospitals in preparation for the establishment of homeland departments of health. Radikobo Ntsimane, of the University of KwaZulu-Natal's School of Religion and Theology, studied the history of mission hospitals. See Radikobo P. Ntsimane, "Amandla Awekho Emuthini, Asenyangeni: A Critical History of the Lutheran Medical Missions in Southern Africa with Special Emphases on Four Mission Hospitals, 1930s–1978" (Ph.D. diss., University of KwaZulu-Natal, 2010); Welcome Siphamandla Zondi, "Medical Missions and African Demand in KwaZulu-Natal, 1836–1918" (Ph.D. diss., University of Cambridge, 2000).

22. Saldru Community Health Project, *Health and Health Services in the Ciskei*, Saldru Working Papers No. 54 (Cape Town: Saldru, 1983), 21.

23. Ibid., 26. This included the newly built (1975) Cecilia Makiwane Hospital, which was built on the periphery of the Ciskei in the largest township of the region, thus inaccessible to many in remote rural villages.

24. Switzer, *Power and Resistance*, 213, 339.

25. Saldru Community Health Project, *Health and Health Services in the Ciskei*, 28.

26. Luvuyo Wotshela, "Homeland Consolidation, Resettlement and Local Politics in the Border and the Ciskei Region of the Eastern Cape, South Africa, 1960–1996" (Ph.D. diss., Oxford University, 2001), 14; see also 4. According to the Saldru Community Health Project, *Health and Health Services in the Ciskei*, 6, the population almost doubled in the Ciskei between 1973 and 1983, from 350,000 to 630,000 people.

27. Switzer, *Power and Resistance*, 339.

28. See Digby, "Early Black Doctors"; Zondi, "Medical Missions and African Demand"; Alfred B. Xuma, "Native Medical Practitioners," *Leech* (November 1933): 12–14.

29. See Noble, "Doctors Divided"; Vanessa Noble, "A Medical Education with a Difference: A History of the Training of Black Student Doctors in Social, Preventive and Community-Oriented Primary Health Care at the University of Natal Medical School, 1940s–1960," *South African Historical Journal* 61, no. 3 (September 2009): 550–74; Jeeves, "Delivering Primary Health Care"; Karin A. Shapiro, "Doctors or Medical Aids—The Debate over the Training of Black Medical Personnel for the Rural Black Population in South Africa in the 1920s and 1930s," *Journal of Southern African Studies* 13, no. 2 (January 1987): 234–55.

30. By 1960, all of the nearly forty experimental community health centers had been reduced to mere clinics, the University of Natal departments were closed, and the Karks left South Africa for Israel. Nursing education seemingly took

a similar turn, although Nontobeko Moletsane remembered practical field trips to economic and agricultural projects as part of her training at King Edward VIII hospital in the early 1960s. Nontobeko Moletsane, interview by author, May 22, 2008, Amalinda. Moletsane trained slightly earlier than the other nurses and was the only one of those whom I interviewed and who worked at Zanempilo to remember these things. Others who commented on these issues included Novayi Vitta Jekwa (interview by author, March 13, 2008, Beacon Bay, East London) and Xoliswa Qodi Nqangweni (interview by author, November 23, 2008, Bhisho).

31. Dr. Siyolo Solombela, interview by author, May 25, 2008, Bonnie Doon, East London.

32. See Magaziner's discussion of activists' decision to engage in Black Theology versus African Theology in Daniel R. Magaziner, *Law and the Prophets: Black Consciousness in South Africa, 1968—1977* (Athens: Ohio University Press, 2010), chap. 5.

33. This echoes the definition of the World Health Organization. See BCP Limited, "Projects and People," 1977, AAS20, UNISA Archives (hereafter cited as UNISA), 9. When asked about the relation between health and Black Consciousness, Dr. Dubs Msauli stated that a community cannot be fully developed if it does not have good health or access to health care. Dr. Lawrence Menzeleli "Dubs" Msauli, interview by author and Lindani Ntenteni, July 21, 2008, Mdantsane. See also Farmer, *Pathologies of Power*.

34. Bennie Khoapa, interview by author, November 3, 2008, Durban. Khoapa put the total donation at R30,000, while Ramphele wrote that the sum was R20,000. The BCP yearly report for 1975 puts the start-up costs at R30,000 but does not indicate from where the money came. Ramphele, *Across Boundaries*, 95. See also BCP, "1975 Report," n.d., 4 AAS20, UNISA.

35. BCP Brochure, "Zanempilo Community Health Centre," n.d., AAS20, UNISA; see also Dr. Nomonde Xundu (granddaughter of Benjamin Tyamzashe), interview by author, July 26, 2008, Johannesburg. Zinyoka also absorbed people from surrounding areas. Stanley Roji came from a white farm and Nonzwakazi Dl'ebusuku from neighboring villages to work at the Tyamzashe home. Some Zinyoka residents said the village has only become a "location" within the past thirty years.

36. Nontobeko Moletsane interview, May 22, 2008. See also Ramphele, *Across Boundaries*, 89.

37. Dr. Lawrence Menzeleli "Dubs" Msauli, interview by author, June 24, 2008, Mdantsane. Msauli served as a board member of the Eastern Cape BCP. Later, in return for the church's help, Biko and the BCP arranged for a new chapel to be built.

38. Biographical information for B. Tyamzashe comes from Deirdre D. Hansen, *The Life and Work of Benjamin Tyamzashe: A Contemporary Xhosa Composer*, Institute of Social and Economic Research Occasional Paper No. 11 (Grahamstown: Rhodes University, 1968), 17; Xolela Mangcu, *To the Brink: The State of Democracy in South Africa* (Scottsville: University of KwaZulu-Natal Press, 2008), 20–21; "A Life through Music," *Kei Mercury*, October 3, 1996. For more on the role of the educated elite, see Lungisile Ntsebeza, *Democracy Compromised: Chiefs and the Politics of the Land in South Africa* (Leiden: Brill, 2005), 5–6, and Timothy Gibbs, *Mandela's Kinsmen: Nationalist Elites and Apartheid's First Bantustan* (Johannesburg: James Currey, 2014), especially the first two chapters.

39. Nomonde Xundu interview. This was Freehold land, so available for black ownership. It is unclear how James acquired the land and if it had any connection to the family's previous position in the King Sandile court.

40. Hansen, *Life and Work of Benjamin Tyamzashe*, 18; Mangcu, *To the Brink*, 20–21.

41. Nomonde Xundu interview; Mandisa Xundu, interview by author and Lindani Ntenteni, August 12, 2008, Duncan Village; Mathew N. Seyisi, interview by author and Lindani Ntenteni, August 20, 2008, Zinyoka; Mjondo and Miti interview.

42. Bennet Sizindzo Gulwa, interview by author and Lindani Ntenteni, June 25, 2008, Bhisho; Nombeko Marjorie Tyamzashe, interview by author, April 3, 2008, Zinyoka; interviews from the Ginsberg Social History Project such as T. Mbilini, interview by Mfundo Ngele and Andile Jack, July 9, 2002, Ginsberg; Mhlobo Zihlangu, interview by Lindani Ntenteni and Thembisa Mtyongwe, July 7, 2002, Ginsberg; Skwanti Nano, interview by Lindani Ntenteni, n.d., Ginsberg.

43. Benjamin Tyamzashe, "New Clinic in Zinyoka Is a Boon," *Indaba Supplement, Daily Dispatch*, January 3, 1975.

44. Ramphele, *Across Boundaries*; Stubbs, "Martyr of Hope."

45. Ramphele, *Across Boundaries*, 95–96.

46. Solombela interview; Ramphele, *Across Boundaries*, 111–16. Msauli remembered a prison warden's surprise at the amount of paperwork brought for him to sign while Msauli was held in police custody in King William's Town. Palweni later assumed the position of head medical officer at the BCP's Solempilo health center in Natal.

47. Nontobeko Moletsane, interview by author, August 12, 2008, Amalinda.

48. "Community Project Dedicated," *Crozier*, November 1975, 4.

49. BCP, "1975 Report," 4.

50. "Black Self-Help Centre Launched," April 19, 1975, *Daily Dispatch*. Malusi Mpumlwana confirmed that the minister did not attend the function. Malusi

Mpumlwana, telephone interview by author, May 5, 2010. Khoapa speculated that the BCP would have invited Siyo in an effort to show Ciskei leaders it did not want to compete negatively with local authorities, but sought to work together to improve the health and health care of the villagers. Bennie Khoapa, telephone interview by author, May 3, 2010.

51. Manyela interview; Mjondo and Miti interview.

52. Switzer, *Power and Resistance*, 330; Wotshela, "Homeland Consolidation," 18. See also Jeff Peires, "Ethnicity and Pseudo-Ethnicity in the Ciskei," in *Segregation and Apartheid in Twentieth-Century South Africa*, ed. William Beinart and Saul Dubow (London: Routledge, 1995), 256–84; Bernard Magubane et al., "Resistance and Repression in the Bantustans," in *The Road to Democracy*, vol. 2, ed. SADET (Pretoria: University of South Africa, 2006), 758–61; and Gibbs, *Mandela's Kinsmen*, for some similar politics in the neighboring homeland of the Transkei.

53. Switzer, *Power and Resistance*, 330–35; Magubane et al., "Resistance and Repression in the Bantustans," 767–74; Peires, "Ethnicity and Pseudo-Ethnicity."

54. "East Cape Head of BCP Denies Plan to Kill Homeland Leaders," *Daily Dispatch*, May 13, 1975; Magubane et al., "Resistance and Repression in the Bantustans," 774.

55. "Minister Blames Saso for Fort Hare Unrest," *Daily Dispatch*, March 28, 1974; "East Cape Head of BCP Denies Plan to Kill Homeland Leaders." Sebe also claimed that Black Consciousness activists misunderstood the real needs of the black people. "Sebe Lashes Saso, BPC," *Daily Dispatch*, May 24, 1978.

56. "BCP Hit at Sebe Speech," *Daily Dispatch,* February 19, 1976; "This Death Could Have Been Avoided Says Sebe," *Daily Dispatch,* September 21, 1977.

57. It ended up in Natal. For more on the relationship between Black Consciousness and the university and theological students, see Philippe Denis, "Seminary Networks and Black Consciousness in South Africa in the 1970s," *South African Historical Journal* 62, no. 1 (2010): 162–82. See also Philippe Denis, "'Men of the Cloth': The Federal Theological Seminary of Southern Africa, Inkatha and the Struggle against Apartheid," *Journal of Southern African Studies* 34, no. 2 (June 2008): 305–24; and Gibbs, *Mandela's Kinsmen*, chap. 2. Also in that chapter, Gibbs describes the changing relationships between Black Consciousness activists working in the Transkei and Transkei politicians.

58. Sijama interview. Other headmen included Luqolo, Sijama's predecessor; Misani; and Kewuthi, who came after Sijama. Leslie Xinwa wrote that F. Kekeni was the headman in "One Clinic Too Many" (*Daily Dispatch*, January 23, 1976), but I did not come across this name in interviews, such

as Fuzile Ndaba, interview by author and Lindani Ntenteni, June 25, 2008, Zinyoka; Manyela interview; Seyisi interview; Stanley Roji, interview by author and Lindani Ntenteni, May 8, 2008, Zinyoka; Tyamzashe interview. For more on changes to land policies, see Wotshela, "Homeland Consolidation," especially chap. 3. Aran Mackinnon highlights the way betterment sparked changes in the relationships between community members and political leaders in his work, though in the case of the Nquthu District in Zululand, the chief was able to mobilize people against the state. Aran S. MacKinnon, "Chiefs, Cattle, and 'Betterment': Contesting Zuluness and Segregation in the Reserves," in *Zulu Identities: Being Zulu, Past and Present*, eds. Benedict Carton, John Laband, and Jabulani Sithole (Scottsville: University of KwaZulu-Natal Press, 2009), 250–55; Aran S. MacKinnon, "Negotiating the Practice of the State: Reclamation, Resistance, and 'Betterment' in the Zululand Reserves," in *The Culture of Power in Southern Africa: Essays on State Formation and the Political Imagination*, ed. Clifton Crais (Portsmouth, N.H.: Heinemann, 2003), 65–90. See also references to betterment in chapter 5.

59. Mjondo and Miti interview.
60. Leslie Xinwa, "One Clinic Too Many," *Daily Dispatch*, January 23, 1976. Xinwa reported that headman F. Kekeni claimed the BCP did not ask his permission to build a clinic in Zinyoka, so pushed the Ciskei to provide a clinic. He also wrote that Kekeni allegedly stood at the stream to discourage people from going to Zanempilo and that the Ciskei secretary for health borrowed Zanempilo's building plans to build clinics elsewhere.
61. Nontobeko Moletsane, interview by author, June 16, 2006, Amalinda; Nontobeko Moletsane interview, May 22, 2008; Msauli interview, June 24, 2008; Thenjiwe Nondalana, interview by author and Lindani Ntenteni, May 29, 2008, Zinyoka; Sijama interview.
62. Peter Jones, interview by author, April 22, 2006, Athens, Ohio; Msauli, interview, June 24, 2008.
63. Thenjiwe Nondalana, interview by author and Lindani Ntenteni, February 27, 2008, Zinyoka.
64. Nontobeko Moletsane interview, June 16, 2006.
65. Ramphele, *Across Boundaries*, 99.
66. Roji interview.
67. Msauli interview, June 24, 2008.
68. Nondalana interview, February 27, 2008; Thenjiwe Nondalana, interview by author, June 9, 2006, Zinyoka.
69. The state took over the clinic when it shut down the BCP in October 1977, although the Anglican Church fought for control over the land. The South

African government later turned Zanempilo over to the Ciskei government in 1981.

70. Nontobeko Moletsane interview, August 12, 2008.

71. Ibid. See also Nontobeko Moletsane interview, June 16, 2006. Moletsane remembered that a Mr. Mazibuko made the demonstration.

72. Nonzwakazi Dl'ebusuku, interview by author and Lindani Ntenteni, April 10, 2008, Zinyoka.

73. BCP Limited, "1976 Report," 5.

74. She reported that some Zinyoka residents were given money from the clinic for schooling their children in the form of a bursary. Nonzwakazi Dl'ebusuku, interview by author, March 10, 2008, Zinyoka; Dl'ebusuku interview, April 10, 2008.

75. Nontobeko Moletsane interview, June 16, 2006.

76. BCP, "1975 Report," 5.

77. BCP Limited, "Projects and People"; BCP Limited, "BCP 1976 Report," 6–7. The building was finished at the end of 1977, but never opened. The BCP was shut down by the government as Dr. Chapman Palweni traveled en route from Kimberly to Natal with his family to assume the post of director.

78. Msauli interview, June 24, 2008.

79. Because of her involvement with Black Consciousness, she was blacklisted and could not find a nursing job once she left Zanempilo to go to Cape Town with her husband, another example of how apartheid stifled some of the best talent in South Africa.

80. See Ramphele, *Across Boundaries*, 103.

81. See Xinwa, "One Clinic Too Many"; Nondalana interview, February 27, 2008; Mpumi Mcilongo, interview by author, November 6, 2008, Roodepoort.

82. Thoko Mbanjwa, ed., *Black Review 1974/1975* (Durban: Black Community Programmes, 1975), 122.

83. Solombela interview.

84. This description of the outstations is taken from Thenjiwe Mtintso, "Giving More Babies Chance to Grow Up Strong," *Indaba Supplement, Daily Dispatch*, January 30, 1976; and the following interviews: Mcilongo interview; Letisha Nonkululeko Dubula, interview by author and Lindani Ntenteni, August 8, 2008, Tamarha; Sydney Moletsane interview; Mziwoxolo Ndzengu, interview by author, August 15, 2008, Zwelitsha; Sido Hlaula, interview by author and Lindani Ntenteni, November 21, 2008, King William's Town; Solombela interview. The mobile clinic run by King William's Town Municipality saw on average 300 patients per month in 1974, equaling 1,200 that year. See National Archives Cape Town Repository KAB 4/KWT 1/1/1/19–21.

85. Ramphele, *Across Boundaries*, 104.

86. Bennie Khoapa, interview by author, June 4, 2008, Durban.

87. Msauli interview, June 24, 2008. Aelred Stubbs was also a fruitful contact. See, for example, Aelred Stubbs, "Second Report on Black Community Programmes and Zimele Trust Fund," November 1976, to friends overseas, Karis-Gerhart Collection in Struggles for Freedom in Southern Africa, Aluka digital library. See also "Maitshe Nchaupe Aubrey Mokoape Testimony," *State v. Cooper et al.*, reel 5, 5000–5003, AD1719, Historical Papers, Cullen Library, University of the Witwatersrand, for more on contacts activists had with European doctors (in this case in Geneva).

88. Financial registers for "Zanempilo Community Health Clinic—1" and "Black Community Programmes (Solempilo Community Centre)—17" provided to me in March 2010 by Tshikululu Social Investments. See also "Anglo Visit Zanempilo," *Daily Dispatch*, February 1, 1977; "Anglo Men Meet BCP Today," *Daily Dispatch*, January 31, 1977.

89. Seyisi interview; Zanempilo Community Committee meeting minutes from July 2007 and August 2008.

90. Nomalizo Felicia Madikane, interview by author and Lindani Ntenteni, October 28, 2008, Zwelitsha. Madikane said her husband believed that their son would bring health to the family because that is what the clinic did for the villages.

91. See introduction to Feierman and Janzen, *Social Basis of Health and Healing*.

92. Beauty Nongauza, interview by author and Lindani Ntenteni, November 19, 2008, King William's Town.

93. Hlaula interview, November 21, 2008.

94. See Ramphele's comments on this in *Across Boundaries*; Sydney Moletsane interview. Beauty Nongauza (interview) said patients would be confused when Dr. Moletsane mistakenly told them to sit on their hip when he wanted them to sit up: "He used to say *Hlala ngeyinxe*—the hip, no, he would see the person trying his best to position himself and he [*laughs*]. So, we had to explain to Moletsane."

95. Ramphele, *Across Boundaries*, 98–99.

96. Siganyati Leleni, interview by author and Lindani Ntenteni, August 20, 2008, Zinyoka.

97. Maria Nomutile Masiki, interview by author and Lindani Ntenteni, September 2, 2008, Zinyoka.

98. Solombela interview. Dr. Solombela also explained that the BCP needed to "look at [health] in its totality, knowing how people live, what's available for them, and what they can use to actually make and be able to feed healthy food to their babies." See also David Baronov, *The African Transformation of*

Western Medicine and the Dynamics of Global Cultural Exchange (Philadelphia: Temple University Press, 2008).

99. Sydney Moletsane interview; Nontobeko Moletsane interview, May 22, 2008. Incidentally, M. M. Nakase, a longtime Njwaxa resident, remembered a particular *sangoma* (diviner) from Zinyoka as being very effective. M. M. Nakase, B. E. Nakase, and Nokukwaka Cola, interview by author and Lindani Ntenteni, July 3, 2008, Njwaxa.

100. Catherine Burns, "A Long Conversation: The Calling of Katie Makanya," *Agenda* 54 (2002): 134.

101. Nongauza interview. On the use of injections and stethoscopes, see Benedict Carton, "'We Are Made Quiet by This Annihilation': Historicizing Concepts of Bodily Pollution and Dangerous Sexuality in South Africa," *International Journal of African Historical Studies* 39, no. 1 (2006): 85–106; Anne Digby, *Diversity and Division in Medicine: Health Care in South Africa from the 1800s* (Oxford: Peter Lang, 2006), 352, 384–403, 259; Karen E. Flint, *Healing Traditions: African Medicine, Cultural Exchange, and Competition in South Africa, 1820–1948* (Athens: Ohio University Press, 2008), 135–43; Feierman and Janzen, *Social Basis of Health and Healing*, 3.

102. Jacob Dlamini, *Native Nostalgia* (Auckland Park: Jacana Media, 2009); Horwitz, *Baragwanath Hospital*.

103. Ndzengu interview.

104. Nondalana interview, February 27, 2008.

105. Masiki interview; Leleni interview; Seyisi interview.

106. Mjondo and Miti interview.

107. Solombela interview.

108. Nondalana interview, February 27, 2008; Nondalana interview, May 29, 2008.

109. Dl'ebusuku interview, April 10, 2008. Dl'ebusuku used the exact word, "apartheid," but one of the Xhosa terms for apartheid, *ucalu-calulo*, is translated as "prejudice" or "racism." It is likely, then, that Dl'ebusuku used the term "apartheid" more generally to talk about a system or practice based on prejudice.

110. Youth and adults were divided into senior and junior groups, and their duties and responsibilities changed as they reached certain stages in life. The dividing lines between these stages were sharper for boys, whose manhood was marked by an initiation that included circumcision and instruction in the laws of behavior for men. Once boys became men, they put away recreational stick-fighting and other childish behaviors, and began to speak soberly and take on leadership responsibilities. See Anne Kelk Mager, *Gender and the*

Making of a South African Bantustan: A Social History of the Ciskei, 1945–1959 (Portsmouth, N.H.: Heinemann, 1999), 128–29.

111. Sijama interview. Mager describes young men and women increasingly disregarding rules of appropriate behavior for their age group in the 1940s and 1950s. As Mager explains, this kind of behavior was often sparked by contests over resources such as money and beer and exacerbated by the fact that with poverty and the absences of middle-aged males in many villages, initiation into manhood would be delayed and youth were left to destructive idleness. See Mager, *Gender and the Making of a South African Bantustan*, chap. 5

112. Ramphele, *Across Boundaries*, 104–5; Mamphela Ramphele, "Dynamics of Gender within Black Consciousness Organisations: A Personal View," in *Bounds of Possibility: The Legacy of Steve Biko and Black Consciousness*, ed. Barney Pityana et al. (Cape Town: David Philip, 1991), 220; Amanda Alexander and Andile Mngxitama, "Interview with Deborah Matshoba," in *Biko Lives!: Contesting the Legacies of Steve Biko*, ed. Andile Mngxitama, Amanda Alexander, and Nigel Gibson (New York: Palgrave Macmillan, 2008), 280.

113. Malusi Mpumlwana interview, December 20, 2008.

114. Nontobeko Moletsane interview, August 12, 2008.

115. Ramphele, *Across Boundaries*, 14–15; Mamphela Ramphele, interview by Mary Marshall Clark, August 2, 1999.

116. Khoapa interview, June 4, 2008; Mjondo and Miti interview.

117. Nqangweni interview; Ndzengu interview; Hlaula interview, November 21, 2008. See Noble's discussion of the gendered aspects of the medical profession and UNB education in "Doctors Divided," chap. 6.

118. Ramphele, "Dynamics of Gender," 221. Black nurses were not novel since they were often the main providers of Western health care in rural black South Africa, and the nursing profession was seen as a women's profession.

119. Malusi Mpumlwana interview, December 20, 2008. Xolela Mangcu expressed a similar sentiment when he talked about their fascination with Ramphele as young children from Ginsberg in an interview by the author, May 3, 2008, King William's Town. Trudi Thomas was a female doctor in the Ciskei region. But she was stationed over 26 miles (42 km) away at the St. Matthews Mission Hospital, so people in Zinoyka most likely would not have interacted with her.

120. Nohle Mohapi, interview by author, October 30, 2008, Port Elizabeth.

121. Sydney Moletsane interview.

122. Sido Hlaula, interview by author and Lindani Ntenteni, December 2, 2008, King William's Town.

123. Ndzengu interview. Incidentally, Ndzengu met his wife at the clinic when she came to work there as a nurse.

124. In his book on HIV/AIDS in the Eastern Cape, Jonny Steinberg argues that rural clinics and health care workers can be empowered to make a significant impact on rural health in addition to urban-centered hospitals. See Jonny Steinberg, *Three-Letter Plague: A Young Man's Journey through a Great Epidemic* (Johannesburg: Jonathan Ball, 2008). See Steinberg's list of further reading on 330, 333.

CHAPTER 5. THE NJWAXA LEATHER HOME INDUSTRY

1. "Reclamation and Settlement of Njwaxa Location No. 18, District of Middledrift," November 3, 1965, Reference no. N2/11/3/27, National Archives SAB BAO 20/615, H128/1431/18.

2. Ibid. See also Meetings of Headmen and People, Victoria East, December 30, 1965 and District Administration Meeting, June 26, 1968, both in Box 38 N1/15/4, Eastern Cape Archives and Records; Sabra Study Group of Fort Hare, *The Ciskei—A Bantu Homeland: A General Survey* (Alice: Fort Hare University Press, 1971); Nontozande Nofence James, interview by author and Lindani Ntenteni, June 26, 2008, Njwaxa; Novayi Vitta Jekwa, interview by author, March 13, 2008, Beacon Bay, East London.

3. See P. J. de Vos et al., *A Socio-economic and Educational Survey of the Bantu Residing in the Victoria-East, Middledrift and Zwelitsha Areas of the Ciskei* (Alice: University of Fort Hare, 1970), 25; M. M. Nakase, B. E. Nakase, and Nokukwaka Cola, interview by author and Lindani Ntenteni, July 3, 2008, Njwaxa; Rev. David Russell, interview by author, May 15, 2008, Cape Town; Jekwa interview; Njwaxa Group interview by author and Lindani Ntenteni, September 18, 2008, Njwaxa. In "Ciskei Farming Problems," *Daily Dispatch*, May 30, 1974, Dr. Tait, a senior lecturer in geography at Fort Hare, said the Ciskei had "possibly the lowest agricultural production per unit area in the world." The most serious problem, in his view, was low production from farming enterprises. It is possible that the betterment policies planned for Njwaxa in the 1960s decreased the ability or interest of residents to rely on crop cultivation and stock for sustenance. The initial plan to change the environmental practices of Njwaxa included a decrease in cultivation to free land for grazing (from 805 to 471 morgens of cultivated land), as well as the culling of stock to be replenished by more sustainable breeds. See "Reclamation and Settlement of Njwaxa Location."

4. Diana Wylie demonstrated this in *Starving on a Full Stomach: Hunger and the Triumph of Cultural Racism in Modern South Africa* (Charlottesville: University Press of Virginia, 2001), chap. 7.

5. P. A. Black wrote that one could argue that "the policy to develop the Ciskei has generally arisen from a realization of the basic untenability of a system which is based on inequalities between individuals, regions, and nations." P. A. Black, "Economic Development for the Ciskei," in *Ciskei: Economics and Politics of Dependence in a South African Homeland*, ed. Nancy Charton (London: Croom Helm, 1980), 16–29, and chaps. 2 and 12. See also Les Switzer, *Power and Resistance in an African Society: The Ciskei Xhosa and the Making of South Africa* (Madison: University of Wisconsin Press, 1993), 340–45; Jeffrey Butler, Robert I. Rotberg, and John Adams, *The Black Homelands of South Africa: The Political and Economic Development of Bophuthatswana and Kwa-Zulu* (Berkeley: University of California Press, 1977); Fred T. Hendricks, *The Pillars of Apartheid: Land Tenure, Rural Planning and the Chieftaincy* (Uppsala: Academiae Ubsaliensis, 1990); Simon Bekker, P. A. Black, and A. D. Roux, *Some Development Issues in Ciskei* (Grahamstown: Rhodes University, 1982). The Tomlinson Commission and Report of 1954, which reported on the poor state of homeland agricultural, insufficient land, and lack of economic development, was meant to assess the homeland situation and thus the possibilities of implementing a policy change. It acknowledged the major challenges the government faced in putting separate development into action, but the government did it anyway.

6. Betterment required that communities fence-off grazing and farm land and group homesteads into one area. It also often included soil, water, and plant conservation, which inspired cattle culling. Certain areas were targeted for this at different times. Historians have shown how this played out differently in these different times and places, have discussed the role of chiefs as middlemen who either supported or resisted this state intervention, and have examined why people in general responded negatively. For betterment in the Ciskei, see Chris de Wet, *Moving Together, Drifting Apart: Betterment Planning and Villagisation in a South African Homeland* (Johannesburg: Witwatersrand University Press, 1995); Chris de Wet and Michael Whisson, eds., *From Reserve to Region: Apartheid and Social Change in the Keiskammahoek District of (Former) Ciskei, 1950–1990* (Grahamstown: Institute for Social and Economic Research, Rhodes University, 1997). See also P. A. McAllister, "Resistance to 'Betterment' in the Transkei: A Case Study from Willowvale District," *Journal of Southern African Studies* 15, no. 2 (January 1989): 346–68; William Beinart, "Introduction: The Politics of Colonial Conservation," *Journal of Southern African Studies* 15, no. 2 (January 1989): 143–62;

Aran S. MacKinnon, "Chiefs, Cattle, and 'Betterment,'" in *Zulu Identities: Being Zulu, Past and Present*, eds. Benedict Carton, John Laband, and Jabulani Sithole (Scottsville: University of KwaZulu-Natal Press, 2009), 250–55; Aran S. MacKinnon, "Negotiating the Practice of the State: Reclamation, Resistance, and 'Betterment' in the Zululand Reserves," in *The Culture of Power in Southern Africa: Essays on State Formation and the Political Imagination*, ed. Clifton Crais (Portsmouth, N.H.: Heinemann, 2003), 65–90.

7. See Bernard Magubane et al., "Resistance and Repression in the Bantustans," in *The Road to Democracy*, vol. 2, ed. SADET (Pretoria: University of South Africa, 2006), 774; Butler, Rotberg, and Adams, *Black Homelands of South Africa*, 181–91; Switzer, *Power and Resistance*, 344; A. J. Raubenheimer, "Homelands Urged to Develop Land," *Daily Dispatch*, December 6, 1973; "R1.35m to Be Spent on Ciskei Agriculture," *Daily Dispatch*, June 6, 1973; "Abraham Appeals to Xhosa Farmers," *Daily Dispatch*, n.d. See also Timothy Gibbs's discussion of betterment and community development in the Transkei in *Mandela's Kinsmen: Nationalist Elites and Apartheid's First Bantustan* (Johannesburg: James Currey, 2014), especially 53–57.

8. The XDC split into the Ciskei and Transkei Development Corporations in 1976. The Tswana and Zulu corporations were formed in 1975 and 1978, respectively. For more on the XDC and Bantu Investment Corporation in Bophuthatswana and KwaZulu, see Butler, Rotberg, and Adams, *Black Homelands of South Africa*, 98–99, chaps. 7 and 8; Roger Southall, "Buthelezi, Inkatha and the Politics of Compromise," *African Affairs* 80, no. 321 (October 1981): 453–81; Charton, *Ciskei*; Sam Nolutshungu, *Changing South Africa: Political Considerations* (Manchester: Manchester University Press, 1982), 82–90; Switzer, *Power and Resistance*, 340–42.

9. The film *Last Grave at Dimbaza* (Chris Curling, Pascoe Macfarlane, Nana Mahomo, Antonia Caccia, Andrew Tsehlana; Brooklyn, N.Y.: First Run/Icarus Films, 1974) played a large role in raising international attention. See also "Border Industries of No Benefit to Ciskei—Siyo," *Daily Dispatch*, October 10, 1973. L. F. Siyo, then Ciskei minister of interior, said they needed to speed up the process of industrial development. "Blacks Want to Share Economy Says Sebe," *Daily Dispatch*, December 4, 1973; "Sebe Sees Mr. O [Oppenheimer]," *Kei Mercury*, May 30, 1974; "Sebe Pleads for More Industry," *Daily Dispatch*, March 11, 1975; "Aid Needed," *Kei Mercury*, August 5, 1976; "New Store Opens," *Kei Mercury*, August 12, 1976.

10. "Sebe Pleads for More Industry"; "Big Industrial Boom Forecast for the Ciskei," *Kei Mercury*, May 9, 1974. "Jobs Boost for Ciskei," *Kei Mercury*, March 28, 1974, as well as "Dr. Meyer Forecasts New Growth in 1976," *Kei*

Mercury, November 13, 1975, reported plans for new factories in Dimbaza, Alice, and Keiskammahoek.

11. Barry Streek, "Sebe: Our Route for the Future," *Indaba Supplement, Daily Dispatch*, January 9, 1973. See also special insert on the XDC, *Daily Dispatch*, December 15, 1973; "New Factories for Dimbaza," *Daily Dispatch*, January 14, 1976.

12. By March 1974, 10,834 black jobs were created, but a 1970 census estimated the population of the Ciskei at 526,000. Charton, *Ciskei*, 230, 10. About 35 percent of the potential workforce was left unemployed by the end of the 1970s. Switzer, *Power and Resistance*, 345. See a contemporary assessment for Bophuthatswana and KwaZulu in Butler, Rotberg, and Adams, *Black Homelands of South Africa*.

13. Black, "Economic Development for the Ciskei," 26.

14. See Catherine Higgs, "Zenzele: African Women's Self-Help Organizations in South Africa 1927–98," *African Studies Review* 47, no. 3 (December 2004): 119–41; Mafika Pascal Gwala, ed., *Black Review 1973* (Durban: Black Community Programmes, 1974), 7–8.

15. For correspondence and records of the Bantu Affairs Commissioners regarding school feeding schemes and the distribution of soup powder in the 1960s, see "Bantu Welfare: Famine Relief Scheme File 1 (1966–1970)," n.d., Box 310 N7/8/2, Eastern Cape Archives and Records; "Relief of distress, Famine Relief Scheme, File 2," n.d., Box 313 N7/8/2, Eastern Cape Archives and Records; "Middledrift Quarterly Meetings with Native Administrators, Monday, 30th September, 1968, and June 30, 1965," n.d., Box 39 N1/15/4, Eastern Cape Archives and Records. These boxes contain similar records from the 1940s and 1950s.

16. Njwaxa Group interview. Other communities were also paid to eradicate noxious weeds or for working on roads and dams. See "Relief of distress, Famine Relief Scheme, File 2."

17. See "Help for Red Cross," *Kei Mercury*, July 13, 1975; "Fund at Nearly R3000," *Kei Mercury*, October 2, 1975; "Ciskei Women Learn New Skills," *Kei Mercury*, November 24, 1977. Mrs. Sebe gained media attention by showing up at events held by some of these organizations, such as a workshop held by the Cape Province Women's Agricultural Association, which taught Ciskeian women various home and cooking skills. "Mrs. Sebe Patron [of Cripple Care Society]," *Kei Mercury*, February 24, 1977. Sebe established her own women's association, in part in opposition to other Zenzele women's organizations.

18. BCP, "1974 Report," n.d., Karis-Gerhart Collection in Struggles for Freedom in Southern Africa, Aluka digital library (hereafter cited as KG-Aluka);

Thoko Mbanjwa, *Black Review 1974/75* (Durban: Black Community Programmes, 1975), 120.

19. Rev. Temba Sibeko and Cybil Sibeko, interview by author, December 15, 2008, Fort Beaufort.
20. Mantuka Maisela, interview by author, July 24, 2008, Santon; see also Philippe Denis, "Seminary Networks and Black Consciousness in South Africa in the 1970s," *South African Historical Journal* 62, no. 1 (2010): 162–82.
21. BCP, "1974 Report," 6; Malusi Mpumlwana, telephone interview by author, December 20, 2008.
22. Fr. Timothy Stanton, email correspondence with author, January 24, 2009. Stanton served as the rector in Alice from 1968 until 1975, when the seminary was "expropriated." Other members of the Community of Resurrection included Aelred Stubbs, friend to Biko and Black Consciousness activists, and Trevor Huddleston, ardent opponent against apartheid and forced removals in Sophiatown in the 1950s and leader of the anti-apartheid movement in Britain in the 1980s. See Robin Denniston, *Trevor Huddleston: A Life* (New York: St. Martin's Press, 1999).
23. Nakase, Nakase, and Cola interview; Njwaxa Group interview.
24. Fr. Timothy Stanton, email correspondence with author, January 24, 2009.
25. T. H. Sibeko to Inter Church Aid administrator, September 9, 1974; T. H. Sibeko to John Reese, April 22, 1976, both in AC 623, file 4.3.3, Historical Papers, Cullen Library, University of the Witwatersrand.
26. Malusi Mpumlwana, interview, December 20, 2008.
27. Vuyo Mpumlwana, interview by author, October 3, 2008, Mthatha.
28. In addition to those pictured in figure 7, Papu also remembered the name of one man, Nstikelelo Cola, and the names of two other women, Jane Khene and Nozukile Sinxo, who were part of the initial group. Sarha Papu, interview by author and Lindani Ntenteni, June 26, 2008, Njwaxa.
29. Papu interview, June 26, 2008.
30. Ibid. While education had not been important to most villagers during Papu's childhood, in the 1970s they saw it as vital for the economic future of their families. Ibid.; Nakase, Nakase, and Cola interview.
31. Nakase, Nakase, and Cola interview.
32. Papu interview.
33. James interview.
34. Ibid.
35. Nontombomhlaba Mamase, interview by author and Lindani Ntenteni, June 26, 2008, Njwaxa.
36. Ibid.

37. See Iris Berger's comments on working women creating bonds in *Threads of Solidarity: Women in South African Industry, 1900–1980* (Bloomington: Indiana University Press, 1992), 5. In many Xhosa villages at the time, there was a hierarchy of women in extended families that could have created tensions between women, though I did not find evidence of this.

38. Mamase interview.

39. James interview.

40. Vuyo Mpumlwana interview; Conversation with Njwaxa women, June 14, 2011. If a person arrived too late for work, she or he forfeited her or his wages for the entire day.

41. Conversation with Njwaxa women, June 14, 2011.

42. Dina Mjondo and Nomnyaka Miti, interview by author and Lindani Ntenteni, August 27, 2008, Zinyoka.

43. Switzer, *Power and Resistance*, 342; Njwaxa Group interview. See also Berger, *Threads of Solidarity*.

44. This was corroborated by some Njwaxa women. Conversation with Njwaxa women, June 14, 2011. See Anne Kelk Mager, *Gender and the Making of a South African Bantustan: A Social History of the Ciskei, 1945–1959* (Portsmouth, N.H.: Heinemann, 1999).

45. This built upon the idea of the Dependents Conference of the Border Council of Churches. Mapetla Mohapi, and later Pumzile Majeke, directed the Zimele Trust Fund. See Ramphele's description in Mamphela Ramphele, "Empowerment and Symbols of Hope: Black Consciousness and Community Development," in *Bounds of Possibility: The Legacy of Steve Biko and Black Consciousness*, ed. Barney Pityana et al. (Cape Town: David Philip, 1991), 168–69.

46. When asked if any villagers or any men were jealous of those who had jobs at the factory, interviewees simply responded that others were planning to work at the factory when the second shift opened. Conversation with Njwaxa women, June 14, 2011. For example, Nokukwaka Cola looked forward to working at the factory when it extended to include an evening shift. Cola lived and worked in East London with her husband but wanted to move back to Njwaxa to help her mother-in-law take care of her children and the homestead. Nakase, Nakase, and Cola interview.

47. Vuyo Mpumlwana interview.

48. Ibid.

49. She eventually ended up in Canada, where she became a clinical psychologist. Vuyo Mpumlwana interview. For some, her work with the ANC may seem to be a major shift in political loyalties since in some areas Black Consciousness political groups clashed with ANC groups. For some Black Consciousness

adherents, like Vuyo's brother, Malusi, however, Black Consciousness tran-
scended political parties. It did not matter which political group one belonged
to, but rather if one was conscientized. See Malusi Mpumlwana, interview by
author, April 16, 2008, Johannesburg.
50. Maisela interview.
51. Voti Samela, interview by author and Lindani Ntenteni, August 6, 2008,
KwaGcina (Sterkspruit).
52. BCP, "1975 Report," n.d., AAS20, UNISA Archives (hereafter cited as
UNISA). It is unclear how much this tanning contributed to the total raw
materials the factory needed to keep up production.
53. Malusi Mpumlwana interview, December 20, 2008.
54. Samela described Njwaxa as "the bundus," or a wild, remote area. Samela
interview.
55. BCP Limited, "1976 Report," n.d., KG-Aluka. This was financed in large
part by the ICCO in Holland, according to Mamphela Ramphele, *Across
Boundaries: The Journey of a South African Woman Leader* (New York: Feminist Press, 1996), 101. Peter Jones also described ICCO's support in Peter
Jones, interview by author, May 14, 2008, Somerset West.
56. BCP Limited, "Projects and People," 1977, AAS20, UNISA. They had been
making fifty pairs per day.
57. Samela interview.
58. Ibid.
59. Vuyo Mpumlwana interview.
60. Papu interview.
61. Samela interview.
62. Vuyo Mpumlwana interview.
63. Yet they also had to beware of police informers. Biko seemed to deal with
disagreements or other staff problems by taking people aside and speaking with them individually. See discussion of the conflict between S'buku
and Samela below. Also, Mziwoxolo Ndzengu reported another incident at
Zanempilo when he suspected an employee of stealing R200. Ndzengu said
that when he conferred with Biko about the missing money, Biko told him
not to worry; he trusted Ndzengu and would take care of the problem. Mziwoxolo Ndzengu, interview by author, August 15, 2008, Zwelitsha.
64. Russell interview.
65. Jones interview.
66. Ibid.; Bennie Khoapa, interview by author, November 3, 2008, Durban.
67. Ramphele, "Empowerment and Symbols of Hope," 167. It is unclear how
Ramphele envisioned this capital injection coming about. It seems unlikely
that Njwaxa residents would have had the capital to buy shares in the factory.

Perhaps the BCP had planned to gift the shares or asked a donor to buy the shares on behalf of the villagers. This may have eventually allowed for a bigger return to villagers, which would have followed the BCP's goals of cultivating local leadership and ownership. However, this assumes that the factory would have been making a profit. Interestingly, Ramphele later would work for the World Bank and sit on a number of corporate boards in South Africa.

68. For example, Dr. Siyolo Solombela, interview by author, May 25, 2008, Bonnie Doon, East London. The Black People's Convention in particular took this issue on. For examples, see reports on BCP meetings in B. A. Khoapa, ed., *Black Review 1972* (Durban: Black Community Programmes, 1973), 12; Asha Rambally, ed., *Black Review 1975–1976* (Durban: Black Community Programmes, 1977), 108–9. See also documents in UNISA: AAS153, "Black Communalism" by H. Rachidi, file 2; the program for the BCP's special seminar on black communalism, file 3; NAHECS: AZAPO/BCM, particularly Box 28; "Azapo Aids Squatters," *Sowetan*, August 8, 1981.

69. The Black Consciousness espoused by the Azanian People's Organization (AZAPO) after 1977 took on a class analysis and became explicitly socialist. The structural challenges activists were up against in community work may have influenced this shift, but greater worker organization and protest in the early to mid-1970s, a rise in Marxism among white radicals, dissatisfaction with apathetic black businesses or the middle class, and a new political terrain have been proven to have played a significant role. See Nurina Ally and Shireen Ally, "Critical Intellectualism," in *Biko Lives!*, ed. Andile Mngxitama, Amanda Alexander, and Nigel Gibson (New York: Palgrave Macmillan, 2008), 171–88; Nigel Gibson, "Black Consciousness after Biko: The Dialectics of Liberation in South Africa, 1977–1987," in Mngxitama, Alexander, and Gibson, *Biko Lives!*, 138; Nolutshungu, *Changing South Africa*; Robert Fatton Jr., *Black Consciousness in South Africa: The Dialectics of Ideological Resistance to White Supremacy* (Albany: State University of New York Press, 1986).

70. As highlighted in chapter 1, Black Consciousness activists stressed the need for those with greater resources to help those without. They also derided those in the black middle class who seemed aloof. But this did not mean activists completely shunned what some have considered middle-class goals of property accumulation or education, for instance. Alan Cobley, *Class and Consciousness: The Black Petty Bourgeoisie in South Africa, 1924–1950* (New York: Greenwood Press, 1990); Sean Redding, "South African Blacks in a Small Town Setting: The Ironies of Control in Umtata, 1878–1955," *Canadian Journal of African Studies* 26, no. 1 (1992): 70–90.

71. Roger Southall, "The ANC & Black Capitalism in South Africa," *Review of African Political Economy* 100 (2004): 313–28; Patrick Bond, *Talk Left,*

Walk Right: South Africa's Frustrated Global Reforms (Scottsville: University of KwaZulu-Natal Press, 2004); Alan Hirsch, *Season of Hope: Economic Reform under Mandela and Mbeki* (Scottsville: University of KwaZulu-Natal Press, 2005); Seekings and Nattrass, *Class, Race, and Inequality*; Bill Freund and Harold Witt, eds., *Development Dilemmas in Post-Apartheid South Africa* (Scottsville: University of KwaZulu-Natal Press, 2010); Hein Marais, *South Africa Pushed to the Limit: The Political Economy of Change* (London: Zed Books, 2011).

72. Papu interview.
73. James interview.
74. Conversation with Malusi Mpumlwana, June 20, 2011, Johannesburg airport.
75. Vuyo Mpumlwana interview.
76. Papu interview.
77. Mamase interview.
78. James interview.
79. Njwaxa Group interview.
80. Samela interview. This was confirmed by Njwaxa residents in the Njwaxa Group interview. For Samela, Njwaxa's distance from Sebe in King William's Town and nearby Zwelitsha (then the location of the Ciskei administrative headquarters) was significant because it made people more inclined to work at a factory and support a BCP project.
81. Njwaxa Group interview.
82. James interview.
83. Nakase, Nakase, and Cola interview. Papu also expressed this in Papu interview.
84. Mamase interview.
85. Njwaxa Group interview.
86. Samela interview. Njwaxa residents also claimed that S'buku took his own tools home, while the government kept the rest. Njwaxa Group interview.
87. Njwaxa Group interview.
88. Samela later heard that S'buku had played a role in the South African security forces' cross-border raids in Lesotho in 1982 and even wondered if he had told the police that Biko and Jones had left for Cape Town, leading to Biko's last arrest. Samela interview. Former security policeman Donald Card told of how he bribed a student at Fort Hare to become a SASO member and feed him with information, indicating that it is highly likely that S'buku was a police plant. Donald Card, interview by author, October 15, 2008, Gonubie, East London.
89. Ramphele, "Empowerment and Symbols of Hope," 167.

90. See, in particular, Lindani Ntenteni, Mark Mandita, and author discussion with Mr. and Mrs. James, Mr. and Mrs. Nakase, Sarha Papu, and Nontombomhlaba Mamase, June 18, 2008, Njwaxa; Njwaxa Group interview.

CONCLUSION

1. See Mangcu's description of the Cape Town meetings and events leading to Biko's death in Xolela Mangcu, *Biko: A Biography* (Cape Town: Tafelburg, 2012), 252–63. For a description of the death and torture of Biko and the Truth and Reconciliation Commission hearings regarding his death, see Leslie Hadfield, "The Death of Stephen Biko," essay on the website, *Overcoming Apartheid, Building Democracy*; Amnesty Hearing Transcripts, "Killing of Steve Biko," Port Elizabeth-1 (September 8–11, 1997), Port Elizabeth-7 (December 8–11, 1997), and Cape Town-10 (March 30–31, 1998), Amnesty Hearings and Decisions on South African Department of Justice TRC website. See also Donald Woods, *Biko*, 3rd ed. (New York: Henry Holt, 1991), where Woods describes the initial inquest into Biko's death and includes Peter Jones's account of his own experience.

2. Bennie Khoapa, interview by author, June 4, 2008, Durban.

3. Dr. Sydney Moletsane, interview by author, November 4, 2008, Port Shepstone.

4. Sido Hlaula, interview by author and Lindani Ntenteni, November 21, 2008, King William's Town. Whether or not the police actually took the cutlery, the fact that some interviewees said they did signifies how complete the police raid was in their eyes.

5. And after some conflict with the Anglican Church over the land ownership. See "Church-State Tussle over Zanempilo Land," *Daily Dispatch,* December 8, 1977; "BCP Clinic Now Belongs to Church," *Daily Dispatch,* February 2, 1978; "Zanempilo Clinic to Be Handed to Ciskei," *Daily Dispatch,* July 1, 1981.

6. Thenjiwe Nondalana, interview by author and Lindani Ntenteni, May 29, 2008, Zinyoka.

7. Voti Samela, interview by author and Lindani Ntenteni, August 6, 2008, Kwa Gcina (Sterkspruit).

8. The BCP was run by a relatively close-knit group of activists. The organization undoubtedly would have changed with further growth and new circumstances. For example, Khoapa spoke repeatedly about the unresolved question of how the BCP would have incorporated new groups and programs,

pointing out that the BCP did not have anything like a constitution that other groups could reproduce or be incorporated into. The way post-1977 organizations involved new people indicates that the BCP could have become an umbrella organization, sponsored new local programs, or engaged in training and coordinating conferences as it hoped to in the beginning.

9. Mamphela Ramphele, *Across Boundaries: The Journey of a South African Woman Leader* (New York: Feminist Press, 1996), 141. The rest of the information about Ithuseng comes from Ramphele, *Across Boundaries*, 138–44, and Lindy Wilson, *Out of Despair—Ithuseng*, VHS/DVD (Cape Town: Lindy Wilson Productions, 1984).

10. Malusi Mpumlwana, telephone interview by author, December 20, 2008.

11. It could not be registered as a welfare organization, so its funding options were limited. Teresa Barnes and Thandiwe Haya, "Educational Resistance in Context: Zingisa Educational Project in the Eastern Cape, 1975–1993," in *The History of Education Under Apartheid, 1948–1994: The Doors of Learning and Culture Shall Be Opened*, ed. Peter Kallaway (New York: Peter Lang, 2002), 150.

12. This could help secure greater funding for Zingisa from the South African Council of Churches. Malusi Mpumlwana interview.

13. See TCOE Annual Report for 2007 and TCOE website. See also Nohle Mohapi, interview by author, October 30, 2008, Port Elizabeth. In 2008, Nontobeko Moletsane still conducted sessions with rural women's groups under TCOE, even though she was in her late sixties and had been in a coma earlier that year.

14. Most of this information comes from a meeting I had with Deena Soliar in Durban at Umtapo, June 5, 2008. On AZAPO projects, see Pandelani Nefolovhodwe, interview by author, November 5, 2008, Midrand; records in the NAHECS archives, AZAPO/BCM collection.

15. See Patrick Mkhize, interview by David Wiley, May 8, 2006, Durban, *South Africa: Overcoming Apartheid, Building Democracy* website.

16. Nefolovhodwe interview; Is'Baya Development Trust website; Monique Vanek, "Wilgespruit Fellowship Centre: Part of Our Struggle for Freedom," in *From National Liberation to Democratic Renaissance in Southern Africa*, ed. Cheryl Hendriks and Lwazi Lushaba (Dakar: CODESRIA, 2005), 152–70.

17. Thirty-eight villages have been put on the path to commercialization, and nearly 800 farmers have been identified as lead farmers for cooperative groups. See Peter Jones and Rosemary du Preez, "Uvuselelo Integrated Village Renewal Programme," Is'Baya and ARC-LNR Report, provided by Peter Jones, September 6, 2013. See also the Is'baya Development Trust website.

18. Jones and du Preez, "Uvuselelo."

19. Amartya Sen, *Development as Freedom* (New York: Alfred A. Knopf, 1999), 3. See also L. R. Gordon, "Fanon and Development: A Philosophical Look," *Africa Development* 29, no. 1 (2004): 71–93. Gordon argues that the term should be "liberation" because liberation indicates a historical trajectory and is existential. For him, the focus should be on building a people's ability to influence and operate in a social world.

20. Andrew Kirkendall, *Paulo Freire and the Cold War Politics of Literacy* (Chapel Hill: University of North Carolina Press, 2010), 168.

21. Archbishop Njongonkulu Ndungane, "Spirituality and the Development Agenda," paper presented at the Steve Biko Foundation Thirtieth Anniversary Commemorative International Conference: Consciousness, Agency, and the African Development Agenda, September 10–12, 2007, University of Cape Town. This sentiment is echoed in Steve de Gruchy, Nico Koopman, and Sytse Strijbos, eds., *From Our Side: Emerging Perspectives on Development and Ethics* (Amsterdam: Rozenberg, 2008).

22. Mamphela Ramphele, "Empowerment and Symbols of Hope: Black Consciousness and Community Development," in *Bounds of Possibility: The Legacy of Steve Biko and Black Consciousness*, ed. Barney Pityana et al. (Cape Town: David Philip, 1991), 171. See also Andrea Cornwall, "Whose Voices? Whose Choices? Reflections on Gender and Participatory Development," *World Development* 31, no. 8 (August 2003): 1325–42; Jane L. Parpart, "Rethinking Participation, Empowerment, and Development from a Gender Perspective," in *Transforming Development: Foreign Aid for a Changing World*, ed. Jim Freedman (Toronto: University of Toronto Press, 2000), 222–34.

23. Ramphele, "Empowerment and Symbols of Hope," 172–73.

24. Ibid., 174.

25. Mamphela Ramphele, *Laying Ghosts to Rest: Dilemmas of the Transformation in South Africa* (Cape Town: Tafelberg, 2008), chap. 7; see also chap. 16. Although Ramphele seemed to have gone against her own ideas when she teamed up with the Democratic Alliance without consulting her political party, Agang, in 2014, she does make a good point here.

26. Bennie Khoapa, conversation with author, June 2, 2011.

27. Mangcu, *Biko*, 275, 285.

28. The following few references show that the effectiveness of participatory approaches to development and Freire's conscientization methods are still debated, theorized, and applied: Bill Cooke and Uma Kothari, eds., *Participation: The New Tyranny?* (London: Zed Books, 2001); Samuel Hickey and Giles Mohan, eds., *Participation: From Tyranny to Transformation? Exploring New Approaches to Participation in Development* (London: Zed Books, 2004); Ghazala Mansuri and Vijayendra Rao, "Community-Based and -Driven

Development: A Critical Review," *World Bank Research Observer* 19, no. 1 (Spring 2004): 1–39; Andrea Cornwall, "Historical Perspectives on Participation Development," *Commonwealth and Comparative Politics* 44, no. 1 (March 2006): 49–65; Margaret Ledwith and Jane Springett, *Participatory Practice: Community-based Action for Transformative Change* (Bristol, U.K.: Policy Press, 2010).

29. Kirkendall, *Paulo Freire*, 97.

30. This approach would have been more effective in Guinea-Bissau, where, Linda Harisim has argued, a literacy program was irrelevant (as discussed in ibid., 106–13).

31. Interestingly, Freire worked with a number of governments while at the same time using methods geared toward reforming the very social, political, and economic systems the governments perpetuated. Kirkendall writes that in Chile, Eduardo Frei's government "sought to both liberate and to control, and at its best and worst, it exemplified the promise and the contradictions of 1960s reform." Ibid., 61. For a discussion on the effect the state has on development and how scholars have looked at this in the past, see John Martinussen, *Society, State and Market: A Guide to Competing Theories of Development* (London: Zed Books, 2005), chap. 19; David Hulme and Mark Turner, *Governance, Administration, and Development: Making the State Work* (West Hartford, Conn.: Kumarian Press, 1997).

32. Daniel R. Magaziner, *The Law and the Prophets: Black Consciousness in South Africa, 1968—1977* (Athens: Ohio University Press, 2010), 129–33. Some have used oppressive methods to conscientize people to a certain way of thinking, as evidenced in Guinea-Bissau where Freire worked in the 1970s. He worked in newly independent countries such as Guinea Bissau and São Tomé and Príncipe, and later Nicaragua, though these were one-party states and often disregarded his democratic educational practices. See Kirkendall, *Paulo Freire*.

33. For example: Dambisa Moyo, *Dead Aid: Why Aid Is Not Working and How There Is a Better Way for Africa* (New York: Farrar, Straus and Giroux, 2009); William Easterly, *Reinventing Foreign Aid* (Cambridge, Mass.: MIT Press, 2008); William Easterly, *White Man's Burden: Why the West's Efforts to Aid the Rest Have Done So Much Ill and So Little Good* (New York: Penguin Press, 2006).

34. Ramphele, "Empowerment and Symbols of Hope," 170.

35. Patrick Bond, *Talk Left, Walk Right: South Africa's Frustrated Global Reforms* (Scottsville: University of KwaZulu-Natal Press, 2004); Hein Marais, *South Africa Pushed to the Limit: The Political Economy of Change* (London: Zed Books, 2011).

36. Roger Southall, "The ANC & Black Capitalism in South Africa," *Review of African Political Economy* 100 (2004): 313–28; Alan Hirsch, *Season of Hope: Economic Reform under Mandela and Mbeki* (Scottsville: University of KwaZulu-Natal Press, 2005); Jeremy Seekings and Nicoli Nattrass, *Class, Race, and Inequality in South Africa* (New Haven, Conn.: Yale University Press, 2005); Bill Freund and Harold Witt, eds., *Development Dilemmas in Post-Apartheid South Africa* (Scottsville: University of KwaZulu-Natal Press, 2010).

37. "Walking Together for Health: A Pathfinder Programme for the Health Reform in the Eastern Cape," Letsema Circle pamphlet, 2011, 5. The organization promises to help people work with and hold accountable their "community partners"—the government, the private sector, nongovernmental organizations—in order to reach their goals.

Bibliography

ARCHIVAL COLLECTIONS

African Studies Documentation Centre, University of South Africa Library (UNISA)
    AAS 20   Black Community Programmes
    AAS 127   SASO and BPC
    AAS 153   Black Consciousness, misc.

Cory Library for Historical Research, Rhodes University

Digital Innovation South Africa digital library, www.disa.ukzn.ac.za (DISA)

Eastern Cape Department of Agriculture and Rural Development, Land Use Management Office, Bhisho

Eastern Cape Department of Sport, Recreation, Arts, and Culture, Records and Archives Services, King William's Town

Historical Papers, William Cullen Library, University of the Witwatersrand (Cullen)
    A835   Spro-cas 1969–1973
    A1888   Benjamin Pogrund Papers
    A2176   South African Students Organization
    A2177   Black People's Convention
    A2675   Karis-Gerhart Collection
    AB2414   St. Peter's Theological College, Federal Theological Seminary
    AC623   South African Council of Churches
    AD1126   University Christian Movement
    AD1719   *State v. Cooper et al.*

Karis-Gerhart Collection: From Protest to Challenge, 1964–1990, Microfilmed for Cooperative Africana Microform Project (CAMP) of the Center for Research Libraries (KG)

National Archives and Records of South Africa
    Cape Town Archives Repository
    National Archives Repository, Pretoria

National Heritage and Cultural Studies Centre, University of Fort Hare
    Azanian People's Organization / Black Consciousness Movement (AZAPO/
    BCM)

South Africa: Overcoming Apartheid, Building Democracy, http://overcomingapartheid
.msu.edu/interview.php
    Interviews with Ben Khoapa, Patrick Mkhize, Nchaupe Aubrey Mokoape

South African National Intelligence Agency, intelligence reports and confiscated
documents related to Black Community Programmes, Ltd., as requested under the
Promotion of Access to Information Act 2000 (PAIA)

Steve Biko Foundation, Johannesburg
    Department of Justice files
    Bruce Haigh Collection
    King William's Town files
    University of Witwatersrand, Karis-Gerhart Collection copies

Struggles for Freedom in Southern Africa, Aluka digital library, www.aluka.org
(Aluka)

The Black Consciousness Movement of South Africa—Material from the collection
of Gail Gerhart, filmed for CAMP (GG)

NEWSPAPERS AND PERIODICALS

Black Review	1972–1975/76
Daily Dispatch	1969–1978, boxes filed by subject
Kei Mercury	1960, 1974–1977
SASO Newsletter	1970–1977
The Crozier (Diocese of Grahamstown)	1973–1977

INTERVIEWS BY THE AUTHOR (LN INDICATES
WITH LINDANI NTENTENI)

Biko, Nobandile, September 9, 2008, Cape Town
Biko, Ntsiki, April 24, 2008, King William's Town
Card, Donald, October 15, 2008, Gonubie, East London
Dubula, Letisha Nonkululeko, August 8, 2008, Tamarha Location, LN
Gulwa, Bennet S., June 25, 2008, Bhisho, LN
Hlaula, Sido, November 21, 2008; December 2, 2008, King William's Town, LN
Hope, Anne, May 16, 2008, Lakeside
Jekwa, Dr. Mncedisi Winston, May 11, 2008, Beacon Bay, East London
Jekwa, Novayi Vitta, March 13, 2008; March 27, 2008, Beacon Bay, East London
Jones, Peter, April 22, 2006, Athens, Ohio, USA; September 4, 2004; May 14, 2008, Somerset West
ka Msumza, Luyanda, December 2, 2008, Mdantsane, LN
Khoapa, Bennie, June 4, 2008; November 3, 2008, Durban; October 8, 2009, May 3, 2010, telephone
Madikane, Nomalizo Felicia, October 28, 2008, Zwelitsha, LN
Mafuna, Bokwe, November 6, 2008, Roodepoort
Magida, Nokuzola, December 12, 2008, telephone
Magida, Ray, February 26, 2008; March 26, 2008, King William's Town
Maisela, Mantuka, July 24, 2008, Sandton
Mangcu, Xolela, May 3, 2008, King William's Town
Mangena, Oshadi, May 26, 2011, Johannesburg
Mcako, Nomazotsho Nyakati and Ntsiki Biko, December 2, 2008, Ginsberg
Mcilongo, Nompumelelo (Mpumi), November 6, 2008, Roodepoort
Mohapi, Nohle, October 30, 2008, Port Elizabeth
Moletsane, Dr. Sydney, November 4, 2008, Port Shepstone
Moletsane, Nontobeko, June 16, 2006; May 22, 2008; August 12, 2008, Amalinda, LN
Moodley, Asha Rambally, August 3, 2011, telephone
Mpumlwana, Malusi, April 16, 2008, Johannesburg; December 20, 2008; May 5, 2010, telephone
Mpumlwana, Thoko, July 24, 2008, Pretoria
Mpumlwana, Vuyo, October 3, 2008, Mthatha
Msauli, Dr. Lawrence Menzeleli "Dubs," June 24, 2008; July 21, 2008, Mdantsane, LN
Ndzengu, Mziwoxolo, August 15, 2008, Zwelitsha
Ndzengu, Yoliswa, December 19, 2008, telephone

Nefolovhodwe, Pandelani, November 5, 2008, Midrand
Nengwekhulu, Harry, July 31, 2008, Pretoria
Nongauza, Beauty, November 19, 2008, King William's Town, LN
Palweni, Chapman, November 11, 2008, Pretoria
Pityana, Barney, March 20, 2008, East London
Qodi (now Nqangweni), Xoliswa, November 23, 2008, Bhisho
Ramokgopa, Ramsey, November 10, 2008, Johannesburg
Randall, Peter, May 13, 2009, telephone
Russell, David, May 15, 2008, Rosebank, Cape Town
Samela, Voti, August 6, 2008, Kwa Gcina (Sterkspruit), LN
Sibeko, Temba and Cybil, December 15, 2008, Fort Beaufort
Solombela, Dr. Siyolo, May 25, 2008, Bonnie Doon, East London
Solombela, Pinkie, April 10, 2008, Bonnie Doon, East London
Xundu, Mandisa E., August 12, 2008, Duncan Village, LN
Xundu, Nomonde, July 25, 2008, Johannesburg
Xundu, Rev. Mcebisi, October 30, 2008, Port Elizabeth

Interviews Conducted in Zinyoka

Dl'ebusuku, Nonzwakazi, March 10, 2008; April 10, 2008; July 2, 2008, LN
Leleni, Siganyati, August 20, 2008, LN
Manyela, Mzwandile, August 20, 2008, LN
Masiki, Maria N., September 2, 2008, LN
Mjondo, Dina, and Nomnyaka Miti, August 27, 2008, LN
Ndaba, Fuzile, June 25, 2008, LN
Nondalana, Thenjiwe Evelyn, June 9, 2006; February 27, 2008; May 29, 2008, LN
Roji, Stanley, March 10, 2008; May 8, 2008; July 2, 2008, LN
Seyisi, Ndodana M., August 20, 2008, LN
Sijama, Nosingile, September 17, 2008, LN
Tyamzashe, Nombeko Marjorie, March 10, 2008, April 13, 2008, LN

Interviews Conducted in Njwaxa

James, Nontozande Nofence, June 26, 2008, LN
Mamase, Nontombomhlaba, June 26, 2008, LN
Nakase, M. M., B. E. Nakase, and Nokukwaka Cola, July 3, 2008, LN
Papu, Sarha S., June 26, 2008, LN

Group Meeting with Nontozande James, Nontonbomhlaba Mamase, M. M. Nakase, B. E. Nakase, Nokukwaka Cola, and Sarha Papu, August 22, 2008, LN

Group Interview, September 18, 2008, LN:
Bonisile Sinxo
D. J. Makinana
Kholeka Mamase
Lily Ndlebe
Maggie Mamase
Mildred L. Yoyo
M. Kalawe
Mlindeli Cola
M. S. Kenene
Mvuzo Papu
Myali Nakase
N. H. Makinana
N. J. Mamase
Nofence James
Nontobeko Jali
Nomachina Mamase
Nozinzile Nakase
Thamsanqa Sinxo

ARTICLES, BOOKS, DISSERTATIONS, REPORTS, AND UNPUBLISHED PAPERS

Abbink, Jon, and Ineke van Kessel, eds. *Vanguard or Vandals: Youth, Politics, and Conflict in Africa.* Boston: Brill, 2005.

Achebe, Nwando. *Farmers, Traders, Warriors, and Kings: Female Power and Authority in Northern Igboland, 1900–1960.* Portsmouth, N.H.: Heinemann, 2005.

Aerni-Flessner, John. "'If We Govern Ourselves, Whose Son Is to Govern Us?': Youth, Independence and the 1960s in Lesotho." Ph.D. diss., Washington University, 2011.

Akyeampong, Emmanuel Kwaku. *Between the Sea & the Lagoon: An Eco-social History of the Anlo of Southeastern Ghana, c. 1850 to Recent Times.* Athens: Ohio University Press, 2001.

Anderson, Benedict. *Imagined Communities: Reflections on the Origin and Spread of Nationalism.* London: Verso, 1991.

Andersson, Neil, and Shula Marks. "Industrialization, Rural Health, and the 1944 National Health Services Commission in South Africa." In *The Social Basis of Health and Healing in Africa*, edited by Steven Feierman and John M. Janzen, 131–61. Berkeley: University of California Press, 1992.

Arnold, Millard. *The Testimony of Steve Biko*. London: M. Temple Smith, 1979.

Attwell, David. *Rewriting Modernity: Studies in Black South African Literary History*. Athens: Ohio University Press, 2005.

Babou, Cheikh Anta. *Fighting the Greater Jihad: Amadu Bamba and the Founding of the Muridiyya of Senegal, 1853–1913*. Athens: Ohio University Press, 2007.

Badat, Saleem. *Black Student Politics, Higher Education and Apartheid: from SASO to SANSCO, 1968–1990*. Pretoria: Human Science Research Council, 1999.

Barber, Karin. *Africa's Hidden Histories: Everyday Literacy and Making the Self*. Bloomington: Indiana University Press, 2006.

Barker, Hannah, and Simon Burrows, eds. *Press, Politics, and the Public Sphere in Europe and North America, 1760–1820*. Cambridge: Cambridge University Press, 2002.

Baronov, David. *The African Transformation of Western Medicine and the Dynamics of Global Cultural Exchange*. Philadelphia: Temple University Press, 2008.

Bay, Edna G., and Donald L. Donham, eds. *States of Violence: Politics, Youth, and Memory in Contemporary Africa*. Charlottesville: University of Virginia Press, 2006.

Beinart, William. "Introduction: The Politics of Colonial Conservation." *Journal of Southern African Studies* 15, no. 2 (January 1989): 143–62.

Beinart, William, and Saul Dubow, eds. *Segregation and Apartheid in Twentieth-Century South Africa*. London: Routledge, 1995.

Bekker, Simon, P. A. Black, and A. D. Roux. *Some Development Issues in Ciskei*. Grahamstown: Rhodes University, 1982.

Berger, Iris. *Threads of Solidarity: Women in South African Industry, 1900–1980*. Bloomington: Indiana University Press, 1992.

Bernstein, Hilda. *No. 46—Steve Biko*. London: International Defence and Aid Fund, 1978.

Biko, Steve. *Black Viewpoint*. Durban: Spro-cas/BCP, 1972.

———. *I Write What I Like*. Randburg: Ravan Press, 1996.

Bond, Patrick. *Talk Left, Walk Right: South Africa's Frustrated Global Reforms*. Scottsville: University of KwaZulu-Natal Press, 2004.

Bonner Philip, Peter Delius, and Deborah Posel, eds. *Apartheid's Genesis: 1935–1962*. Johannesburg and Braamfontein: Ravan Press and Witwatersrand University Press, 1993.

Bonnin, Debby, Louise Haysom, Lungi Lingishi, Asha Moodley, and Veni Soobrayan. "Editorial: Celebrating 10 Years." *Agenda*, no. 34 (1997): 2–3.

Bornat, Joanna. "Remembering and Reworking Emotions: The Reanalysis of Emotion in an Interview." *Oral History* 38, no. 2 (2010): 43–52.

Bozzoli, Belinda. *Class, Community, and Conflict: South African Perspectives*. Johannesburg: Ravan Press, 1987.

Brown, Julian. "An Experiment in Confrontation: The Pro-Frelimo Rallies of 1974." *Journal of Southern African Studies* 38, no. 1 (March 2012): 55–71.

Brown, Karen. "'Trees, Forests and Communities': Some Historiographical Approaches to Environmental History on Africa." *Area* 35, no. 4 (December 2003): 343–56.

Bundy, Colin. "Street Sociology and Pavement Politics: Aspects of Youth and Student Resistance in Cape Town, 1985." *Journal of Southern African Studies* 13, no. 3 (April 1987): 303–30.

Burns, Catherine. "A Long Conversation: The Calling of Katie Makanya." *Agenda* 54 (2002): 133–40.

Burton, Andrew, and Helene Charton-Bigot, eds. *Generations Past: Youth in East African History*. Athens: Ohio University Press, 2010.

Butler, Jeffrey, Robert I. Rotberg, and John Adams. *The Black Homelands of South Africa: The Political and Economic Development of Bophuthatswana and Kwa-Zulu*. Berkeley: University of California Press, 1977.

Calderisi, Robert. *The Trouble with Africa: Why Foreign Aid Isn't Working*. London: Zed Books, 2006.

Campbell, James T. *Songs of Zion: The African Methodist Episcopal Church in the United States and South Africa*. New York: Oxford University Press, 1995.

Carruthers, Jane. "Africa: Histories, Ecologies and Societies." *Environment and History* 10, no. 4 (November 2004): 379–406.

Carton, Benedict. *Blood from Your Children: The Colonial Origins of Generational Conflict in South Africa*. Charlottesville: University of Virginia Press, 2000.

———. "'We Are Made Quiet by This Annihilation': Historicizing Concepts of Bodily Pollution and Dangerous Sexuality in South Africa." *International Journal of African Historical Studies* 39, no. 1 (2006): 85–106.

Chambers, Robert. *Managing Rural Development: Ideas and Experience from East Africa*. Uppsala: Scandinavian Institute of African Studies, 1974.

———. *Rural Development: Putting the Last First*. London: Longman, 1983.

Chapman, Audrey R., and Leonard S. Rubenstein, eds. *Human Rights and Health: The Legacy of Apartheid*. Washington, D.C.: American Association for the Advancement of Science and Physicians for Human Rights, 1998.

Charney, Craig. "Civil Society vs. the State: Identity, Institutions, and the Black Consciousness Movement in South Africa." Ph.D. diss., Yale University, 2000.

Charton, Nancy, ed. *Ciskei: Economics and Politics of Dependence in a South African Homeland*. London: Croom Helm, 1980.

Cherry, Janet. "'We Were Not Afraid': The Role of Women in the 1980s' Township Uprising in the Eastern Cape." In *Women in South African History*, edited by Nomboniso Gasa, 281–313. Cape Town: Human Science Research Council Press, 2007.

Chirenje, J. Mutero. *Ethiopianism and Afro-Americans in Southern Africa, 1883–1916*. Baton Rouge: Louisiana State University Press, 1987.

Clark, Nancy L. *Manufacturing Apartheid: State Corporations in South Africa*. New Haven, Conn.: Yale University Press, 1994.

Clark, Nancy L., and William H. Worger. *South Africa: The Rise and Fall of Apartheid*. New York: Longman, 2004.

Clarke, Bob. *Anglicans Against Apartheid, 1936–1996*. Pietermaritzburg: Cluster, 2008.

Cobley, Alan Gregor. *Class and Consciousness: The Black Petty Bourgeoisie in South Africa, 1924–1950*. New York: Greenwood Press, 1990.

———. *The Rules of the Game: Struggles in Black Recreation and Social Welfare Policy in South Africa*. London: Greenwood Press, 1997.

Cooke, Bill, and Uma Kothari, eds. *Participation: The New Tyranny?* London: Zed Books, 2001.

Cooper, Frederick. *Africa since 1940: The Past of the Present*. Cambridge: Cambridge University Press, 2002.

Cooper, Frederick, and Randall M. Packard, eds. *International Development and the Social Sciences: Essays on the History and Politics of Knowledge*. Berkeley: University of California Press, 1997.

Cornwall, Andrea. "Historical Perspectives on Participation Development." *Commonwealth and Comparative Politics* 44, no. 1 (March 2006): 49–65.

———. "Whose Voices? Whose Choices? Reflections on Gender and Participatory Development." *World Development* 31, no. 8 (August 2003): 1325–42.

Couzens, Tim. *The New African: A Study of the Life and Work of H. I. E. Dhlomo*. Johannesburg: Ravan Press, 1985.

Dagron, Alfonso Gumucio. "Playing with Fire: Power, Participation, and Communication for Development." *Development in Practice* 19, no. 4–5 (June 2009): 453–65.

Davenport, Rodney, and Richard Elphick, eds. *Christianity in South Africa: A Political, Social, and Cultural History*. Berkeley: University of California Press, 1997.

Davies, Grace. "Strength in Numbers: The Durban Student Wages Commission, Dockworkers and the Poverty Datum Line, 1971–1973." *Journal of Southern African Studies* 33, no. 2 (2007): 401–20.

de Beer, Cedric. *The South African Disease: Apartheid Health and Health Services*. Trenton, N.J.: Africa World Press, 1986.

Decker, Corrie. "Reading, Writing, and Respectability: How Schoolgirls Developed

Modern Literacies in Colonial Zanzibar." *International Journal of African Historical Studies* 43, no. 1 (2010): 89–114.

de Gruchy, John, and Steve de Gruchy. *The Church Struggle in South Africa*. Minneapolis: Fortress Press, 2005.

de Gruchy, Steve, Nico Koopman and Sytse Strijbos, eds. *From Our Side: Emerging Perspectives on Development and Ethics*. Amsterdam: Rozenberg, 2008.

Denis, Philippe. "'Men of the Cloth': The Federal Theological Seminary of Southern Africa, Inkatha and the Struggle against Apartheid." *Journal of Southern African Studies* 34, no. 2 (June 2008): 305–24.

———. "Seminary Networks and Black Consciousness in South Africa in the 1970s." *South African Historical Journal* 62, no. 1 (2010): 162–82.

Denniston, Robin. *Trevor Huddleston: A Life*. New York: St. Martin's Press, 1999.

de Villiers, G. E., ed. *Ravan—Twenty-five Years (1972–1997): A Commemorative Volume of New Writing*. Randburg: Ravan Press, 1997.

de Vos, P. J., et al, *A Socio-economic and Educational Survey of the Bantu Residing in the Victoria-East, Middledrift and Zwelitsha Areas of the Ciskei*. Alice: University of Fort Hare, 1970.

de Wet, Chris. *Moving Together, Drifting Apart: Betterment Planning and Villagisation in a South African Homeland*. Johannesburg: Witwatersrand University Press, 1995.

de Wet, Chris, and Michael Whisson, eds. *From Reserve to Region: Apartheid and Social Change in the Keiskammahoek District of (former) Ciskei, 1950–1990*. Grahamstown: Institute for Social and Economic Research, Rhodes University, 1997.

Digby, Anne. *Diversity and Division in Medicine: Health Care in South Africa from the 1800s*. Oxford: Peter Lang, 2006.

———. "Early Black Doctors in South Africa." *Journal of African History* 46, no. 3 (November 2005): 427–54.

Digby, Anne, and Howard Phillips. *At the Heart of Healing: Groote Schuur Hospital 1938–2008*. Auckland Park: Jacana Media, 2008.

Dlamini, Jacob. *Native Nostalgia*. Auckland Park: Jacana Media, 2009.

Easterly, William. *Reinventing Foreign Aid*. Cambridge, Mass.: MIT Press, 2008.

———. *White Man's Burden: Why the West's Efforts to Aid the Rest Have Done So Much Ill and So Little Good*. New York: Penguin Press, 2006.

Edgar, Robert, and Luyanda ka Msumza, eds. *Freedom in Our Lifetime: The Collected Writings of Anton Muziwakhe Lembede*. Athens: Ohio University Press, 1996.

Etherington, Norman. "African Economic Experiments in Colonial Natal 1845–1880." *African Economic History* 5 (Spring 1978): 1–14.

Evans, Ivan. *Bureaucracy and Race: Native Administration in South Africa*. Berkeley: University of California Press, 1997.

Evans, Nicholas, and Monica Seeber, eds. *The Politics of Publishing in South Africa.* London and Scottsville: Holger Ehling Publishing and University of Natal Press, 2000.

Farmer, Paul. *Partner to the Poor: A Paul Farmer Reader.* Edited by Haun Saussy. Berkeley: University of California Press, 2010.

———. *Pathologies of Power: Health, Human Rights, and the New War on the Poor.* Berkeley: University of California Press, 2003.

Fatton, Robert, Jr. *Black Consciousness in South Africa: The Dialectics of Ideological Resistance to White Supremacy.* Albany: State University of New York Press, 1986.

Feierman, Steven, and John M. Janzen, eds. *The Social Basis of Health and Healing in Africa.* Berkeley: University of California Press, 1992.

Feit, Edward. "Generational Conflict and African Nationalism in South Africa: The African National Congress, 1949–1959." *International Journal of African Historical Studies* 5, no. 2 (1972): 181–202.

Ferguson, James. *The Anti-politics Machine: "Development," Depoliticization, and Bureaucratic Power in Lesotho.* Cambridge: Cambridge University Press, 1990.

———. *Expectations of Modernity: Myths and Meanings of Urban Life on the Zambian Copperbelt.* Berkeley: University of California Press, 1999.

Field, Sean. "Beyond 'Healing': Trauma, Oral History and Regeneration." *Oral History* 34, no. 1 (Spring 2006): 31–42.

———. *Oral History, Community, and Displacement: Imagining Memories in Post-Apartheid South Africa.* New York: Palgrave Macmillan, 2012.

Flint, Karen E. *Healing Traditions: African Medicine, Cultural Exchange, and Competition in South Africa, 1820–1948.* Athens: Ohio University Press, 2008.

Freire, Paulo. *Cultural Action for Freedom.* Harmondsworth: Penguin, 1970.

———. *Education for Critical Consciousness.* New York: Continuum, 1973.

———. *Letters to Cristina: Reflections on My Life and Work.* Translated by Donaldo Macedo et al. New York: Routledge, 1996.

———. *Pedagogy of the Oppressed.* Translated by Myra Bergman Ramos. New York: Herder and Herder, 1971.

Freund, Bill, and Harold Witt, eds. *Development Dilemmas in Post-Apartheid South Africa.* Scottsville: University of KwaZulu-Natal Press, 2010.

Gasa, Nomboniso, ed. *Women in South African History: Basus'iimbokodo, Bawel'imilambo/They Remove Boulders and Cross Rivers.* Cape Town: Human Science Research Council Press, 2007.

Gerhart, Gail M. *Black Power in South Africa: The Evolution of an Ideology.* Berkeley: University of California Press, 1978.

Gibbs, Timothy. *Mandela's Kinsmen: Nationalist Elites and Apartheid's First Bantustan.* Johannesburg: James Currey, 2014.

Glaser, Clive. *Bo-Tsotsi: The Youth Gangs of Soweto, 1935–1976.* Portsmouth, N.H.: Heinemann, 2000.

Glennie, Jonathan. *The Trouble with Aid: Why Less Could Mean More for Africa.* London and New York: Zed Books and Palgrave, Macmillan, 2008.

Gonzáles, Ondina E. *Christianity in Latin America: A History.* Cambridge: Cambridge University Press, 2008.

Gordon, L. R. "Fanon and Development: A Philosophical Look." *Africa Development* 29, no. 1 (2004): 71–93.

Gqola, Pumla. "Black Woman, You Are on Your Own: Images of Black Women in Staffrider Short Stories, 1978–1982." Master's thesis, University of Cape Town, 1999.

———. "Contradictory Locations: Blackwomen and the Discourse of the Black Consciousness Movement (BCM) in South Africa." *Meridians* 2, no. 1 (2001): 130–52.

Gran, Guy. *Development by People: Citizen Construction of a Just World.* New York: Praeger, 1983.

Gwala, Mafika Pascal, ed. *Black Review 1973.* Durban: Black Community Programmes, 1974.

Hadfield, Leslie. "Biko, Black Consciousness, and 'the System' eZinyoka: Oral History and Black Consciousness in Practice in a Rural Ciskei Village." *South African Historical Journal* 62, no. 1 (2010): 78–99.

———. "The Death of Stephen Biko." In *Overcoming Apartheid, Building Democracy.* www.overcomingapartheid.msu.edu.

———. "Restoring Human Dignity and Building Self-Reliance: Youth, Women, and Churches and Black Consciousness Community Development, South Africa, 1969–1977." Ph.D. diss., Michigan State University, 2010.

———. "We Salute a Hero of the Nation: Steve Biko's Place in South Africa's History." Master's thesis, Ohio University, 2005.

Halisi, C. R. D. *Black Political Thought in the Making of South African Democracy.* Bloomington: Indiana University Press, 1999.

Hansen, Deirdre D. *The Life and Work of Benjamin Tyamzashe: A Contemporary Xhosa Composer.* Institute of Social and Economic Research Occasional Paper No. 11. Grahamstown: Rhodes University, 1968.

Hansen, L. D. *The Legacy of Beyers Naudé.* Stellenbosch: SUN Press, 2005.

Harries, Jane. "Women in Production in the Ciskei." B.A. Honors thesis, University of Cape Town, 1979.

Harries, Patrick. *Work, Culture, and Identity: Migrant Laborers in Mozambique and South Africa, c. 1860–1910.* Portsmouth, N.H.: Heinemann, 1994.

Hassim, Shireen. *Women's Organizations and Democracy in South Africa: Contesting Authority.* Madison: University of Wisconsin Press, 2006.

Healy, Meghan. "Women and the Problem of Family in Early African Nationalist History and Historiography." *South African Historical Journal* 64, no. 3 (September 2012): 450–71.

Hendricks, Fred T. *The Pillars of Apartheid: Land Tenure, Rural Planning and the Chieftancy.* Uppsala: Academiae Ubsaliensis, 1990.

Hickey, Samuel, and Giles Mohan, eds. *Participation: From Tyranny to Transformation? Exploring New Approaches to Participation in Development.* London: Zed Books, 2004.

Higgs, Catherine. "Zenzele: African Women's Self-Help Organizations in South Africa 1927–98." *African Studies Review* 47, no. 3 (December 2004): 119–41.

Hilliard, David, ed. *The Black Panther Party Service to the People Programs.* Albuquerque: University of New Mexico Press, 2008.

Hirsch, Alan. *Season of Hope: Economic Reform under Mandela and Mbeki.* Scottsville: University of KwaZulu-Natal Press, 2005.

Hodge, Joseph M., Gerald Hödl, and Martina Kopf, eds. *Developing Africa: Concepts and Practices in Twentieth-Century Colonialism.* Manchester: Manchester University Press, 2014.

Hodgson, Dorothy Louise. *Once Intrepid Warriors: Gender, Ethnicity, and the Cultural Politics of Maasai Development.* Bloomington: Indiana University Press, 2001.

Honwana, Alcinda, and Filip De Boeck, eds. *Makers and Breakers: Children and Youth in Postcolonial Africa.* Oxford: James Currey, 2005.

Hopkins, Dwight. *Black Theology USA and South Africa: Politics, Culture, and Liberation.* Maryknoll, N.Y.: Orbis Books, 1989.

Horwitz, Simonne. *Baragwanath Hospital, Soweto: A History of Medical Care 1941–1990.* Johannesburg: Wits University Press, 2013.

Hulme, David, and Mark Turner. *Governance, Administration, and Development: Making the State Work.* West Hartford, Conn.: Kumarian Press, 1997.

Hyden, Goran. *Beyond Ujamaa in Tanzania: Underdevelopment and an Uncaptured Peasantry.* London: Heinemann, 1980.

Hyslop, Jonathan. *The Classroom Struggle: Policy and Resistance in South Africa, 1940–1990.* Pietermaritzburg: University of Natal Press, 1999.

Iliffe, John. *The African Poor: A History.* Cambridge: Cambridge University Press, 1987.

Isaacman, Allen F. *Cotton Is the Mother of Poverty: Peasants, Work, and Rural Struggle in Colonial Mozambique, 1938–1961.* Portsmouth, N.H.: Heinemann, 1996.

Jeeves, Alan. "Delivering Primary Health Care in Impoverished Urban and Rural Communities: The Institute of Family and Community Health in the 1940s." In *South Africa's 1940s: Worlds of Possibilities,* edited by Saul Dubow and Alan Jeeves, 87–107. Cape Town: Double Storey Books, 2005.

————. "Health, Surveillance and Community: South Africa's Experiment with Medical Reform in the 1940s and 1950s." *South African Historical Journal* 43, no. 1 (November 2000): 244–66.

Johnstone, Frederick. *Class Race and Gold: A Study of Class Relations and Racial Discrimination in South Africa.* London: Routledge and K. Paul, 1976.

Joseph, Peniel E., ed. *The Black Power Movement: Rethinking the Civil Rights–Black Power Era.* New York: Routledge, 2006.

————, ed. *Neighborhood Rebels: Black Power at the Local Level.* New York: Palgrave Macmillan, 2010.

Kallaway, Peter, ed. *The History of Education Under Apartheid, 1948–1994: The Doors of Learning and Culture Shall Be Opened.* New York: Peter Lang, 2002.

ka Msumza, Luyanda. "From Half-way Station to Permanent Settlement: A Study in the Evolution of Ginsberg Township, 1939 to 1964." Honors thesis, University of Cape Town, 1993.

Karis, Thomas, and Gail M. Gerhart. *From Protest to Challenge: A Documentary History of African Politics in South Africa, 1882–1990.* Vol. 5, *Nadir and Resurgence, 1964–1979.* Bloomington: Indiana University Press, 1997.

Keaney, Matthew P. "'I Can Feel My Grin Turn to a Grimace': From the Sophiatown Shebeens to the Streets of Soweto on the Pages of *Drum, The Classic, New Classic,* and *Staffrider.*" Master's thesis, George Mason University, 2010.

Kemp, Amanda, Noziziwe Madlala, Asha Moodley, and Elaine Salo. "The Dawn of a New Day: Redefining South African Feminism." In *The Challenge of Local Feminisms: Women's Movements in Global Perspective,* edited by Amrita Basu, 131–62. Boulder, Colo.: Westview Press, 1995.

Khoapa, B. A., ed., *Black Review 1972.* Durban: Black Community Programmes, 1973.

Kirkendall, Andrew. *Paulo Freire and the Cold War Politics of Literacy.* Chapel Hill: University of North Carolina Press, 2010.

————. "Reentering History: Paulo Freire and the Politics of the Brazilian Northeast, 1958–1964." *Luso-Brazilian Review* 41, no. 1 (2004): 168–89.

Lal, Priya. "Self-reliance and the State: The Multiple Meanings of Development in Early Post Colonial Tanzania." *Africa: The Journal of the International African Institute* 82, no. 2 (2012): 213–34.

Ledwith, Margaret, and Jane Springett. *Participatory Practice: Community-based Action for Transformative Change.* Bristol, U.K.: Policy Press, 2010.

Limb, Peter. *The ANC's Early Years: Nation, Class and Place in South Africa before 1940.* Pretoria: Unisa Press, 2010.

————. *The People's Paper: A Centenary History and Anthology of Abantu-Batho.* Johannesburg: Wits University Press, 2012.

Maathai, Wangari. *The Green Belt Movement: Sharing the Approach and the Experience.* Nairobi: Environment Liaison Centre International, 1998.

————. *Unbowed*. New York: Alfred A. Knopf, 2006.

MacKinnon, Aran S. "Chiefs, Cattle, and 'Betterment': Contesting Zuluness and Segregation in the Reserves." In *Zulu Identities: Being Zulu, Past and Present*, edited by Benedict Carton, John Laband, and Jabulani Sithole, 250–55. Scottsville: University of KwaZulu-Natal Press, 2009.

————. "Negotiating the Practice of the State: Reclamation, Resistance, and 'Betterment' in the Zululand Reserves." In *The Culture of Power in Southern Africa: Essays on State Formation and the Political Imagination*, edited by Clifton Crais, 65–90. Portsmouth, N.H.: Heinemann, 2003.

Macqueen, Ian. "Re-imagining South Africa: Black Consciousness, Radical Christianity and the New Left, 1967–1977." Ph.D. diss., University of Sussex, 2011.

————. "Students, Apartheid and the Ecumenical Movement in South Africa, 1960–1975." *Journal of Southern African Studies* 39, no. 2 (2013): 447–63.

M-Afrika, Andile. *The Eyes That Lit Our Lives: A Tribute to Steve Biko*. King William's Town: Eyeball Publishers, 2010.

Magaziner, Daniel. "Christ in Context: Developing a Political Faith in Apartheid South Africa." *Radical History Review*, no. 99 (2007): 80–106.

————. *The Law and the Prophets: Black Consciousness in South Africa, 1968–1977*. Athens: Ohio University Press, 2010.

Mager, Anne Kelk. *Gender and the Making of a South African Bantustan: A Social History of the Ciskei, 1945–1959*. Portsmouth, N.H.: Heinemann, James Currey, David Philip, 1999.

Magubane, Bernard, et al. "Resistance and Repression in the Bantustans." In *The Road to Democracy in South Africa*. Vol. 2, edited by SADET, 749–802. Pretoria: Unisa Press, 2006.

Magubane, Zine. "Attitudes towards Feminism Among Women in the ANC, 1950–1990: A Theoretical Re-interpretation." In *Road to Democracy*. Vol. 4, *1980–1990*, edited by SADET, 975–1034. Pretoria: Unisa Press, 2010.

Mainwaring, Scott. *The Catholic Church and Politics in Brazil, 1916–1985*. Stanford, Calif.: Stanford University Press, 1986.

Mamdani, Mahmood. *Citizen and Subject: Contemporary Africa and the Legacy of Late Colonialism*. Princeton, N.J.: Princeton University Press, 1996.

Mangcu, Xolela. *Biko: A Biography*. Cape Town: Tafelberg, 2012.

————. *To the Brink: The State of Democracy in South Africa*. Scottsville: University of KwaZulu-Natal Press, 2008.

Mangena, Mosibudi. *On Your Own: Evolution of Black Consciousness in South Africa/Azania*. Braamfontein: Skotaville, 1989.

Mansuri, Ghazala, and Vijayendra Rao. "Community-Based and -Driven Development: A Critical Review." *World Bank Research Observer* 19, no. 1 (Spring 2004): 1–39.

Marais, Hein. *South Africa Pushed to the Limit: The Political Economy of Change.* London: Zed Books, 2011

Marks, Shula. *Divided Sisterhood: Race, Class, and Gender in the South African Nursing Profession.* New York: St. Martin's Press, 1994.

———. "South Africa's Early Experiment in Social Medicine: Its Pioneers and Politics." *American Journal of Public Health* 87, no. 3 (March 1997): 452–59.

Marks, Shula, and Richard Rathbone, eds. *Industrialization and Social Change in South Africa: African Class Formation, Culture and Consciousness 1870–1930.* New York: Longman, 1982.

Martinussen, John. *Society, State and Market: A Guide to Competing Theories of Development.* London: Zed Books, 2005.

Mashaba, Grace. *Rising to the Challenge of Change: A History of Black Nursing in South Africa.* Kenwyn: Juta Press, 1995.

Massey, Daniel. *Under Protest: The Rise of Student Resistance at the University of Fort Hare.* Hidden Histories. Pretoria: Unisa Press, 2010.

Mbanjwa, Thoko, ed. *Black Review 1974/1975.* Durban: Black Community Programmes, 1975.

———, ed. *Black Viewpoint Number 2: Détente.* Durban: BCP, 1975.

———, ed. *Black Viewpoint Number 3: Apartheid: Hope or Despair for Blacks?* Durban: BCP, 1976.

Mbeki, Govan. *Let's Do It Together: What Cooperative Societies Are and Do.* Cape Town: African Bookman, 1944.

McAllister, P. A. "Resistance to 'Betterment' in the Transkei: A Case Study from Willowvale District." *Journal of Southern African Studies* 15, no. 2 (January 1989): 346–68.

Miescher, Stephan F. "Building the City of the Future: Visions and Experiences of Modernity in Ghana's Akasombo Township." *Journal of African History* 53, no. 3 (2012): 367–90.

Miller, Debra A., ed. *Aid to Africa.* Detroit: Greenhaven Press, 2009.

Mngxitama, Andile, Amanda Alexander, and Nigel Gibson, eds. *Biko Lives!: Contesting the Legacies of Steve Biko.* New York: Palgrave Macmillan, 2008.

Moodie, Dunbar. *Going for Gold: Men, Mines and Migration.* Berkeley: University of California Press, 1994.

Mosala, Itumeleng J., and Buti Tlhagale, eds. *The Unquestionable Right to Be Free: Black Theology from South Africa.* Maryknoll, N.Y.: Orbis Press, 1986.

Moskowitz, Kara. "'Are You Planting Trees or Are You Planting People?' Squatter Resistance and International Development in the Making of a Kenyan Postcolonial Political Order (c. 1963–78)." *Journal of African History* 56, no. 1 (March 2015): 99–118.

Moyo, Dambisa. *Dead Aid: Why Aid Is Not Working and How There Is a Better Way for Africa.* New York: Farrar, Straus and Giroux, 2009.

Mzamane, Mbulelo V., Bavusile Maaba, and Nkosinathi Biko. "The Black Consciousness Movement." In *The Road to Democracy in South Africa*. Vol. 2, edited by SADET, 99–159. Pretoria: Unisa Press, 2006.

Naidoo, Kumi. "The Politics of Youth Resistance in the 1980s: The Dilemmas of a Differentiated Durban." *Journal of Southern African Studies*, Special Issue: Social History of Resistance in South Africa, 18, no. 1 (March 1992): 143–65.

Ndlovu, Sifiso. "The Soweto Uprising." In *The Road to Democracy in South Africa*. Vol. 2, edited by SADET, 317–50. Pretoria: Unisa Press, 2006.

———. *The Soweto Uprisings: Counter-Memories of June 1976*. Randburg: Ravan Press, 1998.

Ndungane, Njongonkulu. "Spirituality and the Development Agenda." Paper presented at the Steve Biko Foundation Thirtieth Anniversary Commemorative International Conference: Consciousness, Agency, and the African Development Agenda, September 10–12, 2007, University of Cape Town.

Nekhwevha, Fhulu. "The Influence of Paulo Freire's 'Pedagogy of Knowing' in South African Education Struggle in the 1970s and 1980s." In *The History of Education Under Apartheid, 1948–1994: The Doors of Learning and Culture Shall Be Opened*, edited by Peter Kallaway, 134–44. New York: Peter Lang, 2002.

Nkrumah, Kwame. *I Speak of Freedom: A Statement of African Ideology*. London: William Heinemann, 1961.

Noble, Vanessa. "Doctors Divided: Gender, Race, and Class Anomalies in the Production of Black Medical Doctors in Apartheid South Africa, 1948–1994." Ph.D. diss, University of Michigan, 2005.

———. "A Medical Education with a Difference: A History of the Training of Black Student Doctors in Social, Preventive and Community-Oriented Primary Health Care at the University of Natal Medical School, 1940s-1960." *South African Historical Journal* 61, no. 3 (September 2009): 550–74.

Nolutshungu, Sam. *Changing South Africa: Political Considerations*. Manchester: Manchester University Press, 1982.

Nqakula, Charles. "1(b): 15 Leopold Street." In *Umhlaba Wethu: A Historical Indictment*, edited by Mothobi Mutloatse, 21–24. Johannesburg: Skotaville, 1987.

Ntsebeza, Lungisile. *Democracy Compromised: Chiefs and the Politics of the Land in South Africa*. Leiden: Brill, 2005.

Ntsimane, Radikobo P. "Amandla Awekho Emuthini, Asenyangeni: A Critical History of the Lutheran Medical Missions in Southern Africa with Special Emphases on Four Mission Hospitals, 1930s–1978." Ph.D. diss., University of KwaZulu-Natal, 2010.

Nuttall, Sarah, and Carli Coetzee eds. *Negotiating the Past: The Making of Memory in South Africa*. Cape Town: Oxford University Press, 1998.

Nyerere, Julius K. *Freedom and Socialism: A Selection from Writings and Speeches, 1965–1967.* Dar es Salaam: Oxford University Press, 1968.

———. *Freedom and Unity: A Selection from Writings and Speeches.* London: Oxford University Press, 1967.

O'Meara, Dan. *Forty Lost Years: The Apartheid State and the Politics of the National Party, 1948–1994.* Athens: Ohio University Press, 1996.

Opliphant, Andries Walter, and Ivan Vladislavic, eds. *Ten Years of Staffrider, 1978–1988.* Johannesburg: Ravan Press, 1988.

Packard, Randall M. *White Plague, Black Labor: Tuberculosis and the Political Economy of Health and Disease in South Africa.* Berkeley: University of California Press, 1989.

Parpart, Jane L. "Rethinking Participation, Empowerment, and Development from a Gender Perspective." In *Transforming Development: Foreign Aid for a Changing World,* edited by Jim Freedman, 222–34. Toronto: University of Toronto Press, 2000.

Peires, Jeff. "Ethnicity and Pseudo-Ethnicity in the Ciskei." In *Segregation and Apartheid in Twentieth-Century South Africa,* edited by William Beinart and Saul Dubow, 256–84. London: Routledge, 1995.

———. "The Lovedale Press: Literature for the Bantu Revisited." *History in Africa* 6 (1979): 155–75.

Peterson, Bhekizizwe. "Culture, Resistance and Representation." In *The Road to Democracy in South Africa.* Vol. 2, edited by SADET, 161–85. Pretoria: Unisa Press, 2006.

Peterson, Derek R. *Creative Writing: Translation, Bookkeeping, and the Work of Imagination in Colonial Kenya.* Portsmouth, N.H.: Heinemann, 2004.

Phillips, Howard. "The Grassy Park Health Centre: A Peri-Urban Pholela?" In *South Africa's 1940s: Worlds of Possibilities,* edited by Saul Dubow and Alan Jeeves, 108–28. Cape Town: Double Storey Books, 2005.

Pityana, Barney. "Power and Social Change." In *Student Perspectives on South Africa,* edited by David Welsh and Hendrik W. van der Merwe, 174–89. Cape Town: David Philip, 1972.

Pityana, Barney, Mamphela Ramphele, Malusi Mpumlwana, and Lindy Wilson, eds. *Bounds of Possibility: The Legacy of Steve Biko and Black Consciousness.* Cape Town: David Philip, 1991.

Platzky, Laurine, and Cherryl Walker. *The Surplus People: Forced Removals in South Africa.* Johannesburg: Ravan Press, 1985.

Pohlandt-McCormick, Helena. *I Saw a Nightmare: Doing Violence to Memory: The Soweto Uprising, June 16, 1976.* New York: Columbia University Press, 2006.

———. "'I Saw a Nightmare . . .': Violence and the Construction of Memory (Soweto, June 16, 1976)." *History and Theory* 39, no. 4 (2000): 23–44.

Posel, Deborah. *The Making of Apartheid, 1948–1961: Conflict and Compromise.* Oxford: Oxford University Press, 1991.

———. "Race as Common Sense: Racial Classification in Twentieth-Century South Africa." *African Studies Review* 44, no. 2 (2001): 87–113.

Prozesky, Martin, ed. *Christianity Amidst Apartheid: Selected Perspectives on the Church in South Africa.* New York: St. Martin's Press, 1990.

Rambally, Asha, ed. *Black Review 1975–1976.* Durban: Black Community Programmes, 1977.

Ramphele, Mamphela. *Across Boundaries: The Journey of a South African Woman Leader.* New York: Feminist Press, 1996.

———. *Laying Ghosts to Rest: Dilemmas of the Transformation in South Africa.* Cape Town: Tafelberg, 2008.

Randall, Peter. *Taste of Power.* Johannesburg: Spro-cas, 1973.

Raum, O. F. "Self-Help Associations." *African Studies Review* 28, no. 2 (1969): 119–41.

Redding, Sean. "South African Blacks in a Small Town Setting: The Ironies of Control in Umtata, 1878–1955." *Canadian Journal of African Studies* 26, no. 1 (1992): 70–90.

Rich, Paul. *Hope and Despair: English-Speaking Intellectuals and South African Politics, 1896–1976.* London: British Academic Press, 1993.

———. *White Power and the Liberal Conscience: Racial Segregation and South African Liberalism, 1921–60.* Manchester: Manchester University Press, 1984.

Rist, Gilbert. *The History of Development: From Western Origins to Global Faith.* London: Zed Books, 2002.

Rodney, Walter. *How Europe Underdeveloped Africa.* London: Bogle-L'Ouverture Publications, 1972.

Romero, Patricia. *Profiles in Diversity: Women in the New South Africa.* East Lansing: Michigan State University Press, 1998.

Sabra Study Group of Fort Hare. *The Ciskei—A Bantu Homeland: A General Survey.* Alice: Fort Hare University Press, 1971.

Saldru Community Health Project. *Health and Health Services in the Ciskei.* Saldru Working Papers No. 54. Cape Town: Saldru, 1983.

Saunders, Christopher, ed. *From Apartheid to Democracy: Localities and Liberation.* Cape Town: Department of Historical Studies, UCT, 2007.

———. *The Making of the South African Past.* Cape Town: David Philip, 1988.

Schneider, Leander. "Colonial Legacies and Postcolonial Authoritarianism: Connects and Disconnects." *African Studies Review* 49, no. 1 (2006): 93–118.

———. "High on Modernity? Explaining the Failings of Tanzanian Villagisation." *African Studies* 66, no. 1 (2007): 9–38.

Scott, James C. *Seeing Like a State: How Certain Schemes to Improve the Human Condition Have Failed.* New Haven, Conn.: Yale University Press, 1998.

Scully, Pamela, and Denise Walsh. "Altering Politics, Contesting Gender." *Journal of Southern African Studies* 32, no. 1 (2006): 1–12.

Seekings, Jeremy. "Whose Voices? Politics and Methodology in the Study of Political Organisation and Protest in the Final Phase of the 'Struggle' in South Africa." *South African Historical Journal* 62, no. 1 (2010): 7–28.

Seekings, Jeremy, and Nicoli Nattrass. *Class, Race, and Inequality in South Africa.* New Haven, Conn.: Yale University Press, 2005.

Sellström, Tor. "Sweden and the Nordic Countries: Official Solidarity and Assistance from the West." In *The Road to Democracy in South Africa.* Vol. 3, *International Solidarity,* edited by SADET, 421–531. Pretoria: Unisa Press, 2008.

Sen, Amartya. *Development as Freedom.* New York: Alfred A. Knopf, 1999.

Shapiro, Karin A. "Doctors or Medical Aids—The Debate over the Training of Black Medical Personnel for the Rural Black Population in South Africa in the 1920s and 1930s." *Journal of Southern African Studies* 13, no. 2 (January 1987): 234–55.

Smith, Christian. *The Emergence of Liberation Theology: Radical Religion and Social Movement Theory.* Chicago: University of Chicago Press, 1991.

South African Democracy Education Trust (SADET). *The Road to Democracy in South Africa.* Vols. 1–4. Pretoria: Unisa Press, 2006–10.

Southall, Roger. "The ANC & Black Capitalism in South Africa." *Review of African Political Economy* 100 (2004): 313–28.

———. "Buthelezi, Inkatha and the Politics of Compromise." *African Affairs* 80, no. 321 (October 1981): 453–81.

Steinberg, Jonny. *Three-Letter Plague: A Young Man's Journey through a Great Epidemic.* Johannesburg: Jonathan Ball, 2008.

Suttner, Raymond. *The ANC Underground in South Africa, 1950–1976: A Social and Historical Study.* Auckland Park: Jacana Media, 2008.

———. "Women in the ANC-led Underground." In *Women in South African History,* edited by Nomboniso Gasa, 233–255. Cape Town: Human Science Research Council Press, 2007.

Switzer, Les. *Media and Dependency in South Africa.* Africa Series 47. Athens: Ohio University Monographs in International Studies, 1985.

———. "Politics and Communication in the Ciskei, An African Homeland in South Africa." Occasional Papers (Rhodes University. Institute of Social and Economic Research) 23. Grahamstown: Institute for Social and Economic Research, Rhodes University, 1979.

———. *Power and Resistance in an African Society: The Ciskei Xhosa and the Making of South Africa.* Madison: University of Wisconsin Press, 1993.

———, ed. *South Africa's Alternative Press: Voices of Protest and Resistance, 1880s-1960s.* Cambridge: Cambridge University Press, 1997.

Switzer, Les, and Mohamed Adhikari, eds. *South Africa's Resistance Press: Alternative Voices in the Last Generation Under Apartheid.* Athens: Ohio University Center for International Studies, 2000.

Thomas, Cornelius. "Disaffection, Identity, Black Consciousness and a New Rector: An Exploratory Take on Student Activism at the University of the Western Cape 1966–1976." *South African Historical Journal* 54 (2005): 72–90.

———. *Tangling the Lion's Tale: Donald Card, from Apartheid Era Cop to Crusader for Justice.* East London: Donald Card, 2007.

Thomas, Trudi. *The Children Of Apartheid: A Study of the Effects of Migratory Labour on Family Life in the Ciskei.* London: Africa Publications Trust, 1974.

Tollman, Steve, and Derek Yach. "Public Health Initiatives in South Africa in the 1940s and 1950s: Lessons for a Post-Apartheid Era." *American Journal of Public Health* 83, no. 7 (July 1993): 1043–50.

Tomaselli, Keyan, and P. Eric Louw, eds. *The Alternative Press in South Africa.* Bellville: Anthropos and James Currey, 1991.

Tropp, Jacob. *Natures of Colonial Change: Environmental Relations in the Making of the Transkei.* Athens: Ohio University Press, 2006.

Turner, Richard. *The Eye of the Needle: An Essay on Participatory Democracy.* Johannesburg: Spro-cas, 1972.

Vanek, Monique. "Wilgespruit Fellowship Centre: Part of Our Struggle for Freedom." In *From National Liberation to Democratic Renaissance in Southern Africa,* edited by Cheryl Hendriks and Lwazi Lushaba, 152–70. Dakar: CODESRIA, 2005.

van Kessel, Ineke. *"Beyond Our Wildest Dreams": The United Democratic Front and the Transformation of South Africa.* Charlottesville: University Press of Virginia, 2000.

van Onselen, Charles. *Studies in the Social and Economic History of Witwatersrand, 1886 1914.* New York: Longman, 1982.

van Wyk ed., Chris. *We Write What We Like: Celebrating Steve Biko.* Johannesburg: Wits University Press, 2007.

Victor, Stephanie. "Segregated Housing and Contested Identities: The Case of the King William's Town Coloured Community, 1895–1946." M.Sc. thesis, Rhodes University, 2007.

Vinson, Robert Trent. *The Americans Are Coming!: Dreams of African American Liberation in Segregationist South Africa.* Athens: Ohio University Press, 2012.

Walker, Cherryl, ed. *Women and Gender in Southern Africa to 1945.* Cape Town: David Philip and James Currey, 1990.

———. "Women and Resistance: In Search of South African Feminism." *Work in Progress,* no. 36 (April 1985): 25–30.

———. *Women and Resistance in South Africa.* New York: Monthly Review Press, 1991.

Wallerstein, Immanuel. "The Three Stages of African Involvement in the World Economy." In *Political Economy of Contemporary Africa*. Beverly Hills, Calif.: Sage Press, 1986.

Walshe, Peter. *Prophetic Christianity and the Liberation Movement in South Africa*. Pietermaritzburg: Cluster Publications, 1995.

———. "South Africa: Prophetic Christianity and the Liberation Movement." *Journal of Modern African Studies* 29, no. 1 (March 1991): 27–60.

White, Luise, Stephan F. Miescher, and David William Cohen, eds. *African Words, African Voices: Critical Practices in Oral History*. Bloomington: Indiana University Press, 2001.

Wilde, Melissa J. *Vatican II: A Sociological Analysis of Religious Change*. Princeton, N.J.: Princeton University Press, 2007.

Woods, Donald. *Biko*. 3rd ed. New York: Henry Holt, 1991.

Wotshela, Luvuyo. "Homeland Consolidation, Resettlement and Local Politics in the Border and the Ciskei Region of the Eastern Cape, South Africa, 1960–1996." Ph.D. diss., Oxford University, 2001.

Wylie, Diana. *Art + Revolution: The Life and Death of Thami Mnyele, South African Artist*. Charlottesville: University of Virginia Press, 2008.

———. *Starving on a Full Stomach: Hunger and the Triumph of Cultural Racism in Modern South Africa*. Charlottesville: University Press of Virginia, 2001.

Zondi, Welcome Siphamandla. "Medical Missions and African Demand in KwaZulu-Natal, 1836–1918." Ph.D. diss., University of Cambridge, 2000.

Index